TELL ME THE STORY OF HOW
I CONQUERED YOU

TELL ME THE STORY OF HOW I CONQUERED YOU

Elsewheres *and* Ethnosuicide *in the Colonial Mesoamerican World*

BY JOSÉ RABASA

UNIVERSITY OF TEXAS PRESS
Austin

♾ The paper used in this book meets the minimum requirements of
ANSI/NISO Z39.48–1992 (R1997) (Permanence of Paper).

LIBRARY OF CONGRESS CATALOGING-IN-PUBLICATION DATA
Rabasa, José.
  Tell me the story of how I conquered you : elsewheres and
ethnosuicide in the colonial Mesoamerican world / by José Rabasa.
    p.   cm. — (Joe R. and Teresa Lozano Long series in Latin
American and Latino art and culture)
  Includes bibliographical references and index.
  ISBN 978-0-292-74761-6
  1. Codex Telleriano-Remensis.   2. Mexico—History—Spanish
colony, 1540–1810.   3. Aztec art.   4. Nahuatl language—Writing.
5. Aztecs—Missions.   6. Franciscans—Missions—Mexico—History.
7. Dominicans—Missions—Mexico—History.   8. Mexico—History—
Spanish colony, 1540–1810.   9. Spain—Colonies—z America—
Administration.   I. Title.
F1219.56.C627R33   2011
972′.02—dc22

                                            2011003824

Para Santiago Illapa

CONTENTS

ACKNOWLEDGMENTS

I first explored the project of reading folio 46r of the Codex Telleriano-Remensis in the workshop "Catholicism Reads Veiled Bodies" at the conference "The Rhetorics and Rituals of (Un)veiling in Early Modern Europe" at the University of Michigan in 1997. In my 1998 Morrison Library Inaugural Address at Berkeley, "Franciscans and Dominicans under the Gaze of a *Tlacuilo*: Plural-World Dwelling in an Indian Pictorial Codex," I lectured on the possibility of learning how to read the colonial world from the standpoint of the *tlacuilo*, a native painter and scribe, who had been drafted into the production of an album of Mesoamerican forms of writing that were collected in what is known today as the Codex Telleriano-Remensis. The Morrison Library program of inaugural addresses at Berkeley provides a forum where new faculty expose their research to the community at large. When Charles Faulhaber, the director of the Bancroft Library, invited me to deliver a lecture, he gave me the choice of presenting recent work or delineating the beginnings of a new line of research. I chose the latter.

In the ensuing years, I have shared my work on folio 46r with undergraduate and graduate students at Harvard and Berkeley, who not only have provided a space to present my ideas and receive invaluable criticism but have also shared my interest in learning to read colonial Nahuatl documents in tandem with Mesoamerican pictography. At Berkeley and Harvard, I also had the opportunity to present my work to my colleagues in Spanish and Portuguese; Ethnic Studies; the Townsend Center at Berkeley, where I served as Senior Fellow in 2003–2004; the gatherings and colloquia of SEMMYCOLON (Seminario de Estudios Medievales, Modernos y Coloniales) that I codirected with my medievalist friend Jesús Rodríguez Velasco; and the Seminario de Culturas Hispánicas, Barker Humanities Center at Harvard. I thank my students and colleagues at Berkeley and Harvard for sharing my enthusiasm for the world the *tlacuilo* of the Codex Telleriano-Remensis revealed to me. It has always surprised me that I could sustain the interest of students and colleagues on what I learned to say about the colonial world from a single page in this colonial codex. Two University of California Humanities Research Fellowships (2001–2002, 2008–2009) allowed me to concentrate full time on the writing of this book.

The richness and complexities of folio 46r led to many lectures in which I have presented earlier versions of the chapters that now make up this book. I begin by acknowledging my debt to those close to Berkeley. I thank Gordon Brotherston and Lucia Sá for inviting me on several occasions to present my work in the Department of Spanish and Portuguese at Stanford University. Also at Stanford, in connection with the University of Pennsylvania, I had the opportunity to develop my ideas on the colonial divide at the symposium "Medieval/Renaissance: Rethinking Periodization" in 2006; Jennifer Summit and David Wallace's invitation to deliver one of the keynote addresses provided me with ample time to present my thoughts. I thank Roland Greene for his generous comments and suggestions during this symposium. Other occasions and institutions where I exposed my readings of folio 46r include the conference "Cryptic Cartographies," University of Oregon, 2002; the 36th Annual Comparative Literature Symposium at Texas Tech University, "(In)versions of the New World: Writing Race, Religion, and Sex in Colonial Latin America," 2003; the conference "Theorizing Scriptures," Institute for the Study of Signifying Scriptures, Claremont Graduate University, 2004; the conference "In Comparable Americas: Colonial Studies after the Hemispheric Turn," Newberry Library and the University of Chicago, April 30–May 1, 2004; the conference on the Subaltern and the Popular, University of California at Santa Barbara, 2006; the seminar on Postcolonial Medievalisms, 2006 meeting of ACLA; the conference on Early Modern Eyes, University of Wisconsin, 2007; and the Seminario de Discursos, Legitimación y Memoria, Universidad de Salamanca, 2007. More recently, June 1–4, 2010, I discussed several chapters of the book in a series of seminars at the Universidad Javeriana, Bogotá, Colombia.

These conferences and seminars have been extremely productive, and I cannot do justice to all those with whom I have had conversations. I will limit myself to mentioning the following friends and critics: María Piedad Quevedo, Mónica María del Valle, Juan Carlos Segura, Daniel Castelblanco, Cristo Figueroa, Javier Sanjinés, Leonardo García Pabón, Analisa Taylor, William Hanks, William Taylor, José Saldívar, Michael Taussig, Ileana Rodríguez, Doris Sommer, Heather McMichael, Stephanie Schmidt, Ana Pulido, Deirdre Snyder, Magali Rabasa, Arturo Dávila, Johannes Neurath, Alberto Mendo, Victoriano de la Cruz Cruz, John

Sullivan, Estelle Tarica, Michael Iarocci, Dan Nemser, Vincent Wimbush, Camilo Vergara, Galen Brokaw, Nelson Maldonado, Lisa Voigt, David Lloyd, Francine Masiello, Walter Mellion, Lee Palmer Wandel, Kathleen Davis, Swati Chattopadhyay, Bhaskar Sarkhar, Cristina Venegas, Bishnupriya Gosh, Kamala Visweswaran, Gauri Viswanathan, Ivonne del Valle, Seth Kimmel, Alfonso Mendiola, Perla Chinchilla Pawling, Sudipta Sen, Parama Roy, Gyanendra Pandey, Stephanie Wood, Walter Mignolo, Fernando Coronil, John Beverley, Enrique Dussel, Aníbal Quijano, Laura Pérez, Ramón Grosfogel, Patricia Penn Hilden, Timothy Reiss, Santiago Colás, Catherine Brown, Tom Conley, Neil Whitehead, Jorge Cañizares Esguerra, James Clifford, William Paulson, Felipe Rojas, Sylvia García-Sellers, Sarah Schoellkopf, Tara Daly, Sara Castro-Klarén, Santa Arias, Luis Fernando Restrepo, Abdul Karim Mustapha, Germán Labrador, Fernando R. de la Flor, Nicole Legnani, Anna More, Daniel Woolf, Nadia Altschult, Yuri Herrera, Sergio Rivera-Ayala, Manolo Callahan, Joseph Morales, Chrissy Arce, Byron Barahona, David Rojinski, Salvador Velazco, Agustín Palacios, Erika Helgen, Viviana Díaz Balsera, Yolanda Martínez-San Miguel, Josefina Saldaña, Ralph Bauer, Rosa Yáñez, and many others whose names I cannot recollect now but who have left an imprint on my thought. My special thanks go to Laurence Cuelenaere, who read the manuscript several times and offered invaluable criticism.

I remain particularly thankful to the anonymous readers who offered critical comments and substantial suggestions in the rounds of revisions the manuscript went through. I also thank Theresa J. May for her support at the University of Texas Press. Nancy Warrington edited the manuscript with care. However, I remain solely responsible for the final version.

Given the nature of this project, a continuous reading of folio 46r, there has been a certain amount of repetition in the essays I have published over the years, for which I apologize to my "loyal" readers who have learned to skip through the known in pursuit of the new. The chapters contain borrowed small and large parts from my previous publications, selections that have enabled me to build a theoretic-political experiment that I have defined as *elsewheres*. Early versions and parts of these chapters appeared under these titles in the following places:

"Franciscans and Dominicans under the Gaze of a *Tlacuilo*: Plural-World Dwelling in an Indian Pictorial Codex." Morrison Inaugural Lecture Series, University of California at Berkeley, Berkeley: Dow Library, 1998.

"Elsewheres: Radical Relativism and the Limits of Empire," *Qui Parle* 16:1 (2006): 71–96.

"The Colonial Divide," special issue on "Medieval/Renaissance: Re-thinking Periodization," ed. Jennifer Summit and David Wallace, *Journal of Medieval and Early Modern Studies* (Fall 2007): 511–529.

"Thinking Europe in Indian Categories; or, 'Tell Me the Story of How I Conquered You'," in *Coloniality at Large*, ed. Mabel Moraña and Enrique Dussel. Durheim: Duke University Press, 2008. Copyright © 2008, Duke University Press. All rights reserved. Reprinted by permission of the publisher.

"Decolonizing Medieval Mexico," in *Medievalism in the Postcolonial World*, ed. Kathleen Davis and Nadia Altschult. Baltimore: Johns Hopkins University Press, 2009. Copyright © 2009, Johns Hopkins University Press. All rights reserved. Reprinted by permission of the publisher.

"Depicting Perspective: The Return of the Gaze in Codex Telleriano-Remensis (c. 1563)," in *Early Modern Eyes*, ed. Walter S. Melion and Lee Palmer Wandel. Leiden: Intersections/Brill, 2009.

I thank the publishers for permission to use parts of these essays in this form.

TELL ME THE STORY OF HOW
I CONQUERED YOU

In reading folio 46r of the Codex Telleriano-Remensis (ca. 1563), I face a *tlacuilo*, a native scribe, who painted the colonial world from an *elsewhere* (Figure 1).[1] The performative force of folio 46r resides in placing me under a threatening empiricism that reveals a world that escapes categorization and the assurance of universals.

By the concept of *elsewheres*, I understand spaces and temporalities that define a world that remains exterior to the spatio-temporal location of any given observer. This definition has enabled me to intuit a spatio-temporal difference that cannot be conflated with the knowledge we Western-trained academics construe about objects and subjects (in this case, Meso-american) that remain—in fact, must remain—outside the languages and methods we privilege in our positive knowledge, hermeneutics, or onto-logical definition of the world.

Elsewheres are not merely spatial locations. They consist of forms of affect, knowledge, and perception underlying what a given individual in a given culture can *say* and *show* about the world. The concept of *else-where* enables me to think in terms of a neuter, that is, of a pure negation, a *not* that lacks any reference to a previous state of affairs or even a posi-tive entity. *Elsewheres* are ineffable though intuitable. *Elsewheres* demand the recognition that objects have a life of their own, but also a life for the Mesoamerican subjects whose affective and practical relation to ob-jects cannot be reduced to those of the foreign or—for that matter—native scholar conducting excavations or archival retrieval or pinching bits and pieces from objects for laboratory testing. In this regard, this book should be read less as a hermeneutic of a Mesoamerican system of writing one may attribute to the *tlacuilo* and more as a philosophical or theoretical re-flection on the revelation of the existence of *elsewheres* that disrupt the as-sumption that Western thought exhausts what can be said and thought—or, by extension, what must remain unsaid and unthought—about the experience humans may have of the world.

Beyond the role of scribes, the *tlacuiloque* in ancient Mesoamerica were

FIGURE I   *Codex Telleriano-Remensis, fol. 46r. Courtesy of the Bibliothèque Nationale de France, Paris.*

wise men and women responsible for transmitting the knowledge they painted in their *amoxtli* (native books made of bark). In this book, I speak of the *tlacuilo* as a she to call attention to the fact that in Mesoamerica, painters included women and men, as evidenced in folio 30r of Telleriano-Remensis, which depicts a female *tlacuilo* that a Spanish gloss identifies as *La pintora*, supposedly a spouse or a concubine of Huitzilihuitl, the first ruler of Mexico-Tenochtitlan (Figure 2). This folio offers a point of entry for envisioning *tlacuiloque* at work, as it is, perhaps, a self-portrait, or minimally an image that captures the conventions used in depicting the posture, instrument, and symbolic language of a female *tlacuilo*. This is the sole image of native painters the *tlacuilo* produced for posterity. But, then again, she probably had a long disquisition on *La pintora* about which the Spanish glossator was apparently oblivious. We don't know and probably will never know if the *tlacuilo* of Telleriano-Remensis was in fact a woman, but in memory of the anonymous *La pintora*, I have chosen to generalize the references to the *tlacuilo* as *she*, even if for the mere rhetorical effect that should keep us from generalizing the male identity of all *tlacuiloque*. In the colonial world, their knowledge extended to the native and Spanish legal, political, and religious institutions that interpellated the Nahuas in the daily life of the colony. The *tlacuilo*, working under the supervision of Dominican friars, had to adapt the traditional Mesoamerican genres to European materials and formats. She modified the use of screenfolds by painting the content on European paper, on discrete sheets to be compiled into a book. The supervisors also demanded that she leave spaces blank for the annotation of glosses.[2]

The notion of *elsewhere* that I develop in this book has affinities with what Doris Sommer calls the "rhetoric of particularism"—that is, the strategies minority writers have developed to produce spaces that bar majority readers from entering. A brief discussion of Sommer's project should prove useful for further defining what I understand by *elsewhere*. In Sommer's argument, it is not a question of majority readers not understanding what is being said (or, in the case of folio 46r, depicted) but of minority writers constructing autonomous spaces by drawing limits of interpretation that must be respected. Having said this, I would underscore that the setting, positioning, and practice of painting cannot be subsumed under minority and resistant practices. The case of the *tlacuilo* differs from the literatures Sommer examines in that it is not necessarily an instance of

FIGURE 2   *Codex Telleriano-Remensis, fol. 30r. Courtesy of the Bibliothèque Nationale de France, Paris.*

a resistance text in which "a target audience is constructed as outsider and another as complicitous in the exclusion."[3] The *tlacuilo*, however, does not paint from the position of a minority writer who writes from within the dominant language, system of representation, and writing system—Latin script in English or Spanish, as in Sommer's cases. The *tlacuilo* follows the instructions of the supervisors and yet paints from a place they cannot access. I am less interested in what the *tlacuilo* keeps the audience from learning, though one might identify signs of no trespassing, than in what was communicated to the missionaries that disrupted their certainty by offering a view of their world that made manifest epistemological fissures and doctrinal inconsistencies between the two main orders in Mexico, the Franciscans and the Dominicans—corresponding to the right- and left-hand top corners of the page. This is to mention just one aspect of folio 46r that disrupted the world of the Dominican missionaries that solicited and supervised the painting of Telleriano-Remensis. What interests me in folio 46r is not so much the *tlacuilo*'s construction of inaccessible *elsewheres* that demand respect, but her creation of a pictorial vocabulary consistent with the ancient Mesoamerican life-forms (i.e., the *elsewhere*) with which and from which she makes sense of the colonial world. Although I am barred from *seeing* the world with the eyes of the *tlacuilo*, I can certainly recognize and be affected by what she *shows* me.

In this book, at the expense of positive knowledge about Codex Telleriano-Remensis or of ancient and colonial pictorial texts, I take the intuition of the *elsewhere* as a point of departure for a theoretic-political experiment on what we may learn to *say* and *see* about the colonial world from native painters. I offer a reminder of the significance of intuition, speculation, and thought experiments when reading history. In this regard, this is not "history" in the strict sense of the term (few historians would recognize what I do as history), and yet it is a historical inquiry. In creating a theoretic-political experiment, I am also less concerned with offering conventional historical evidence (documents) drawn from existing archives than in exploring the possibility of building new forms of historical evidence that place an emphasis on the historical imagination. The notion of *elsewhere* enables me to recognize the existence of a self that produced the painting while drawing the limits of what I can say about this self.

The theoretical virtue of conceptualizing *elsewheres* is that it offers a neuter space that avoids the mirroring effect the category of the Other always carries with respect to a Same. As such, my method allows the *tlacuilo* to teach me how to see and understand the colonial world. In this

way, this book works against the grain of much work in colonial and imperial studies that over the last two or three decades has placed an emphasis on the relationship of power and knowledge (and the expected allowance for resistance). If the end of this book bears many affinities with calls
for decolonization and deconstruction, it underscores that in the *de-* of
deconstruct, decolonial, and demystify, we recognize our participation in
the construct, the colonial, and the mythical. My project also involves the
pursuit of an *elsewhere* to the will for mastery and dominion from within
the tradition of Western thought in which we scholars today cannot but
dwell.[4]

If the end of producing Telleriano-Remensis was to have the *tlacuilo*
create an album of Mesoamerican writing systems to facilitate the indoctrination of the Nahuas, the Dominicans who directed the project became
one more item in the painting of the colonial world. As I will argue in this
book, they were distraught at the depiction of their self and the realization that the painter came from a world they couldn't contain. Although
there are other instances in colonial verbal and pictorial texts in which
missionaries and lay officials bemoan the limits of their mastery, the force
of folio 46r, however, resides in the threat the *tlacuilo* posed by capturing the world of the missionaries in terms that they couldn't anticipate or
fully decipher. The missionaries' recognition of an *elsewhere* refers to the
experience of a subject that is surprised, amazed, or terrified by the realization that he or she cannot understand, experience, or engage the world
of an observer—in this case, the observed (the *tlacuilo*) looking back at the
observer (the missionaries). I share this malaise as I imagine myself under
the gaze of the *tlacuilo*.

In fact, the depiction of colonial objects, institutions, and personages
affects those who come to the paintings from an *elsewhere*, from a *habitus*, that couldn't anticipate the dislocation provoked by a gaze that shows
itself in looking back at those who requested the pictorial text. The eye
of the modern inquisitor finds its match in the eye of the *tlacuilo* who depicts the colonial order from an *elsewhere* that remains inaccessible to the
missionary. In the depiction of the Franciscan missionary (right hand),
we discover a symbolic use of three-dimensional perspective that enables
the *tlacuilo* to record in the frontal depiction the order's preference for
the sacrament of penance and the inquisitorial powers the Franciscan
Fray Juan de Zumárraga, the first bishop of Mexico, assumed in the early
1530s. The frontal perspective is used only on two occasions in Codex
Telleriano-Remensis, for the image of Zumárraga on folio 44v (Figure 3)
and for the Franciscan on folio 46r (see Figure 1); otherwise, the *tlacuilo*

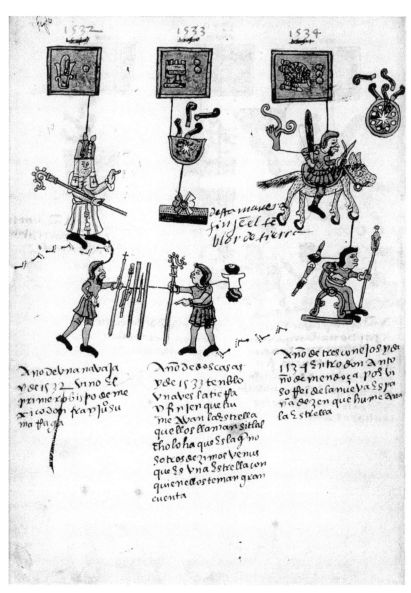

FIGURE 3 *Codex Telleriano-Remensis, fol. 44v. Courtesy of the Bibliothèque Nationale de France, Paris.*

remains faithful to the tradition of picturing the profile of subjects even when inventing new pictorial vocabularies. The doctrine or confession manual held by the Franciscan records the imparting of the doctrine that followed multitudinous baptisms on demand. At the other end of the page, we find the depiction of a Dominican in full ceremonial dress, suggesting the preference of this order for thorough catechization prior to imparting baptism and for strict abidance to the required liturgy. In the act of depicting the essential characteristics of the Dominican and Franciscan orders, the *tlacuilo* shatters the certainty of the missionary by mirroring the ethnographer-missionary. In the *tlacuilo*'s depiction of the missionaries' world, the missionary is led to realize that he is not the only observer. They see themselves through her eyes. In the mirroring, the missionaries learn to recognize their evangelical and ethnographic practices. The *tlacuilo* thus forces them to yield their position as observers to she who now observes them from a place and time that remains opaque in the act of showing itself. The *tlacuilo*'s picturing of readily recognizable colonial subjects manifests an irreducible excess in signification that cannot be exhausted by positive knowledge of the subjects, and yet it has revealed itself as a saturated phenomenon that has enabled me to ask questions about the depicted subjects that I wouldn't have entertained if I had not learned from the *tlacuilo* to see the colonial world differently. The tlacuilo *showed* me a world that altered my seeing, which in turn led me to see the colonial world differently. Given the centrality of folio 46r in this book, I return to this folio in the chapters that follow to elaborate a series of takes that address different questions the *tlacuilo* has taught me to ask.

As I look at the folio and intuit a place of difference from which the *tlacuilo* painted, I am surprised by her ability to dwell in a plurality of worlds. While she partakes of a "modern" subjectivity in conversing with the missionaries—thereby participating in their temporality—and in understanding their request to objectify her culture by creating an album that reproduced and compiled several genres of pictographic writings (*amoxtli* that specialized in the recording of the feasts, calendars, rites, deities, and history), she partakes of a (nonmodern) Mesoamerican subjectivity that captures the colonial world from a habitus or background that is not that of the missionaries, nor that of us modern scholars for that matter. By joining the terms *habitus* and *background*, I want to underscore a collective understanding of these terms rather than an individual manifestation of them. Obviously, the *tlacuilo* didn't use the terms *habitus* or *background* to reflect on her paintings or on the Mesoamerican world in which she dwelled. There are no corresponding terms in Nahuatl that I know of. Having said this, I would assume that the *tlacuilo* and sixteenth-century Nahuas in general were particularly aware (arguably more so than the Spaniards) of the different habitus that differentiated their ways of making the world from those the Spaniards sought to implant. As such, the terms *habitus* and *background* fulfill a heuristic function for approaching the concept of *elsewheres* as comprising the affective, logical, and ethical forms that ground what Mesoamerican subjects *show* or *say*. When I speak of the *tlacuilo*'s habitus, then, it shouldn't be understood as a particular instance of a collective spirit that I could pretend to know and define, but as the ground from which she paints and speaks in showing a world that eludes and yet records Western categories. Her showing affects the assumptions that ground Western thought. This book offers a theoretic-political experiment on the possibility of learning from the *tlacuilo* ways of seeing the world that dislocate the predominance of the West—namely, Christian revealed truth, universal history, ontological claims on the real, three-dimensional perspective, et cetera.

My understanding of the term *habitus* builds on definitions I draw from two classic sources. First, from the Scholastic meaning, most rigorously defined by Thomas Aquinas, that speaks of developing technologies of the self and soul, such as would prepare the soul for the reception of the sacraments and the corresponding infusion of the habitus of grace. The Scholastic definition also concerns the soil that missionaries and secular officials were to prepare (tilling for planting the seeds of Christianity are the preferred metaphors) for implanting spiritual as well as material habitus. This involves a transformation—if not a wholesale replacement—of the indigenous habitus for the reception and incorporation of Christian doctrine, as well as for the development of a work ethic that would turn Indians into productive laborers under proto-capitalist enterprises.

Although both the Dominican and the Franciscan theologians and missionaries make use of the concept of habitus, it is a particular staple of the Thomist theology. It plays a lesser role among Franciscan theologians, who tend to emphasize the function of the will. As we will see in later chapters, for the Franciscans, the central explanation of what was perceived by the mid-sixteenth century as failed conversion was the notion that the Nahuas had lied and deceived the first missionaries about their willingness to embrace the tenets of the Christian dogma. The Dominicans attributed the failed conversion to the impossibility of replacing the old habitus that infused with superstitious meanings the material and spiritual objects introduced by the Spaniards. These two understandings define radically different ethnographic projects and evangelical practices.

The brilliance of the *tlacuilo*, in turn, consists in capturing the habitus of the two orders; her recording of their habitus manages to link the habit (the elegant ceremonial white dress of the Dominican vis-à-vis the rough woolen robe of the Franciscan) with their theological-ethnographic preferences. It is as if the habit itself shaped their evangelic-ethnographic dispositions. In pointing out this difference between habit and ethos, the *tlacuilo* was not alone among sixteenth-century Nahuas.

Second, I find particularly significant Pierre Bourdieu's transformation and redefinition of the term *habitus* in his "Postface to Erwin Panofsky, *Gothic Architecture and Scholasticism.*" My reading of Bourdieu is less concerned with interpreting what Bourdieu understood by *habitus* or with practicing the sociology he defined on the basis of this term, than with taking his insights to expand Scholastic understandings I have outlined above that were part of the intellectual frame of sixteenth-century missionaries. The definition I will develop from Bourdieu, as I have already suggested above, fulfills a heuristic function that enables me to recognize, without exhausting their meaning, the different backgrounds from which and against which the *tlacuilo*, the missionaries, and scholars today make and unmake worlds. The term *habitus* in Bourdieu pertains to the form "through which the creator partakes of his community and time, and that guides and directs, unbeknownst to him, his apparently most unique creative acts."[5] In *Outline of a Theory of Practice*, Bourdieu speaks of *positions* and *dispositions*, terms one could apply to the *tlacuilo* if one were to study her particular mode of being a native painter.[6] I will not carry out this task, for which archaeologists and art historians are much better equipped and have already done extensive, if not definitive, manuscript studies of Codex Telleriano-Remensis, but also because an exhaustive definition of her habitus would be contrary to the principle of *elsewhere* I privilege in this book.[7]

The key word in the cited passage from "Postface" is *unbeknownst*. Arguably the *tlacuilo* could know her position as painter and could evaluate her disposition in terms of the missionaries' recognition of her talent as a painter. But she would remain blind to *the forms through which she participates in her community and time*. I wouldn't want to suggest, however, that her production of the paintings that make up Telleriano-Remensis adopts the colonial structures imposed by the Dominican ethnographic project. I would even complicate this observation by saying that the missionaries were interested in having her make manifest the Mesoamerican pictorial forms rather than in having her reproduce Western Christian forms. The missionaries, however, did not anticipate her invention of a vocabulary that captures European objects from a habitus that was not their own. If in certain formulations of evangelization one finds the call for a wholesale replacement and destruction of the Mesoamerican habitus, the demand that she produce an album of writing systems was conceived as the process of collecting data for the extirpation of what they conceived as superstitions and idolatries. This effort assumes the possibility that the Mesoamerican world could be frozen, made readily available. This effort seems paradoxical, given the continuous complaint, especially among the Dominicans, of a generalized syncretism of European objects and pagan beliefs. Beyond objectifying her habitus, she demonstrated her ability to generate new images that, even if Western in appearance, *show* worlds that cannot be reduced to Western forms.

Given the colonial situation in which the *tlacuilo* paints, I must account for the limits of evangelical practices. The first limit resides, of course, in the fact that she paints from an *elsewhere* that makes sense of what the friars demanded but also of the Western categories they privileged in their request that she produce an album of writing systems. The Nahuas, of course, were born with the capacity to embody a habitus or to speak a language, which for the missionaries should be wholly substituted by the Christian worldview. However, the substitution of Spanish for Nahuatl was not a central objective among missionaries, even in those instances when the Spanish Crown legislated Hispanicization. In fact, the missionaries entertained the dream of *Nahuatlizing* Christianity and in some instances assumed the risk that the schemas structuring their habitus could be radically transformed in the process of translation and dialogue.[8] The art of ethnography, when conducted in earnest, cannot but involve jeopardy, an *ieu parti*—an "(evenly) divided game," according to the *Oxford English Dictionary*.

In the paintings in Telleriano-Remensis, in particular those on folio 46r, I recognize semantic excess that cannot be exhausted by the knowledge and identification of the personages, colonial institutions, situations, glyphs, or spatial arrangement of the depicted subjects. Archaeological knowledge of the codex and its system of writing provides the key for the identification of its signifying forms. But the language that transmitted the stories, incantations, chants, and discourses associated with the depicted subjects in Mesoamerican codices is not, clearly, the language of science that scholars have produced since colonial times. In the case of Telleriano-Remensis, the marginal glosses are in Spanish and on rare occasions quote (in Spanish) native speech that further documents the knowledge recorded in iconic script.[9] Spanish accounts by missionaries and lay officials provide information about historical events, calendars, ceremonies, or rites. It is perhaps because of the urgency to record knowledge about Nahuatl institutions and practices for the purpose of their extirpation that missionaries consulted and diligently recorded verbal performances by informants. It is in native texts using alphabetical script, which record voices in Nahuatl, where we find the sorts of speeches (songs, discourses, chants, incantations, narratives) that would have been enunciated to verbally supplement iconic depictions of historical or ceremonial events. These alphabetically scripted supplements are independent texts rather than verbal descriptions of the pictograms, as is the case in studies by modern archaeologists and art historians. Moreover, archaeologists often perceive colonial texts as contaminated by Spanish ideology. Missionaries rarely if ever privileged "pure" objects.

In this book I am particularly interested in hybrid verbal and pictorial texts in which we can trace the incorporation of European forms. As we read folio 46r, we realize not only that the habitus of the *tlacuilo* is not our own, but also that her pictorial vocabulary produces a new textuality that builds on the remains of the ancient Mesoamerican pictorial systems while incorporating European artifacts and scriptural technologies. It is certainly a hybrid text (as in mixed) but not a mestizo text (as in no longer Mesoamerican). If the analogy does not offend, we may state that in the "same way" that Europe remains Europe after the incorporation of Mesoamerica (chocolate, cacao, cochineal, silver, gold, but also the concepts of the noble savage, cannibalism, wildness, New World, America) into its systems of thought and everyday life, Mesoamerica remains Mesoamerica after the incorporation of European life-forms. The processes of appropriation, expropriation, and exappropriation involve a two-way street.

Along with the texts jointly produced by missionaries and native informants, we also find indigenous intellectuals, such as Fernando de Alva Ixtlixochitl and Domingo de San Antón Muñón Chimalpahin Quauhtlehuanitzin, who collected and critically archived the stories the elders would tell when reading pictorial texts in an effort to preserve their voices for posterity.[10] I speak of verbal performances to underscore that they are singular renditions of narratives, discourses, rites, or incantations rather than faithful repetitions of scripted texts. The native informant possessed the key for both the production and the interpretation of the pictorial texts, even when their voices were silenced in texts such as Codex Telleriano-Remensis. If the missionary supervising the production of Telleriano-Remensis silenced his sources, this codex offers a point of entry into questions that can be further explored with colonial instances of Nahuatl texts that combine iconic and Latin script. Among the notable examples I will address in this book, I can mention here the *Historia Tolteca-Chichimeca* and the corpus of texts collected by the great Franciscan ethnographer Bernardino de Sahagún—namely, *Primeros memoriales* (1561), *Historia general de las cosas de Nueva España* or *Florentine Codex* (ca. 1579), and *Colloquios y doctrina christiana* (1564).

I will refer to Sahagún's texts less for the purpose of documenting speech that could be associated with pictograms in Codex Telleriano-Remensis than for further exploring the implications of producing texts in conjunction with Indian informants where the end was to lead the Nahuas to objectify their own culture. This objectification entailed telling stories that implemented their own ethnosuicide. One clear instance of paradigmatic texts for ethnosuicide is the bilingual confessional manuals that required Indians to tell the story of their conversion, of expressing their attrition and subsequent contrition for having honored false gods in their pagan pasts.[11] Another instance is the ethnographic inquests that demand that Indians tell the story of how they were conquered. These second kinds of stories range from the acknowledgment of the epistemological limits of discourses of magic (magical incantations have no effect on Spaniards) to the internalization of the ontological truths supposedly manifest in learning to reproduce three-dimensional pictorial perspective. In telling these stories, Indians were asked to narrate and show how they had turned themselves into normalized Western subjects. Telling these stories also entails the production of linguistic and cognitive instruments (grammars, vocabularies, and *cartillas*—reading primers—for teaching writing and reading; confession manuals; catechisms; sermons) for the destruction of native culture.[12] Codex Telleriano-Remensis belongs to this genre of texts that promoted ethnosuicide in assuming that the *tlacuilo* has internalized the superiority of Western epistemological and ontological values. And this is precisely the missionaries' assurance of control that the *tlacuilo* disrupts. The evangelical and epistemological instruments for ethnosuicide proved (and continue to prove) to be ineffectual when introduced to an *elsewhere* that exposes the limits of empire.

One may further expand the concept of ethnosuicide to include the participation in the collection of objects as an instance of desecration. There is defacement in the production of copies of ancient texts dislocated from the role images played in ceremonies or in the remembrance of ancestors. The production of scientific truths and the collection of artifacts in museums, whether in modern institutions or the cabinets of the sixteenth century, assume the potential to sap life from objects by turning them into historical evidence. Indian workers dig, translate, copy, and retrieve objects whose significance they would learn in the articles or the museum tags archaeologists and historians produce. By delegating the task of producing meaning to the specialists, native informants contribute to the desecration of their cultures. As such, participation in the historical and archaeological inquiries already constitutes an act of ethnosuicide. Obviously, indigenous subjects can be trained in scientific methods, in the technologies of conversion to Christianity, and to adopt Western protocols of interpretation.

One needs, however, to keep in mind that if ethnosuicide is an objective diligently pursued by missionaries in their production of catechistic instruments and the administration of the sacraments, these same instruments and processes, which took on a life of their own in versions produced by Nahua scribes, enabled Nahuas to develop a distance and critical consciousness with respect to the missionaries' contradictory conceptualization and definitions of evangelical methods. If the *tlacuilo* participates in ethnosuicide by producing copies of the ancient books that sap the life these objects had in the communities, her objectification of the missionaries, in turn, saps the force of the evangelical instruments that were to lead to her self-destruction. Lest one wants to reduce all missionaries to a uniform ideology, one ought to allow for missionaries who produced catechistic instruments that developed skills that would enable Nahuas to act in the legal, political, and cultural life of the colony. The call to commit ethnosuicide is perplexing, for it led the Nahuas to wonder why they were asked to destroy their culture and selves, but also to conceptualize the call to ethnosuicide from an *elsewhere* that by remaining inaccessible to the missionary observer — or, for that matter, to scholars today bent on insisting on the efficacy of colonial techniques of governmentality — makes its success all too dubious. In the production of knowledge for extirpation we witness the production of cultural artifacts that manifest an intentionality, in both the *tlacuilo* (or more generally the informant) and the objects themselves, that turns the call for ethnosuicide into ethnogenesis. The "new" objects the *tlacuilo* produces in responding to the missionaries become *actors* that elude the mastery of both missionary and *tlacuilo*. As such, the objects as *actors* form part of an ethnogenetic process that future generations take on and modify while remaining determined by them. We witness the paradoxical turn of ethnosuicide into ethnogenesis. In the objectification of culture and history in images remains the slippage that leads from self-destruction into healing and invention.[13]

These observations build on the ethical turn in anthropology and archaeology that has systematically insisted since the 1980s on vigilance for the violence one inflicts in the production of knowledge. However, scholars today tend to be too cavalier about the ethnosuicide involved in the training of informants for ethnography and labor for excavations—and thus in requesting natives' participation in the mummification of their culture in museums. Even though the awareness of mummification dates back to the 1980s, we scholars remain caught in the legacies of the disciplinary categories and often manifest a naïveté regarding the transparency of our informants. Beyond the awareness of being caught in institutional and authoritative binds, this book places an emphasis on the performativity of the informants and the objects they produce.

In the case of Codex Telleriano-Remensis, one faces the task of understanding a habitus that investigates another habitus, of observers who mutually place each other within a field of vision and hearing. It is worth recalling here that Aquinas's understanding of habitus, whether intellectual or spiritual, resides in and results from specific disciplines that in colonial practices would include the inculcation of logical attitudes and ways of caring for the soul in opposition to the *ancient wisdom* Indians are called to *ruin*. Those tasked with colonizing a Mesoamerican habitus, that is, of reeducating Indian subjects by means of the catechism, alphabetical writing, and pictorial perspective, ultimately faced the daunting prospect of producing a wholesale replacement of one habitus with another. It clearly escaped the missionaries that the "neophytes" could, as it were, cultivate the new habitus alongside the previous one without necessarily affecting the integrity of what made those subjects distinctively Mesoamerican: clearly colonial ladinos drew from different cultures but hardly merely reproduced medieval, Renaissance, or modern subjectivities. As we examine the uses of perspective and alphabetical writing, we come to realize the existence of wild or savage literacy, that is, uses of the alphabet outside the supervision and control of missionaries and lay officials. If perspective and the alphabet wished to colonize the mind of the Nahuas, these grassroots forms of literacy take on a life of their own in the passage from ethnosuicide to ethnogenesis. Some of these practices could be seen as mestizo, hybrid, or transcultural instances of appropriation that retain their specific form alongside indigenous forms. The quality of ladino need not be exclusively or predominantly or preferably that of mixed, in-between, borderlike, or hybrid forms; rather, ladino experience and practice can be understood as straddling discrete cultural forms, practices, and habitus. If the goal of colonization is to destroy the indigenous habitus either through imposition of a new habitus or simply by making the indigenous habitus inoperative, the categories of the mixed, the hybrid, the borderline, and the in-between would testify to the success of colonization. To paraphrase Homi Bhabha, though perhaps against the gist of Bhabha's argument, the colonial order seeks to engender natives that are "almost, but not quite," "almost, but not white."[14] This amounts to subjects seeking recognition not for their indigenous culture but for their ability to mimic the dominant one or, perhaps, for their ability to articulate equivalences between native and dominant culture (as in the dating systems in Telleriano-Remensis). As a result, the indigenous subjects become bound to perpetual tutelage under the semblance of "almost, but not quite." The *tlacuilo*'s return of the gaze exposes gaps in the constitution of a subject at fault. Her lessons reach beyond the immediate colonial world that sought to circumscribe her.

It is perhaps in the nature of *elsewheres* to introduce suffering, confusion, nihilism, and the end of history. It was an *elsewhere* that introduced havoc into Mesoamerica in the sixteenth century, but it is also an *elsewhere* that now (but already in the sixteenth century) has led the West to its own destruction (of metaphysics, capitalism, globalization), often by recruiting agents from these same *elsewheres* who have learned to dwell in plural worlds without abdicating their own. Given the exploitation of globalization, of capitalism, of terrorist administration of law, invasions from *elsewheres* to the West cannot but be saluted and adopted as a philosophical end. Arguably the best minds in philosophy today (Wittgenstein, Heidegger, Derrida, Nancy, Marion, but I would add sixteenth-century thinkers like Las Casas) have been busy bringing forth this destruction. With Nancy, we may characterize this destruction (indeed, the destruction of destruction) as revolutionary destruction: "It is permanent revolution, the possibility, at every moment, of opening space."[15] In this respect I view the *tlacuilo*'s return of the gaze as a moment in which revolutionary destruction comes to complicate the West's destiny from an *elsewhere*.

It is a reminder that in the face of current processes of globalization, whose beginnings may date from the invention of the Americas in the sixteenth century, we should be cautious not to assume the existence of a single world and history. Even when conceiving the task in terms of an open horizon of meaning or in terms of the undesirability of pursuing univocal sense, we must resist assuming that modernity is an all-encompassing historical reality. But then again, we must also resist the call to explain differences by inventing alternative modernities. The modern in its alternative modalities calls forth the denial of all exteriority to capital and globalization. Theories of alternative modernities have underscored that heterogeneous temporalities to capital are in fact products of the latter rather than rem(a)inders of precapitalist societies that dominant forms of modernity invent in decrying their obsolescence in a generalized call to abandon them.[16] Both the dominant and the alternative definitions of modernity entail the built-in teleology of the *pre-* in premodern as well as the supposition that the nonmodern in its coexistence with the modern must be static.

The concept of *elsewheres*, as I conceive it in this book, has enabled me to retain the possibility that the modern and the nonmodern coexist in a given culture and subject without incurring contradiction. In fact, the concept of *elsewheres* enables me to step out of the negative *non-* in *non-modern* that binds this concept to a denial or a reversal of the modern. It is in the essence of the modern to underscore the incompatibility of the modern and the nonmodern, indeed, to impose the iron-fisted historical logic that promotes the internalization of values aimed at the disappearance of the nonmodern. If the power of modernity reduces all exterior forms to its categories, we must also recognize—to cognize again, that is, intuit a different habitus, as in the *tlacuilo*'s picturing of the colonial order—the countering effects of the nonmodern as an *elsewhere* from which the modern (and its ability to generate binaries) is observed. The task of thinking a way out of the destructive, appropriative, and dominant forms of globalization demands that we acknowledge the places that determine and circumscribe thought within the history of Western thought.

The nominalization of the adverbial *elsewhere*—in the plural form *elsewheres* in the subtitle of this book—allows me to reflect on forms of difference that are not bound by a Same/Other paradigm. Etymologically, *else*, which has its Germanic origins in Middle Dutch *els* and Swedish *eljest*, resonates with the Latin adverbial form *alio* (to another place, elsewhere), from *alius* (another, different), but not with *alter* (other, as in the other of two) nor with *alienus*, the *allos*, everyone's other and the senseless. And yet *alienus* as "alien," or in Spanish *ajeno*, "not one's own," or even the French *ailleurs*, especially in its nominal use, approximate what I want to convey by *elsewheres*. I also use the term to undo binaries such as medieval and modern that create a paradigm that leads scholars to repeat a whole series of truisms about the people and the artifacts that are produced in these reputedly objective periods. *Elsewheres*, then, pose the limits of translation while at the same time point to the task of interrogating the categories, the concepts, and the interpretative strategies that erase and conceal the specificity of historical and cultural phenomena that we scholars may recognize as not our own.

The *tlacuilo*, of course, pertains to radical alterity in her existence as a singular subject, a self that brings forth the showing of the colonial world, and she also remains in radical alterity in her speaking and painting from the space of death. While her paintings bar us from entering her space and time, the intuition of the *elsewhere* from which the *tlacuilo* paints entails the recognition of intentionality, a life of their own for the pictorial forms she invents. But having said this, my reference to the *elsewhere* from which she paints also underscores the habitus she dwells *in* as a member of a collectivity *with* whom she inhabits the world.[17] Although habitus assume specific instances in singular subjects and cultural forms, a habitus always refers to a shared world.

Negation and propriety are fraught with the danger of reproducing the Same/Other paradigm and the kinds of statements one is bound to produce and repeat endlessly. The *not our own* suggests inversion by negation but also the assuredness of ownership. As I have pointed out above, the project of *elsewheres* entails the urgent task of inventing forms of thought not determined by the current habitus in the West that reiterates the will to mastery, appropriation, and domination. This invention would entail being aware of the ethnosuicide that contemporary research projects continue to promote in the production of knowledge. The *elsewheres* to current forms of thought would free us from the violence we scholars exercise when we act as if our categories were transparent. We ought instead to conceive the possibility that words such as *sacred, religion, apostasy, apostleship, art, morality,* or *philosophy* conceal the possibility of dwelling in different semantic spaces. On the other hand, the concepts of *habitus* or *background* have enabled me to intuit spaces of difference rather than to categorize positive referents. In the end, my appeal to different *habitus* or *backgrounds* offers an argument for learning and teaching non-European languages with their potential to lead students to experience, that is, to catch a glimpse into the existence of multiple discrete worlds.

Chapter 2

READING FOLIO 46R

As I sit parsing through Codex Telleriano-Remensis in the reading room at the Bibliothèque Nationale de France (Manuscrit Mexicain 385), I cannot avoid reflecting on the history of the collections of Mexican pictographic manuscripts in European libraries. Unfortunately, for good citizens like me, Mexican co-nationals have a reputation for attempting to remove if not actually removing artifacts from these collections to repatriate ancient and colonial Mesoamerican jewels.[1] Librarians and curators at European collections make a special effort to keep an eye on Mexicans consulting documents. Minimally, it is annoying to be caught in a web of suspicion.

I have been placed right under the librarian who surveys the reading room from a platform—a fine example of a benevolent Foucauldian pan-opticon. I have brought with me Eloise Quiñones Keber's facsimile edition to compare it with the original. Just a few minutes ago, the librarian came to me in a state of agitation, telling me, "Il ne faut pas faire ça!" Surprised, I looked up and asked, "Faire quoi?" He responded, "C'est interdit de le toucher comme ça!" His reprimand was intended to prevent me from mishandling the precious manuscript or, even worse, from mutilating it to repatriate it to Mexico. He was under the impression that I was flipping the pages carelessly, not noticing that I was examining the facsimile.

In spite of this unfortunate event that surprised me but also provoked embarrassment as the zealous librarian interrupted my absorption in comparing the original and facsimile of Telleriano-Remensis, I must add that the director of the collection Manuscrits Orientaux was kind enough to accommodate my request to consult the codex on a day when manuscripts were not available for consultation. Making this appointment involved the facile process of writing a letter to set an appointment. I underscore this because when I was at the Bodleian Library at Oxford, the curator had requested from me a detailed justification for seeing the original Codex Mendoza (ca. 1541), given the excellent recent facsimile edition and thorough documentation of the material aspects, to which he had contributed with an essay.[2] Bruce Barker-Benfield, the curator of Codex Mendoza, did not allow me to handle the manuscript, but was kind enough to sit next to me, in a closed room, for more than four hours examining it page by page. Though I didn't get to touch the original, I was fortunate to have the person most knowledgeable about the material conditions of the codex point out small details ranging from the patches used for its preservation to the folds created by the French corsair who bent it to fit it into his pocket when he first stole it from a Spanish galleon. André Thevet, the cosmographer of the king of France, eventually gifted Codex Mendoza to Richard Hakluyt. At the Bibliothèque Nationale, I am on my own, though in a public space, without the wise guidance of a curator. The earliest mention of Codex Telleriano-Remensis is in 1700, when Charles-Maurice Le Tellier (1642–1710), archbishop of Reims, donated it, along with five hundred other manuscripts, to the Bibliothèque du Roi. However, the manuscript remained lost in the archives until Alexander von Humboldt found it after his return to Europe from his journeys in South America and settlement in Paris in 1804. We owe the name Codex Telleriano-Remensis to Humboldt.[3]

I mention Codex Telleriano-Remensis and Codex Mendoza in tandem because both are colonial Nahuatl manuscripts that have been published recently in gorgeous facsimile editions. These two pictorial manuscripts were intended to reproduce ancient Mesoamerican forms of pictographic writing. As such, they are part of a history of mechanical reproduction that has benefited from technological innovations throughout the centuries. In this regard, Quiñones Keber, the editor of Telleriano-Remensis, rightly points out that her edition is the first instance of a faithful reproduction that benefits from the most advanced photographic technology. Recently the digitalization of documents has taken the art of reproduction one step further, enabling the dispensation of print. The first reproductions of Telleriano-Remensis were by Humboldt in his *Vues des cordillères et monument des peuples de l'Amérique* (1810), which included sixteen images in two plates. The first complete publication was by Edward King, or Lord Kingsborogh, in his *Antiquities of Mexico* (1830–1848), where he used Agostino Aglio's lithographies. The third moment in the reproduction history was E. T. Hamy's edition using chromolithography in *Codex Telleriano-Remensis* (1899).[4] The *tlacuilo*'s replica of the ancient Mesoamerican pictorial system for the Spanish authorities forms part of this history of mechanical reproduction. The *tlacuilo* does not produce a traditional pictorial text but a copy, a replica that provides information and stands for the original religious and historical books that served her as models. In responding to the request to reproduce Mesoamerican forms of pictography, the *tlacuilo* demonstrates her ability to participate in the Spanish system of representation that sought to make the native world visible.

Although the *tlacuilo* participates in the project of representing native culture, we need to avoid a language that reads the *tlacuilo*'s pictures with categories that, even when pertinent to the Renaissance aesthetic and epistemological project of visual appropriation of the American cultural and natural phenomena, would inevitably distort the specifics of Mesoamerican iconic script. For instance, the *tlacuilo*'s use of perspective could not be further from Albrecht Dürer's definition of it as "seeing through": "Item Perspectiva ist ein leteinisch Wort, bedeutt ein Dursehung (*Perspectiva* is a Latin word which means seeing through.)."[5] The *tlacuilo* was knowledgeable about the techniques of linear perspective and chiaroscuro. Her use of perspective, however, must be understood from within her *own* system of painting and writing in which we can trace the incorporation of three-dimensional perspective as one more signifier in a pictorial vocabulary devised for depicting the novelties of the colonial order.

Codex Telleriano-Remensis is the product of at least two subjectivities. On the one hand, we have that of the Dominican friars who requested the production of the codex and annotated it heavily; and on the other, the *tlacuilo* who paints the books comprising at least three genres of Mesoamerican pictorial texts: the *tonalpohualli* (count of the days), the deities associated with the twenty monthly festivities of the agricultural count, and the *xiuhpohualli* (count of the years). The latter record of human events, which also includes natural catastrophes and astronomical phenomena, comprises events that occurred before and after the Spanish invasion—it offers a history of Mexico-Tenochtitlan from its origins to the last date of 1563, forty-four years after Hernán Cortés's landing on the Gulf of Mexico in 1519.

The codex, one of the finest surviving examples of Mesoamerican manuscript painting, features a running pictorial display of these genres with Spanish annotations by different hands. The *tlacuilo* manifests an uncanny ability to invent new pictorial vocabularies for recording Spanish political, religious, and everyday artifacts. Notable is the minimalist use of cultural elements for defining the two main missionary orders of the Franciscans and the Dominicans. Whereas the reproduction of the *tonalamatl*, the festivities, and the record of human events before the conquest respond to the spatialization of native culture, the record of the events in the colonial period responds to the *tlacuilo*'s assignment to tell the story of how the Nahuas had been conquered.[6] Whereas one record seeks to document ancient culture, the other seeks to trace the colonization of the mind of the *tlacuilo*. What is recorded is not the account of the establishment of colonial order, but the incorporation and internalization of the technologies of the self, among which one should include the use of three-dimensional perspective and the Latin alphabet. In producing the requested replicas, the *tlacuilo* was located in the space where informants commit ethnosuicide in the process of objectifying their own culture. Folio 46r is a particularly rich colonial pictorial page for appraising the ethnosuicide at the limits of empire—a central concern of the thought experiment I am elaborating in this book.

Amatl, Liber, Buch

Folio 46r of Codex Telleriano-Remensis may be read in terms of the fragments that compose it as well as in terms of a unity that conveys a connection between the apparently disconnected scenes listed under the discrete years. But the years already pose a problem in that the glosses assume a transparency between the Mesoamerican calendar and the corresponding dating that homogenized time under the supposedly universal system of *anno Domini*. This assumed homogeneous temporality already points to ethnosuicide at the limits of empire in that the significance of the events apparently can be reduced to colonial events at the expense of the significance of the Mesoamerican calendrical entries. All events can be dated using *anno Domini* as if the identification in terms of the Spanish calendar consisted of a mere doubling that didn't entail the erasure of the significance these dates may have from within the Mesoamerican calendar. By considering the inclusion of the European dates as merely doubling the native dates, we would assume that all dating systems fulfill the same function of homogenizing time, but that would even be at the expense of the Judeo-Christian calendar, which, as expressed by the term *anno Domini*, is laden with a teleology. It is as if the *tlacuilo* and the glossator were practicing what has become the universal current practice of dating all events in history in all cultures using the Judeo-Christian calendar. And yet, there is a moment of uncertainty in glossing, in that it proceeds by addition in identifying the two dating systems. Take for instance: "Este año de diez casas y de 1541" [This year of ten houses and of 1541]. The *y/and* entails the possibility of reflecting on the significance of the dates according to the two chronologies.

The materiality of the paper and book format of Telleriano-Remensis also points to the fragmentation of this page and the sequence of folios.

In describing and commenting on this page, I don't follow the sequence of dates. To my mind, its linear conception of time is the least interesting aspect of this page. I find much more compelling the semantic and semiotic connections one may trace in the juxtaposition of apparently disconnected events on the given years of 10 House/1541, 11 Rabbit/1542, and 12 Reed/1543.

If this page retains the conventional structuring of the Mesoamerican annalist tradition, we must note a radical difference between the surfaces on which the ancient (as well as some colonial native) texts were painted and the surfaces on which Codex Telleriano-Remensis was painted. Whereas the former use native paper (*amatl* but also deerskin and cloth) and record the information in strips, large canvases, or folding screens, Telleriano-Remensis was painted on European paper, and the pages were assembled in a book form. The unity is in part the result of the limits imposed by the surface on which the pictographs where painted. The continuities between scenes, for the most part, correspond to the simultaneity of verso and recto folios in our experience of book structures. Whereas the flow from recto to verso entails discontinuity, the juxtaposition verso/ recto may lend itself to creating a continuous text. This sequence—verso/ recto—is particularly manifest in the sections of Telleriano-Remensis dedicated to the *tonalamatl* (book of the days) and the *veintena*, feasts of the twenty months of the agricultural year count. As for the *xiuhamatl*, the book of the years, often referred to as the annals, the strip of year sequences offers an apparently homogeneous series of dates under which events are inscribed.

There are two main sections in the *xiuhamatl* corresponding to Meso-american antiquity. The first series depicts the migration story and humble origins of the Mexicas (Aztecs): although the dates placed at the bottom of the page have a more or less consistent correspondence with place-names, the events are scattered all over the folios and the movement denoted by feet patterns suggests the meandering Chichimecas moving back and forth between recto and verso (Figure 4). Donald Robertson has reconstructed the sequence of events depicted in the discrete pages into a *tira* (a horizontal strip) in which he draws the connections of the footprints between the folios.[7] The dates are not colored with the characteristic use of *xihuitl*, the color turquoise that also means year. Although the strip of dates suggests a *xiuhamatl*, the lack of consistency and the combination of different pictographic forms suggest that the *tlacuilo* drew her information from a variety of sources formatted in diverse pictorial prototypes ranging from events organized according to year lists to events organized in terms of a

FIGURE 4   *Codex Telleriano-Remensis,*
fol. 27r. Courtesy of the Bibliothèque
Nationale de France, Paris.

FIGURE 5   *Codex Telleriano-*
Remensis, fol. 42r. Courtesy of the
Bibliothèque Nationale de France, Paris.

cartographic space. The second series of dates locate the time strip on the top section of the page and use *xihuitl* to color the years (Figure 5). The sequence of events from ancient times flows seamlessly into the colonial period as manifest by the structure of folio 46r (see Figure 1). Formally, the rupture between the migration story of the Mexicas is much more abrupt than the transition to the colonial period. In defining the formal characteristics of pictographic writing before and after the Spanish invasion, we must attend to the invention of new pictorial vocabularies for inscribing events, institutions, and people in consonance with the Mesoamerican tradition. Although I have reservations about a generalized use of the words *book* or *libro* to speak of the painted artifacts on bark, known as *amatl*, we should consider that the history of these European words hardly limits itself to the bound artifacts we know by these terms today, and even less to the Scriptures. Indeed, the etymology of *libro* takes us to *liber* in Latin that originally meant bark, and *book* dates back to the German *Buch*, and perhaps to bark of beech. In their etymologies, *amatl*, *libro*, and *Buch* would be equivalents, though the actual artifacts in the sixteenth century would be radically different. Only *amoxtli* (*amatl* and *oxitl*, paper and glue) correspond to the materiality of books made of bark. Let this observation stand as a warning against the reification of the concept of "book" in sixteenth-century Europe.

Now, if the materiality of the terms *amatl*, *Buch*, and *libro* refer to bark, the structure of the book, in which bound folios alternate, manifests a radical transformation in the experience of reading. I have mentioned the limits the recto/verso structure imposes on narratives that were painted on continuous surfaces of the folding screen, *tira*, or *lienzo* in Mesoamerica, but we must also note that in these Mesoamerican forms the whole "story" is present at one glance. There are folding screens in which there is continuity on the front and back, but even in these cases the totality of the two sides is immediately available. With the advent of the book form in the Middle Ages, the traditions of the scrolls (Jewish or Christian) underwent significant modifications.

Ivan Illich has traced two moments in the transformation of the experience of reading that are a direct result of pages bound in a book form. In his commentary to Hugh of Saint Victor's *Didascalicon*, Illich traces the transition from *lectio divina*, which consisted of a slow, meditative reflection on a given page, to *studium legendi*, which placed an emphasis on the accumulation of knowledge. Scholastics are primarily known for the latter form of reading, in which the page becomes an object for scrutiny. As Illich points out, "Hugh asks the reader to expose himself to the light emanating from the page, *ut agnoscat seisum*, so that he may recognize himself, acknowledge his self. In the light of wisdom that brings the page to glow, the self of the reader to catch fire, and in its light the reader will recognize himself."[8] We can clearly trace this form of reading in devotional texts such as catechisms, confessional manuals, and spiritual exercises, which in fact proliferated in bilingual Nahuatl/Spanish editions in sixteenth-century Mexico. However, the distinction may prove useful for understanding the technology used for the production of Telleriano-Remensis. If my reading of folio 46r has a closer relation to Hugh's emphasis on affect in reading, the objective was to use the book format with ample spaces left out for glosses. For Illich, the *Didascalicon* marks the transition between Hugh's generation that read with tongue and ear and the readers of the *Didascalicon* for whom "the book connoted much more the treasury, the mine, the storage room—the scrutable text."[9] He argues that this transformation in reading habits, and not the printing press, leads to the creation of paratextual technologies (indices, tables of contents, glosses, pagination, etc.) that enable speed, browsing, facile selections of passages, and in general a spiritual economy of reading.[10] Glosses further the objectification of the page as they guide the reader by framing knowledge and construing a connection between the reader and institutions. Whereas the logic behind the production of Telleriano-Remensis partakes of *studium legenda*, as it provides an album for the scrutiny of Mesoamerican forms of life and writing, the phenomenological reading I have been developing in this book remains closer to Hugh's understanding of the luminous page. As a consequence of this phenomenology that opens to the intentionality of the page and recognizes the self of the *tlacuilo*, folio 46r becomes a metaphor for reading the totality of Telleriano-Remensis and, beyond this codex, for reflecting on the colonial world and the postcolonial theoretical issues we bring to bear on the colonial past.[11]

THE EVENTS ON FOLIO 46R

In what follows I first describe the events, the historical personages, the institutions and practices depicted on folio 46r and then move on to discuss the ontological and epistemological implications of the subjectivities involved in its production. However, I will provide in-depth readings of these events and questions in the other chapters composing this book. As I have pointed out, folio 46r provides an entry point for discussing a broad range of indigenous and Spanish colonial texts. I am self-consciously avoiding the term *representation* to avoid a language that reads the *tlacuilo* using categories that might be pertinent to a Renaissance aesthetic and epistemological project of visual appropriation of the world but inevitably distort the specifics of Mesoamerican iconic script. In this sense, the *tlacuilo*'s use of perspective could not be further from Dürer's notion that perspective is a kind of "seeing through."[12] This is not because the *tlacuilo* was not knowledgeable about the techniques used in European three-dimensional perspective, but rather because her use of perspective must be understood from within her *own* system of painting and writing in which, indeed, we can trace the incorporation of European perspectival forms as one type of signifier in a pictorial vocabulary devised for depicting the novelties of colonial order. We may add that perspective is not a technology for "seeing through," as defined by Dürer, but is one element of the world imported by the Spaniards. Thus, the European system of representation assumes a symbolic function in the *tlacuilo*'s pictorial vocabulary that exceeds Erwin Panofsky's typology of perspectival symbolic forms: "Indeed, [perspective] may even be characterized as (to extend Ernst Cassirer's felicitous term to the history of art) one of those 'symbolic forms' in which 'spiritual meaning is attached to a concrete, material sign and intrinsically given to this sign.'" The *tlacuilo* observes the world from an *elsewhere* that dialogues with those perspectival traces of the real that, for Panofsky, entail as much "a consolidation and systematization of the external world, as an extension of the domain of the self."[13] Under one breadth the *tlacuilo* shows us the rudiments of three-dimensional perspective and exposes this European experience of the real as just one form of constituting reality.

A first moment in the reading of folio 46r would entail the recognition of the depicted objects—the annotator identifies some of the events, though he seems to have taken others as self-evident. The most enigmatic among them is the walking figure wearing a European hat, a straw suit, sandals, and carrying a walking stick next to the glyph for Tenochtitlan, the urban center where the Mexicas also known as Aztecs dwelled. Is he returning to or departing from Tenochtitlan? Where from? Where to? Perhaps he is going to or returning from the northern frontier, as part of the Central Mexican Indian contingents who joined the forces of Viceroy Antonio de Mendoza and suppressed the rebellion of the Caxcanes (known as the Mixtón War), as pictured and glossed on the left side of the page. The corpse floating on the top left is Pedro de Alvarado, who, the gloss for 1541 and 10 House tells us, died while fleeing the Indians, "yendose retrayendo de los indios." Among the most salient aspects of the *tlacuilo*'s depiction of the colonial order, I have singled out the succinct yet brilliant pictorial language she elaborates to differentiate the two friars as belonging to the main orders in Mexico. On the top right we face, or rather, a Franciscan friar faces us, dressed in the light gray habit characteristic of the Franciscan order; he wears a cincture, carries the Seraphic rosary, and holds a book, perhaps a *doctrina* or a *confesionario*. On the other side of the page we observe a Dominican, whom we recognize by the emphasis the *tlacuilo* has placed on the formal attire worn while imparting baptism, the preferred sacrament of the Dominican order that demanded thorough catechization before conferring baptism, in opposition to the Franciscan order that baptized multitudes without indoctrination. After baptism, the Franciscans would enforce Christianity by obligating the new Christian subjects to learn the *doctrina* and take confession. The annotator apparently felt no need to gloss these images. He must have felt the significance of the missionaries representative of the two main orders in Mexico, the Dominicans and the Franciscans, was self-evident.

In fact, the depiction of the two orders enables us to conceptualize the ways in which the *tlacuilo* produced pictograms for depicting the essence of the Franciscan and Dominican orders that followed the same pictorial principles used for depicting deities in the sections dedicated to the *tonalamatl* and the *veintena*. The identifying attributes provide a symbolic definition of the Franciscan and the Dominican philosophic-theological habitus, which is in fact encompassed by a Mesoamerican habitus. If the missionaries sought to colonize and dismantle the Mesoamerican habitus, they found themselves circumscribed by the same subjectivity they sought to transform. The taxonomy exceeds the simple identification of the traits that would enable the friars to recognize themselves in the folio. She manifests an uncanny ability to invent forms for depicting their essence in a comic mode. The performative force demonstrates an inexhaustible creativity.

On a most superficial level, the reader of folio 46r will perceive the inclusion of alphabetical writing that glosses the pictorial language. The care one scribe takes in writing the two major commentaries suggests a mestizo rather than a Spaniard; below I will state the reason why the scribe was *not* an Indian. Scholars generally agree that Indian scribes wrote the glosses in a script that replicates print. Consider, for example, the calligraphy in the inscription of "tierra" and "queçalcoatle" on folio 8v (Figure 6). As a sample of glosses by mestizo scribes, note the writing at the top left hand of folio 46r, which states, "Pº de Alvarado," to which another hand adds "cuando murió," when he died, to make sure we understand that the closed eyes denote a corpse. And this same hand was compelled to write "Sol" next to the European sun connected to the corpse. This second hand belongs to Pedro de los Ríos, the Dominican friar who often scratched and scribbled his commentaries in a crude hand on other folios (e.g., see Figures 6 and 7).

The main gloss on folio 46r under the depiction of an indigenous naked insurgent fighting a Spaniard on the other side of a river, written by the same scribe that identified Alvarado, informs us:

> Este año de diez casas y de 1541 se alzaron los indios de jalisco los cuales sujepto don antonio de mendoça murio don pedro de alvarado yendose retrayendo de los yndios al qual llamavan los yndios tonatihu que quiere dezir sol

> [In this year of ten houses and of 1541, the Indians of Jalisco rebelled. Don Antonio de Mendoza subjected them. Don Pedro de Alvarado died when he was fleeing from the Indians, whom the Indians called Tonatiuh, which means sun.]

Reading this, one wonders about the insistence on identifying the sun image with "Sol," since this information had already been supplied in the main gloss. It is self-evident from the addition "cuando murio" that Ríos

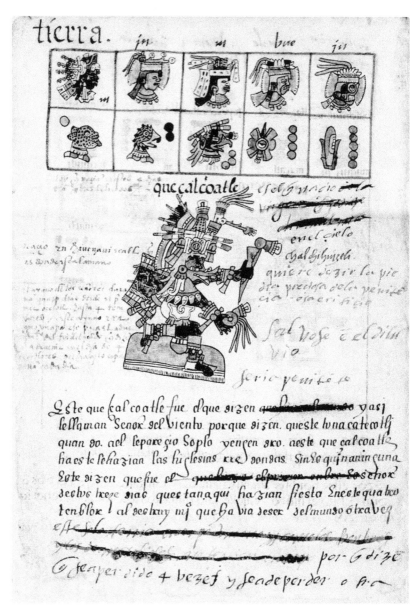

FIGURE 6   *Codex Telleriano-Remensis, fol. 8v. Courtesy of the Bibliothèque Nationale de France, Paris.*

is adding his notations to the gloss that identifies Pedro de Alvarado. I have inserted punctuation in my translation of the Spanish to facilitate reading the English text. The spelling of *tonatiuh* as "tonatihu" indicates that the writer lacked a solid knowledge of Nahuatl orthography; phonetically, the "hu" would erase the glottal stop of the final "h" with an inversion that made no grammatical or phonological sense whatsoever. The reference to "los yndios" calling Alvarado *tonatiuh* suggests that the scribe was not an Indian but a mestizo who limited himself to identifying the Spanish participants in combating the insurrection. Other sources identify the Indian rebel as the Caxcan leader Francisco Tenamaztle.[14]

These events, known as the Mixtón War, consisted of a rebellion in the northern frontier of New Spain that brought together multiple tribes. Spanish documents give the impression that the insurgents came close to driving the Spaniards from the land. There was indeed a generalized fear that all indigenous groups in Mexico would become infected by the rebellion against the Spaniards. This is a phantom that is more revealing about the Spaniards' reduction of a wide variety of ethnic groups with distinct languages, histories, and traditions to the generalized category of "indios." My point is not to diminish the magnitude of the rebellion but to put the scope and fear in perspective. Thousands of Indians from Central Mexico accompanied Viceroy Antonio de Mendoza in his campaign to suppress the uprising.[15] The gloss and other sources speak in terms of a complete defeat and subjection of the rebels. This was hardly the case, since the insurrection lasted for the better part of the sixteenth century, if not longer — one could actually argue that it continues up to our present day.

Pedro de Alvarado made the unfortunate decision to join Mendoza when he learned of the war while procuring food and water on the Pacific coast on his way to the Philippines. Antonio Tello, a Franciscan historian of the seventeenth century, mentions that Alvarado had dismissed the Indian forces by characterizing them as four Indian punks, "cuatro indios gatillo."[16] Alvarado was responsible at the start of Cortés's invasion in 1519 for the massacre of the Mexica elite while they celebrated, unarmed, the feast of the Toxcatl, perhaps the most significant feast in the Mesoamerican calendar. One cannot but hear a mocking tone in the scribe's indication that this most hated Spaniard died while fleeing, "yendose retrayendo de los yndios." In choosing to depict the corpse of Alvarado, the *tlacuilo* seems to celebrate his death in a depiction of the confrontation that lacks the certainty of the gloss's indication that Mendoza succeeded in subjecting them. Although there is no certain reason why a *tlacuilo* from Central Mexico would empathize with the insurgents from Jalisco — the armies accompanying Mendoza to the northern frontier included several thousand Nahuas from different locations from the basin of Mexico-Tenochtitlan— she certainly develops a pictorial vocabulary that places the two warriors on an equal footing. She seems even to favor the force of Tenamaztle, who bears no sign of defeat or death and actually towers over Mendoza. The only corpse is that of the infamous Alvarado.

The *tlacuilo* captures these radically different worlds by separating them with a depiction of a river that at once denotes the geographic feature and a symbolic use of the pictographic convention of water with drops and shells. The feather attire with flint stones on Tenamaztle's back defines the nativistic nature of the rebellion by connecting the insurgency with the god Tezcatlipoca, "Smoking Mirror" in Nahuatl (Figure 7).[17] He is not only a rebel but an apostate who has chosen to bolt from the tutelage of the Church and subordination to the empire. This escape from the universal history of Christianity could not be better emphasized than by juxtaposing the insurgency and the image of a Dominican friar, an apostle, in the process of baptizing and thereby introducing an Indian into universal history. The inclusion of apostle and apostate may be likened to the act of introducing a hand into a glove and then later turning the glove inside out. As such, the *tlacuilo* provides the reader with a topology of conversion and conquest. Note that 1541 corresponds to a period in which Franciscans and Dominicans were engaging in heated debates over the rites of baptism, and that one of the main Dominicans in these debates was Bartolomé de Las Casas. Given that Las Casas is well known for his detailed account of the murders, tortures, and abuses of Native Americans in *Brevísima relación de la destrucción de las Indias* (1552)—known to English readers after the 1656 translation as *Tears of the Indians*—we cannot fail to read this juxtaposition as a statement on the need to catechize Indians thoroughly before baptizing them to avoid apostasy.[18]

Pedro de los Ríos and other members of the Dominican order would have seen this juxtaposition of apostolate and apostasy positively, since it would seemingly confirm the emphasis they placed on thorough indoctrination and the willingness to accept baptism as measures to prevent apostasy. And yet they were troubled by the mirroring implied in the juxtaposition of the apostle and the apostate. Las Casas, however, would not have conceived the rebellion as an apostasy but as a legitimate act of war against the oppressors, as can be appreciated in his entry on the conquest of Jalisco in *Brevísima relación*. He first mentions the atrocities of Nuño de Guzmán, the first conquistador in the region during the 1530s, whose violence led to rebellion, taking refuge in the mountains, and killing some Spaniards,

FIGURE 7 *Codex Telleriano-Remensis, fol. 5r. Courtesy of the Bibliothèque Nationale de France, Paris.*

according to Las Casas, justly and with dignity ("se alzasen y fuesen a los montes y matasen muy justa y dignamente algunos españoles"). Las Casas then goes on to mention the actions of "otros modernos tiranos" [other modern tyrants] that led to the Mixtón War: "se juntaron muchos muchos indios, haciendose fuertes en ciertos peñones" [many Indians got together, making themselves strong in secure crags] (124). Note the very particular use of the term *modernos*; this should complicate a narrative of unambiguous modernization. Also remember that the Crown responded to Las Casas's denunciations of modern tyrants with the publication in 1542 of the *Nuevas Leyes* that demanded the dissolution of slavery and the *encomienda*, and generally sought to rationalize the administration and governance of the Spanish possessions. By pointedly questioning the attributed apostasy of the Indian rebels, Las Casas underscores the legitimacy of their insurgency.

We should also cite, in passing, Las Casas's treatise *De unico vocationis modo omnium gentium ad veram religionem*, which established love as the only valid way of attracting Indians to Christianity. For Las Casas, love is synonymous with reason and understanding, and so conversion motivated by love would have to proceed by appeal to the rationality of the Indians. Thus, in order to attract Indians to the true religion, missionaries had to presuppose and recognize a rational capacity in Indians. To do this, they had to be willing to address Indians in their own languages and categories. As a consequence of proclaiming "love" as the only legitimate motive for converting pagans, Las Casas would have to open himself to the indigenous discursive practices and systems of expression. This would, of course, not be possible if reason and understanding were identified solely with certain European forms, since it would amount to imposing foreign styles of reasoning that might have little impact on the Indians. If an Indian "jumping" into a fountain placed next to a Dominican dressed in full ceremonial dress underscores the centrality of baptism among Dominicans, in following Las Casas, we would have to inquire into the intellectual habitus that prepared the Indian for the reception of baptism and imparting of grace and, beyond this sacramental act, for incorporation into the legal and political administration of church and state.

Insurgency would be a consequence of a poor catechization that left Indians ill prepared not only for the ceremony of baptism but also for the full participation in colonial governance; if the latter were the case, insurgency would also reflect an unjust and poorly administered colonial order that allowed for systematic oppression of its Indian subjects. There is much more going on in this Telleriano-Remensis folio than a mere validation of

Dominican catechistic practices in face of apostasy. Given that Tenamaztle bore the Christian name of Francisco, he would fit into the category of apostate, especially in the literature that underscored the nativist inflection of the rebellion. When is a Christianized rebel an apostate? Would the superficial indoctrination of Tenamaztle's people by Franciscans, during the Nuño de Guzmán years, not count as baptism? Can there be legitimate apostates in Las Casas's view? Dominicans generally opposed conducting wars of extermination, "guerras a sangre y fuego," but would have fallen short of Las Casas's advocacy for restitution of sovereignty to Tenamaztle and reparations for the damages committed against his people.[19] The *tlacuilo* could not but be aware of these tensions and debates within and among the mendicant orders, the secular Church, and the Crown. Nor could the *tlacuilo* be indifferent to the new ladino subject of apostasy— after all, she is a ladino herself. But then again, who's not a ladino after European contact?

Under 1543 we find a depiction of a Franciscan friar holding a book, most likely a catechism or a confessional manual. Given that Dominicans and Franciscans engaged each other during the 1530s in heated debates over the proper preparation of neophytes and the latter's practice of multitudinous baptisms on demand, this image suggests the Franciscan preference for the sacrament of penance, which would ground neophytes in the faith after baptism. The maize plants at the foot of a block of stone topped by a sun may be read as reference to the implanting of the doctrine. The book could refer to Fray Juan de Zumárraga's *Doctrina cristiana cierta y verdadera para gente sin erudicion y letras: en que contiene el catecismo o informacion pa indios con todo lo principal y necessario que el cristiano deue saber y obrar* [*Christian Doctrine, certain and true, for people without erudition and letters: which contains the catechism and information for Indians with everything important and necessary that a Christian must know*]. As implied in this title, for Zumárraga, a *doctrina* should contain the most basic tenets of the faith that illiterate people, more particularly Indians, must know. The objective, clearly, is not to produce a text for thorough indoctrination, but a *doctrina* that would provide the most elemental knowledge in a simple and accessible language, so that "los niños en las escuelas y los indios que se enseñan en las escuelas y los indios que se enseñan en los monasterios comiencen a tartamudear en ella" [the children in the schools and the Indians who are taught in the schools and the Indians taught in the monasteries begin to stutter in it].[20] Observe, however, that Zumárraga's text is not a *doctrina* intended for Indians and children (a telling juxtaposition), but a treatise in which he lays out the rationale for writing minimalist catechisms, so that Indians learn to stutter ("tartamudear") the doctrine.

These radically different positions on catechization before baptism betray deep philosophical differences between the Dominican order and the Franciscan order that reflect their differing allegiances to Thomas Aquinas or Duns Scotus and Ockham. The difference between these schools resides in the primacy the latter places on the will over the intellect. As I have observed above, Las Casas argues that reason and understanding are the only two valid approaches to conversion. For the Franciscans, one baptizes, even by exerting force, so that God may bring forth grace. Such a position is put forth by Motolinía in his 1555 letter to Charles V:

> A V. M. conviene de oficio *darse prisa* que se predique el Santo Evangelio por todas estas tierras, y los que no quisieren oír de grado el Santo Evangelio de Jesucristo, sea por fuerza, que aqui tiene lugar aquel proverbio, más vale bueno por fuerza que malo por grado.

> [It is most pertinent to Your Majesty's office to *rush* the preaching of the Holy Gospel in all these lands, and that for those who do not want to listen to the Holy Gospel willingly, that it be by force, in that the proverb here applies, "better good by force, than evil by choice."][21]

The sense of urgency in "darse prisa" carries, as we will see below, a messianic impulse to bring all peoples into the fold of the Church before the end of time. Multitudinous baptisms would ensure the legitimacy of forcing "converted" Indians to listen to the Holy Gospel, but beyond disapproving of such methods, Las Casas deplores what would amount to forced baptisms, "a veces medio forzado."[22]

In reviewing the main events in this folio, we face the Indian walking in 1542, a year in which the gloss informs us there was an earthquake: "Este año de once Conejos y de 1542 vuo vn tenblor de tierra." This walker carrying a stick has an unusual combination of sandals, a status symbol, and a rudimentary dress made out of grass. He is also wearing a cap. Placed between the place sign for Tenochtitlan (the place of the flowering cactus on a stone) and the sign for earthquake (the glyph of movement on a patch of earth), the significance of the walker escapes us. Does he stand for the thousands of Indians from Central Mexico that relocated on the northern frontier when Mendoza went to suppress the insurrection? What stories of walking would the *tlacuilo* have had in mind when depicting this apparent rambling man? The small trail of feet indicates travel, but where to or where from escapes us.

As I have pointed out, the *tlacuilo* invents a pictorial vocabulary for depicting colonial religious and secular institutions, individuals, European objects, and spiritual economies of conversion. The *tlacuilo* records the sense of being observed and offers a return of the gaze in which the observer (the missionary) is surprised by the *tlacuilo*'s lucid record of the colonial order. I find this sense of reverse observation perhaps nowhere better captured than in the frontal depiction of the Franciscan friar looking out to the viewer of the image. In this looking back, the *tlacuilo* records a self-conscious understanding of three-dimensional perspective that instead of representing the features of an individual friar, as in European portraits, encapsulates the privilege Franciscans gave to the sacrament of penance. This inquisitorial gaze only appears in just one other image: on folio 44v (see Figure 3) depicting Fray Juan de Zumárraga, who held inquisitorial functions in the 1530s (the Holy Inquisition was not officially established in Mexico until 1571). These are the only two instances of frontal perspective in Telleriano-Remensis. If the depictions of the sun in folio 46r also seem frontal, they are clear quotations of a conventional European icon rather than attempts to render perspective itself. One cannot but recognize a symbolic use of perspective—indeed, according to Erwin Panofsky, perspective always carries a symbolic import—that ultimately points to the eyes of the *tlacuilo* looking back at us.

In returning the gaze, the *tlacuilo* captures a particular trait of the Franciscan order that would have made the Dominican observers reflect on how Indians perceived the different orders and their failing to properly evangelize the Nahuas forty years after the introduction of Christianity. In requesting a historical record, a *xiuhamatl* (a book of the years), that included a depiction of the colonial world, the missionaries found themselves portrayed by a subject who reminded them how fragile was the grounding of faith among the new Christians. The penitentiary vigilance of the Franciscans faces the imminent danger of apostasy at a time when missionaries from the different orders wondered whether the neophytes were disguising their old beliefs under the semblance of Christian practices. Missionaries and lay authorities feared apostasy because of the hardened subjects' savvy negotiations of the inner workings of the colonial order. The *tlacuilo*'s virtuous juxtaposition of apostle and apostate, for example, is marked by the Mesoamerican glyph of water. This defines an *inside-inside out* topology of conquest, while at the same time denoting the real water of baptism and raging rivers (as if it were an ironic allegory that stated one thing and meant another). The semblance of ladinos leading Indians into rebellion must have suddenly flashed before the colonial viewer in the *tlacuilo*'s sleight of hand that demonstrated mastery of European forms but for purposes that did not merely testify to effective indoctrination.

Missionaries taught alphabetical writing and perspective to promote reorganization of the Mesoamerican experience and framing of the real. If teaching these technologies was intended to transform Indians at the ontological level of their vision of the world, the missionaries in this pictorial instance faced wild forms of perspectivism; one can make analogous observations regarding wild literacy. Once the principles of three-dimensional perspective and the phonetic script were understood, the Nahuas could use this knowledge outside the teaching of the missionaries. Since there is no standard orthography for writing Nahuatl, the Nahuas use phonetic values in what anthropologists have characterized as wild literacy.[23] By the same token, the use of perspective as a symbol rather than as one mode of recording reality would also suggest unsupervised invention. Wild should be understood as the proliferation of these technologies beyond the semantic and semiotic controls of Spanish religious and secular authorities. Wild forms of perspective and literacy reminded them of how resilient was the habitus that incorporated European forms into a Mesoamerican visual background and techniques of painting. The symbolic use of perspective and general use of European techniques and objects call for a differentiation between the terms *representation* and *depiction*. Whereas the former captures objects in situation, the latter captures types.

In a series of entries in the *Tractatus Logico-Philosophicus*, Ludwig Wittgenstein distinguishes between *depiction* and *representation* in a way that illuminates the "portraits" of the Franciscan and Dominican friars in folio 46r.[1] To my knowledge, Wittgenstein never returned to this distinction, and scholars have ignored it in commentaries of the *Tractatus*, with the notable exception of Roger M. White in his guide to this seminal work. I could very well be taking Wittgenstein's distinction in a direction he didn't anticipate or might not have approved, but my purpose here is not to interpret Wittgenstein but rather to derive definitions of *depiction* and *representation* that lend themselves to a discussion of a broad range of forms, including caricature, political power, stereotypes, ideal types in botanical illustrations in both *natura naturata* and *natura naturans*, ideal social types, particular historical events, and so on. White's discussion amounts to a couple of paragraphs, and the essence of his observation resides in the following statement:

> Wittgenstein is distinguishing two different concepts for which he uses the words "Abbildung" and "Darstellung," both of which are in normal German translatable as "representation," but Wittgenstein's uses are to be differentiated. I follow both the translations of the *Tractatus* in rendering "Abbildung" as "depiction" and "Darstellung" as "representation." The distinction may be further clarified by noting that Wittgenstein always uses these terms with different objects: a picture depicts *reality*, but represents a *situation*.[2]

So much depends on the meaning of *situation* and *reality*. If all representations are also depictions, depictions are not necessarily representations of situations. Wittgenstein's language of representation and depiction, however, implies that such pictures always have a bearing on reality. Beyond the external world, pictures can be self-referential, as in the example of the picture of a clean-shaven Socrates (White's example), which we may judge as a *misrepresentation* on the basis of the standard depictions of Socrates as a bearded man. The domain of reality might range for Wittgenstein from the most naturalistic trompe l'oeil paintings to pictures in which "unrealistic" size serves to depict power, either in the form that Tenamaztle (the Indian leader on the hill in folio 46r) embodies as he towers over Viceroy Mendoza or that the Franciscan missionary preachers assume in relation to their Indian auditors in Fray Diego Valadez's engravings illustrating the *Rhetorica Christiana* (1579).

Wittgenstein's distinction between the terms *depiction* and *representation* enables us to understand the different kinds of pictures that the *tlacuilo* produced. Whereas depiction characterizes the Mesoamerican tradition of pictographic writing, representation corresponds to a particular moment in the history of the West, which in this case involves but neither absorbs nor dissolves the subjectivity of the *tlacuilo*'s picturing of Mesoamerican life-forms.

Let's begin the discussion of Wittgenstein with the following proposition: "A picture can depict any reality whose form it has. A spatial picture can depict anything spatial, a coloured one anything coloured, etc." (2.171). So much can be added to the et cetera. One could envision depiction as comprising formulas, musical scores, historical events and personages, social types, affects, deities, and so on. From there, Wittgenstein proposes: "A picture cannot, however, depict its pictorial form: it displays it" (2.173). We may wonder, however, whether pictures using the perspective construction might be read as depicting the effect of three-dimensional space as a symbolic form by playfully using anamorphosis to expose the rules of linear perspective. The fact that the *tlacuilo* uses European paper to be bound as a book, and that she left space for the inscription of glosses, makes her copy of the Mesoamerican writing system a representation of an ethnographic situation. This does not, however, mean that her invention of a pictorial vocabulary abandons the principles of depiction that we identify with picturing reality without representation.

Clearly pertinent is Wittgenstein's dictum regarding the impossibility that a picture "depict its pictorial form: it displays it" to the extent that what makes the gaze (*a fortiori* reality) visible cannot be made manifest — unless one were to engage and arbitrarily interrupt infinite regress. This proposition could be reformulated in terms of the impossibility of a *grammar of grammar*. We could add the notions of *background* (Ankersmit) and *habitus* (Bordieu) as limits that cannot be expressed without sliding into one more plane ruled by a new encompassing habitus or background. It would then follow that a picture can show a habitus (background or grammar) without depicting the form that makes it intelligible. The pictorial form must ultimately be recognized in depiction, hence Wittgenstein's specification that "what a picture must have in common with reality, in order to depict it—correctly or incorrectly—in the way it does, is its pictorial form" (2.17). The notions of "correct" and "incorrect" would have nothing to do with the sort of distortions one finds in caricatures, where the depiction is correct when the subject is recognized, though ethically questionable (incorrect) when a stereotype is created.

The second set of propositions regarding *representation* opens with: "A picture represents its subject from a position outside it. (Its standpoint is its representational form.) That is why a picture represents its subject correctly or incorrectly" (2.173). If in the case of depiction there is a correspondence between reality and form, Wittgenstein presumes an exteriority between representation and the object, which entails a distinction between a standpoint as representational form and the object of the representation. This exteriority sustains the correct and incorrect representation in terms of the adopted pictorial form. One could then speak of correct and incorrect uses of three-dimensional perspective as a particular adopted standpoint. But by the same token one could consider a picture in which the purpose is to play with multiple forms of perspective, as in a cubist painting. If a stereotype in depiction depends on the possible recognition of a reality, in representation the stereotype would become meaningful in a particular situation that wouldn't exhaust the elements that the depiction of a social type would render. Wittgenstein draws a parallel proposition to the impossibility that a depiction depicts its form: "A picture cannot, however, place itself outside its representational form" (2.174). Pictures that represent subjects would be bound to the adopted standpoint. This leads to the logical consequence that "a picture represents a possible situation in logical space" (2.202). In representation, the standpoint—between subject and object—is bound to the situation or state of affairs, whereas depiction pictures reality without consideration of standpoint, situation, or state of affairs. As such, representation presupposes a separation of the subject and object and thus grounds and enables the appropriation of the world. Wittgenstein would seem to suggest that depiction does not partake of the epistemic chiasmus associated with Descartes. Having said this, we must note that the representation of a *situation* is at once a depiction and a representation, whereas the depiction of *reality* can exist without being a representation.

Would it be accurate to say that *reality* consists of a logical structure that remains undisturbed by the singularity of a *situation*? For example, would a clean-shaven Socrates alter the reality of Socrates as commonly depicted with a beard? Would the singularity of a *situation* turn into a logical form by the fact of repetition, as in the gramophone disc that records a singular musical event but is reproducible without change: "A gramophone record, the musical idea, the written notes, and the sound waves, all stand to one another in the same internal relation of depicting [*abbildenden*] that holds between language and the world" (4.014)?[3] Does this mean that the same object, say Phillip Glass's *Songs and Poems for a Cello Solo* as performed by Wendi Sutter, may record a *situation* but becomes a *reality* in its infinitely possible iteration? It might seem odd that Wittgenstein apparently places the emphasis on the gramophone record capturing the logic of the musical composition rather than its status as an event, but the essence of the gramophone is the infinite iteration of the recorded performance, hence Wittgenstein stresses the picturing of its logic.[4] He further suggests the coexistence of depiction and representation in a picture when he states: "A picture depicts reality by representing a possibility of existence and non-existence of states of affairs" (2.201). Thus, the picture of the cello concerto would depict reality by representing the possible iteration of the singular performance. We can make a similar argument regarding the depiction of an event (a reality) that in a painting would represent the specific situation of a possible state of affairs.

Earlier in the *Tractatus*, Wittgenstein proposes the following sequence of propositions: "*That* is how a picture is attached to reality; it reaches right out to it" (2.151); "It is laid against reality like a measure" (2.1512); "Only the end-points of the graduating line actually *touch* the object that is to be measured" (2.15121). The reaching out defines the how, the *that is how*, while *touch* implies a depiction that can affect the possible situations it comes to represent. I would place the emphasis on possible situations that are potentially *touched* by a depiction of reality, which would differ from the case of representation that is always bound to a situation. Indeed there is a play between depiction and representation, in that the former can teach us how to see the world, and then bring the touching of the real into the specific details of the representation of a situation. The touching would also involve affect, as in the caricature that accentuates or distorts traits, thereby inducing a subject to view the world according to these characteristics, but also as in the affect that results when a subject finds itself mirrored in a depiction.

In the context of Telleriano-Remensis, the request that the *tlacuilo* objectify her culture by reproducing the pictographic system of writing seeks to *touch* Mesoamerican life by confining meaning to an uprooted existence. It conveys a form of controlling the reality by copying it. In this regard, the *tlacuilo* is producing a *representation* that would enable the missionaries to *see* the world. It partakes of the simple structure of such judgments as: "This *is* the Mesoamerican calendar, feasts, and history." In the context of the colonial world, the *tlacuilo*'s representation is caught in a parody that extends the mimetic capture of the power of the deities by including the neutralization of the power of the friars.[5] Bearing this in mind, let us now examine the collection and fabrication of pictographs and the inscription of glosses in Telleriano-Remensis.

CODEX TELLERIANO-REMENSIS AS AN ALBUM

We may further clarify the difference between *depiction* and *representation* by considering cases in the history of objectivity. In *Objectivity*, Lorraine Daston and Peter Galison focus their history of objectivity on developments in the art and science of creating images of objects, from the eighteenth to the twenty-first century. Whereas drawings of ideal plant and animal types manifest instances of depiction, photographs and other mechanical recordings of objects in specific settings that include maculae and all kinds of other particularities pertain to representation. Daston and Galison conclude their history of objectivity by marking the transition from representation to presentation that they identify with nanotechnology and nanomanipulation: "In this corner of science, the representation of the real—the use of images to finally get nature straight—may be coming to an end."[6] *Presentation* no longer aspires to copy what exists, but rather (at least in some formulations) to produce images that no one has ever seen, and moreover to produce haptic images as *tools* that enable us to manipulate reality. In their concluding chapter, they call attention to the long tension between representation (most explanatory) and intervention (most efficacious), and the intimate connection between epistemology and fear. Given their insistence on dating the "mental universe in which we moderns are now so at home" to "a scant two hundred years ago," it is perhaps misplaced to insist that this epistemic mutation could be dated earlier than the eighteenth century.[7] At any rate, historical narratives of *first time* remain suspect, and it is worth noting that in the end, Daston and Galison aspire to tell a story that bolsters the ideals of objectivity even while outlining the horizon of *presentation* in the demise of the "re-" that entails repetition. So, too, in their statement that "objectivity fears subjectivity, the core self," we may legitimately observe that this fear is never completely resolved, and we may wish to apply Bruno Latour's conception of *factishes* (beyond fetish and fact as discrete, readily accessible opposites) that reminds us that facts and fetishes *are* and *are not* fabrications:

> "Fetish" and "fact" can be traced to the same root. The *fact* is that which is fabricated and not fabricated . . . But the *fetish* too is that which is fabricated and not fabricated. There is nothing secret about this joint etymology. Everyone says it constantly, explicitly, obsessively: the scientists in their laboratory practice, the adepts of fetish cults in their rites. But we use these words *after* the hammer has broken them in two: The fetish has become nothing but empty stone onto which meaning is mistakenly projected; the fact has become absolute certainty which can be used as a hammer to break away all the delusions of belief.[8]

In fact, the term *fetish* does not figure in the language of the missionaries, but their efforts to expose idolatry and superstition would play a role similar to the breaking of the fetish to shards. The depiction of the gods in Telleriano-Remensis suggests a mode of neutralization that reduces them to album pictures recording their symbolic appurtenances, and forces the *tlacuilo* to paint their semblance in a "purely" secular context. Nothing occurs when "I tear the temples down" or when "I paint them" for purposes of extirpation. The gods would seem to flee from the world. But we twenty-first-century scholars are also immersed in the logic of factuality ruled by objectivity when we condemn the missionaries and refuse to conceive of Christian native subjects, projecting our expectations of a generalized resistance without realizing that the resistant subject of the postcolonial intellectual is the inverted image of the hard-hearted subject of the missionary. In Daston and Galison's invocation of "we moderns," one might hear an allusion to Bruno Latour's *We Have Never Been Moderns*, but in the tension between these two stories of the *self* of science, we will find our*selves* inscribed. Beyond the question of whether it is acceptable to date back the production of *albums* to the early modern era, we find ourselves caught in these *histories* of *objectivity*. For Daston and Galison, it is not just any self that defines "we moderns," but one caught "in a particular mental universe in which all that exists is divided into the opposed and symmetrical provinces of the objective and the subjective"; and yet there is no reason to find consolation in this apparent necessity or in limiting ourselves to the narrative they have chosen to tell.[9]

Following Wittgenstein's definitions of *depiction* and *representation*, I would argue that the project of producing and collecting *objects* by depicting ideal types and representing items in certain situations can be traced back to the encyclopedic texts missionaries and lay historians produced in the sixteenth century. Whereas *ideal types* depict the ideal reality of the given item, *items in situation* represent particulars in a state of affairs. The picturing of an ideal type has little or no concern with setting and situation, but instead aims to picture the general form. It is in this respect that a depiction of an ideal type would touch upon reality by leading the eye to details that might otherwise remain invisible.

I don't want to reduce Wittgenstein to Cartesianism, but there is an echo of Descartes in his discussion of solipsism first motivated by the proposition "I am the world" (5.63), which gains further clarity in the statement "The subject does not belong to the world; rather, it is a limit of the world," and finds full expression in the observation "Here it can be seen that solipsism, when its implications are followed out strictly, coincides with pure realism. The self of solipsism shrinks to a point without extension, and there remains the reality co-ordinated with it" (5.64). This line of thought concludes with the assertion that "the philosophical self is not the human being . . . but rather the metaphysical subject, the limit of the world—not part of it" (5.641). This "philosophical self" comes very close to the always absent subject of such ontological judgments as "the sky is blue," which is grounded in a third person with no connection to the subject of the enunciation. Further developing the insights of the Port-Royal logicians, Louis Marin arrives at a series of insights that resonate with Wittgenstein's proposition regarding the nonexistence of the subject "that thinks or entertains ideas":

> Judgments such as "the sky is blue" or "the earth is round" can thus be rewritten as follows: "it is, blue the sky" or "it is, round the earth." In such utterances "it," the subject of the verb "to be," functions as purely neutral marker of the indescribable emergence of a given thing's being. As a result, "it" excludes all reference to a subject of representation and discourse.[10]

The form "it is, blue the sky" entails a chiasmus between mode and substance that calls forth a system of language that circumscribes the utterance within the field of representation. In Wittgenstein's terms, the utterance "the sky is blue" *stands for* the exterior world. In this respect, judgments and propositional pictures participate in the judicial regimes through which science defines the legitimacy of representation (it follows the rules) and the right to appropriate the represented object (it belongs to the subject—collective or individual—of the judicial ontological statement). The process of defining the object's properness (lawful and property) entails the subject's ownership. The comparative act that establishes the connection between "sky" and "blue" subsumes one entity into another that is constituted as a subject passing judgment on the world.

Of what use are Marin's and Wittgenstein's terms for understanding early modern pictures of the world and, even more specifically, for understanding Mesoamerican pictographs? The Cartesian split between the subject and specifying predicates regarding the centrality of verbs, more particularly of the verb "to be" in the Port-Royal grammars, may very well amount to a formalization of epistemic transformations already applied to describing and classifying what seemed unprecedented about American nature and culture in the sixteenth century. Beyond the question of the ontological status of linear perspective, Louis Marin has reminded us of the connection between the subject of spatial perspective and the subject of linguistic utterances in the grammars of Port-Royal. In spatial perspective, we find in the picture offering a representational window onto the world a split between the subject and object, which is mediated by the picture; such pictures bear the same formal structure as utterances in which verbs function as nominative judgments about the world that constitute the being of things—for example, "the sky is blue" entails a subject passing judgment on an object, for which the mediation and status of truth resides in the utterance-judgment that functions as a representation. The commonality between pictures and verbal judgments would entail what Jacques Lacan defines as the "subject of science."[11] This regime of science vis-à-vis magic, myth, the religion of the "other" (for sixteenth-century missionaries, Christianity is identified with science in opposition to superstition and idolatry) posits a (potentially) colonized subject that would now police his or her connection to the gods, as well as to spiritual agents, animal and human, that are defined as deceptions. The science that defines myth, idolatry, and superstition constitutes a position for countering the influence of Satan. The subject of science underlies and enables the application of perspective and the imposition of judgments, defining the technological discourse of the self that was implemented in written discourses as well as in the confessional. In depicting the Franciscan in a frontal view as seeing us, the *tlacuilo* indeed captures the friars' powers of observation.

In reading Codex Telleriano-Remensis, we have to attend to the differences between the process of appropriation in the depiction of ancient and colonial Mesoamerican *things* and the glosses that define the "it is" of the *things*, e.g., "otra vez la fiesta de Tezcatlipoca porque se hazia tres veces en el año" [once more the feast of Tezcatlipoca because it was celebrated three times in the year] (fol. 5r; see Figure 7). Do we witness incompatible forms of appropriation and incommensurable modes of signification not only between the systems of painting and writing, but also between the uses of writing and painting in different sections of Telleriano-Remensis? From all appearances, Ríos was satisfied with the paintings to the extent that he does not intervene; however, he often found the written observations wanting or mistaken. In addition to glosses that identify the pictures, we find a disagreement between the different annotators, most visible in the erasures of Ríos, who scratches out words, sentences, and whole passages but also destroys the aesthetic and epistemological integrity of the folios with careless calligraphy that we cannot attribute just to bad handwriting, but must instead see as invasive and perhaps also indicative of an attitude of condescension toward the class of indigenous and mestizo scribes who cultivated their handwriting (see Figures 6 and 7).[12] The Spanish nobility notoriously prided themselves on their inability to write clearly, thus distinguishing themselves from scribes and *letrados*. We can assume that mestizos or Indians trained by the Dominicans wrote the carefully drafted inscriptions that sometimes approximate print. However, the intellectual content of the glosses does not necessarily reflect their ideas or native tongue.

The scratches, corrections, and additions may very well be indicative of tensions within the Dominican order: the neutral descriptions would imply an affinity with Las Casas's views on the compatibility of Mesoamerican life-forms with Christianity, which was opposed by other members of the order who advocated the need for the complete extirpation of the native habitus. I would argue that the pictures of the Dominican and the Franciscan friars on folio 46r are indicative of the *tlacuilo*'s grasp of the irreconcilable philosophical differences between the two orders; being responsive to the sensibility of the Dominican faction led to interrupting production four folios later and to correcting retrospectively the content of the glosses. For instance, the identification of the god Xolotl with twins and everything born in pairs, "dizen que era el señor de los melliços y todas las cosas que nacian juntas" [they say that he was the lord of twins and all things born in pairs], carries addenda by Ríos, "que nosotros llamamos mellizos o cuando la naturaleza obra alguna cosa monstruosa, fuera de lo acostumbrado" [that we call twins or when nature produces something monstrous, out of the common]. Ríos adds that those born on the days ruled by Xolotl, "serian mal fin y bellaco" [would end bad and be evildoers] (fol. 13v). Ríos's second round of annotations interpolates information to further define the significance of the dates beyond the initial description. These hands correcting each other suggest not only an internal disagreement among the Dominican friars supervising the production of Telleriano-Remensis, but also semantic and semiotic slippages in the paintings whose significations were not readily grasped by the annotators. It is not a question of insufficient knowledge or skills on the part of the *tlacuilo* or the indigenous or mestizo scribes but of the force the images capture manifesting a life of their own. Nor is it a question of a resistant *tlacuilo*, though her playfulness may be taken as such, but rather of the paradox the friars faced when they were surprised by the *tlacuilo*, who responded in ways they did not expect. I say paradox because the Dominicans were particularly keen on the idea that the Nahuas were subjects immersed in a habitus that continually produced new significations (superstitions, idolatries) out of recently introduced European objects and practices. Why shouldn't they have anticipated the playfulness of the *tlacuilo*?

The impulse to appropriate Mesoamerican culture by pictorially representing it carries a burden: the representation and the subject of the representation exceed the meaning the glosses would like to establish as a way of reducing *things* to a judicial regime. The *tlacuilo*'s forced participation in the subject of science, that is, her ability to paint the semblance of the gods for the purpose of objectifying her own culture, results in the unexpected effect that the *tlacuilo* objectifies the colonial order and thereby, even if only slightly, eludes its power of representation by codifying the system that was intended to further the erasure of the Mesoamerican habitus. There is a striking similarity in the ways the *tlacuilo* writes the pictographs of the deities and the depictions of the Dominican and Franciscan orders. The latter are made up of traits that define their spiritual power in a manner not unlike the deities whose appurtenances codify their spheres of influence.

The Codex Telleriano-Remensis and a wide range of similar collections of information on pre-Columbian cultures must be understood as early instances, in the history of objectivity, of albums that collect images of the world. These album-codices include pictures of deities, plants, animals, and everyday objects, but also verbal prototypes of songs, incantations, prayers, historical narratives, and creation stories pertaining to Mesoamerican cultures.

If coordinated by a European missionary or lay official, native informants (as in the case of Telleriano-Remensis) often produced the pictures and verbal records. As such, the paintings and written glosses not only offer a glimpse of the depicted subject matter but also manifest the habitus of those who requested the materials as well as of those who produced the actual albums and chronicles. In the process, the *tlacuilo* included in the album pictures of missionary and lay officials, as well as various European objects, animals, attitudes, and standpoints that those who requested them didn't seem to have anticipated. Thus, the observer found himself observed. One cannot but see in the depiction of a frontal Franciscan a return of the *tlacuilo*'s gaze that exposes the gaze of the missionary.

The depictions of the Franciscan and the Dominican constitute them as items in an album that would in the end be more meaningful for the Nahuas than for the missionaries that supervised its production. Indeed, for the latter, the depictions might have seemed offensive, given the caricaturesque simplicity that captured the essence of the orders. In these portraits of the friars, the *tlacuilo* neutralizes the power these orders exercise, each in its own style of evangelization, on the Nahua subjects. This is a form of exerting power by means of mimetic mirroring in which the observer finds himself observed, indeed captured, by the objectification of the system of belief and evangelical practice (as well as the intense disputes regarding the administration of baptism and their implied relativism manifest in the differences between their philosophic-theological traditions) that the friars would have preferred to remain invisible to the Nahuas. And then again, the *tlacuilo* power of depiction could very well reside in a field of vision located *elsewhere* than the points of view of the missionaries.

The Dominican friar wearing a highly stylized white costume in folio 46r, which looks more like baggy pantaloons fastened below the calf than the Dominican habit, lends the image a joyful playfulness that connects to the joy of the nude Nahua, wearing just a *tilma*, receiving the waters of baptism. One cannot but think of the Nahua as appearing to jump into the baptismal font just as the friar seems ready to burst into a dance. There would be motives for celebrations, since baptism was the final step in a long process of indoctrination that involved the Nahuas' recognizing fully the consequences and significance of accepting baptism. The ceremonial dress, which along with the white pantaloons includes a liturgical stole, would have been conspicuous to the friar supervising the production of Telleriano-Remensis. One may assume that it rubbed him the wrong way, considering that the *tlacuilo* was removed from her task a few pages later, where coarse scribbling by Pedro de los Ríos replaced the pictures of the *tlacuilo* (see Figure 8). The semblance suggests the economy of a caricature that accentuates the spiritual traits of the depicted subject. The pantaloon-like attire reproduces the finery of the Dominican white tunic, which would lead Nahuas to observe the exquisite attire of the order in everyday catechizing, imparting mass, baptizing, or just walking on the streets of towns.

The semblance of the Dominican contrasts starkly with the Franciscan sitting on the right side of folio 46r (see Figure 1) under 12 Reed and above a monolith with a European image of the sun, a motif also used to name Pedro de Alvarado (known as Tonatiuh, "sun" in Nahuatl), who appears as a corpse suspended behind the Dominican friar. At the base of the monolith we find two maize plants, perhaps wilted by excessive heat and hence an allusion to the strength of the sun—scholars may further document that the date 12 Reed was a year of drought in the Central Mexican calendar. I am inclined, however, to associate the two maize plants (wilted or not) with the planting of the faith symbolized by the sun atop the monolith. Otherwise how do we explain the monolith? It would make sense to associate the stalks with the imparting of the catechism, given that the Franciscan is holding a *doctrina* or *confesionario*, both instruments for evangelization. The habit of the Franciscan consists of the traditional full-length robe made of rough wool, a huge Seraphic rosary, and the triple-knotted cincture emblematic of the vows of poverty, humility, and contemplation. The Franciscan and the Dominican surface as ideal types defined by their habits, religious paraphernalia, and preferred sacraments (penance vis-à-vis baptism), attributes that distill the identities of the two orders. But there is one more element that distinguishes the Franciscan and merits a detailed discussion, namely, the use of perspective.

TO NEUTRALIZE THE FRIAR'S EVIL EYE

In *Perspective as Symbolic Form*, Erwin Panofsky drew an exhaustive inventory of the symbolic forms perspective has assumed in the West at different historical moments ranging from Greco-Roman Antiquity to the Quattrocento and Cinquecento. He derives from Albrecht Dürer a definition of perspective that places the emphasis on seeing through: "Item Perspectiva ist ein lateinisches Wort, bedeutet eine Durchsehung (*Perspectiva* is a Latin word which means 'seeing through')."[13] Panofsky goes on to emphasize his understanding of perspective as a window: "We are meant to believe we are looking through this window. . . . The material surface upon which the figures or objects are drawn or painted or carved is thus negated, and instead reinterpreted as a mere 'picture plane.'"[14] Although Panofsky draws examples of projections representative of "an immediate sensory impression or . . . a more or less 'correct' geometrical construction," he argues that theories of perspective as invented in the Quattrocento betray an error: "Perspectival construction ignores the crucial circumstance that this retinal image—entirely apart from its subsequent psychological 'interpretation,' and even apart from the fact that the eyes move—is a projection not on a flat but on a concave surface."[15] Hubert Damisch has argued that Panofsky confuses the theory of optics and the structure of the retinal concavity with the experience of vision: "[Panofsky] confused the effective conditions of vision with the optical process that led to the formation of an image on the internal surface, concave, of the retina; it is evident that his confusion led him to just recognize in the construzione legittima a relative validity."[16] Panofsky and Damisch exemplify opposites in debates over the nature of perspective: perspective as a code that betrays a pictorial convention vs. perspective as a paradigm for apprehending reality. The debate would include Nelson Goodman and E. H. Gombrich as illustrious representatives of the opposing views. Samuel Y. Edgerton sums up the terms of the debate when he writes:

> While it is true that geometric perspective did eventually become a culturally prejudiced encoding system, I stand with Gombrich in believing that this Euclidian construct is *not* inherently culture-bound. Western Renaissance-style pictures still reproduce, as no other art form can, the true surface characteristics of the phenomenal world as they are optically transmitted point by point into the human eye by the reflected ambient light.[17]

Whether the system of perspective provides a window for observing the world or betrays a code that demands habituation to be understood, the representations pass judgments on the world. In the colonial catechistic culture, the subject of perspective and enunciation must respond to regulative doctrinal statements (i.e., God is three and one, or your gods are false deities) and to visual pictures that offer windows onto the natural world and leave no room for depictions of Mesoamerican deities. Such pictures depict a world cleansed of aberrations, even when the same system of representation portrays demons, scenes of hell, and prefigurations of doomsday. If one were to place an emphasis on the conventional nature of perspective, the depiction of a Franciscan in a frontal position sitting on a cube could be seen to manifest the *tlacuilo*'s understanding of techniques of perspective. Perspective would seem to operate as *habituation* (to borrow Nelson Goodman's term), but this ability to portray objects in perspective would be a rather facile acquisition if one simply took the *tlacuilo*'s ability to reproduce perspective as a symbolic marker of confessional and inquisitorial vigilance even if her use of perspective seems faulty. The *tlacuilo* lays out a radically different use of perspective in her uses of perspective-as-a-discursive-fragment rather than as part of a system of representation. We must attend to the ways the *tlacuilo* cites perspective as one more European form embedded in a cluster of symbols. It is, perhaps, not a coincidence that the *tlacuilo* depicted the friar sitting on a cube, the example par excellence in phenomenology of the impossibility of viewing the totality of objects. Does the cube as an instantiation of the concealment of the world provide a symbol for the inaccessibility of the subject under confession? Does it constitute a reminder of the inaccessible *elsewhere* from which the *tlacuilo* observes the friars? For the purpose of examining the depiction of perspective in folio 46r, we must assume that the *tlacuilo* was familiar with geometrical perspective and the *camera obscura* even when her use of perspective might seem faulty. In this regard, it is pertinent to mention Gombrich's observation that if it took centuries to discover the secrets of linear perspective and chiaroscuro, once acquired, these techniques can be transmitted in the span of a few days.[18]

Following Merleau-Ponty, Marin has written that "the third dimension is invisible, for it is nothing but our vision. It cannot be seen because it does not unfold under our gaze, for the simple reason that it is our gaze." Marin goes on to cite Merleau-Ponty to the effect that "what makes depth invisible for me is precisely what makes it visible for the spectator as breadth: the juxtaposition of simultaneous points in one direction, which is that of my gaze." As we read Telleriano-Remensis and other Mesoamerican codices, we may construe the use of profile as a choice for conveying depth as breadth—not as pictorial limitation—as a spatial turn in which the subject has to leave its point of view and "think itself elsewhere, outside its plane of vision."[19] The *tlacuilo*'s juxtaposition of the Dominican in profile, yet depicting the movement of the left arm administering the baptismal waters, and the Franciscan in a frontal view, suggesting both volume and shallow depth, plays with the sense of *elsewheres* that enable subjects to dwell in (as well as shift between[20]) different points of view and planes of vision. Is the Dominican's use of the left arm to impart baptism an indication of calquing as in Caravaggio's *Bacchus*? The debate on the ontological status of perspective has little or no bearing on the *tlacuilo* when she is interpreted not as producing a window "to see through" (Dürer by Panofsky) but rather as depicting perspective as one of the appurtenances that saturate the picture of the Franciscan on fol. 46r with inquisitorial and confessional signification.

Given that the projection of objects and figures onto a picture plane conforms with the creation of stelae before the Spanish invasion, we may assume that the effect of perspectival depth would have been recognized, even though frontal facial views were not a practice in pictography or on vases in which the conventions always called for profile drawing against a flat background as the primary indicator of breadth and amplitude. Pictures in profile can be read as conveyors of depth as breadth in a system of representation that suggests the layering of objects without concealing them (one consequence of perspectival recession). Within the convention of portraying faces in profile, the creation of volume and breadth is something one can appreciate in both Maya and Nahua pictures. This would suggest that the notion of the perspectival window of the world would have been readily understood without requiring that this representational system be learned as a code. I say this because we twenty-first-century observers of photography and painting may find ourselves unable to recognize objects. By drawing a link (but without erasing the difference) between linear perspective and illusionistic perspective, one may further explore the question of whether perspective itself calls for learning a code, hence a habituation. I find unconvincing the argument that the sixteenth-century Nahuas would have been incapable of experiencing deception in trompe l'oeil.[21] After all, Mesoamerica was filled with tricksters and artists who performatively fashioned simulacra.

Rather than mystifying the knowledge of perspective, we should assume that even if perspective was not readily recognizable, its conventions and techniques were quickly learned by the Nahuas. The degree of mastery is perhaps nowhere more manifest than in the *tlacuilo*'s ability to depict perspective as a representational paradigm rather than using it to "see through," as Dürer defined *perspectiva*. Moreover, the apparent limitations we may discern in using flat surfaces rather than spatial depth were equally characteristic of certain Spanish prints and paintings.[22] At the risk of sounding Eurocentric (can this be avoided when using a European language and discourse?), I would cite Edgerton's observation on the global impact of linear perspective and chiaroscuro: "Thus Western Renaissance art has influenced so many non-Western cultures not because it is imperialistically imposed but because it works more convincingly—more like natural perception—than traditional, even locally accepted magic representations."[23] God forbid that sixteenth-century Nahuas should have been fascinated with the art of linear perspective or, for that matter, with phonetic writing. This fascination would, of course, not necessarily mean that they were unaware of the theological implications linking linear perspective to the missionaries' evangelical project by way of the notion that "pictures rendered in perspective permitted human beings to see the world just as God conceived of his creation."[24]

In claiming that the Nahuas recognized perspective, we return once again to the question of the difference between depiction and perspective and observe that on folio 46r the *tlacuilo* has not represented a Franciscan in a particular Franciscan situation; rather, she has utilized perspective as an attribute that serves to capture the Franciscan condition. Beyond the association with the confessional scrutiny and the inquisitorial interrogation, the gaze of the Franciscan further implies a connection between Euclidian geometry and the notion that God the Logos is the source of creation. For missionaries in sixteenth-century Mexico, teaching perspective implied making manifest the nature of reality not only because they assumed linear perspective produced the correct view of the world but also because the implied rationalization of vision would correspond to how God sees and orders the world.[25] Learning to see the world in geometrical forms would constitute one more element in the indoctrination of Indians, something to which the *tlacuilo* would seem to be alluding in the depiction (imperfect as it may be) of a cube that (to my eye) recurs in the form of the cube-shaped head. The frontal view of the Franciscan that captures the friar's gaze would have the additional effect, analyzed by Merleau-Ponty and Lacan, of allowing the viewer to experience the world (painted or not) as if its objects looked at the observers. This is not the place to explain Lacan and Merleau-Ponty, so I will limit myself to noting that Lacan differentiates between the eye, in which "geometrical perspective is simply the mapping of space, not sight," and the gaze as an experience of inversion through which the subject finds itself observed by things in the world. To the trompe l'oeil (the illusion created by the semblance that painting is something other than it is) and the *dompte-l'oeil* (the taming of the gaze that leads to the lowering of the eyes), we must add the *clein-l'oeil*, with which the *tlacuilo* provides a self-reflective statement about her clever depiction of the missionary orders. The *tlacuilo* frustrates the appetite of the eye that must be fed, "the eye filled with voracity, the evil eye."[26] The *tlacuilo* introduces a macula, a speckle, into the missionaries' visual field, into their perception of the album collecting Mesoamerican objects for their observation, classification, and control.

The frontal depiction of the Franciscan has as its complement the profile view of the Dominican. The depiction of the Dominican is not completely devoid of linear perspective, as the image also embodies volume. The apparently awkwardly drawn left arm captures the movement of pouring the holy water. The gait of the Dominican shown in the act of baptizing signifies the joy of sacrament given and received in full cognizance of the doctrinal implications and political obligations of accepting the Christian faith. Whereas the Franciscans would administer baptism before properly catechizing Indians, hence without informing them of their obligations, the Dominican emphasis on proper evangelization prior to baptism implied informing Indians of the doctrinal and political obligations. This is the crux of the difference between these two religious orders that the *tlacuilo* adroitly captures in her depiction of the two orders. It is an image that Las Casas and his followers would have found fascinating but one that his more repressive brothers would have found questionable. The prominence of the left arm pouring the baptismal waters suggests that the depiction of movement was one of the objectives in the artist's application of perspective. Beyond the movement of the arm, the Dominican radiates spiritual joy in the gait. At the risk of sounding anachronistic or ahistorical, I will allude to a passage in which Merleau-Ponty cites Rodin to the effect that one of the differences between photography and painting resides in that the latter seeks to record movement while the former inevitably embalms life: "Painting searches not for the outside of movement but for its secret ciphers, of which there are more subtle than those of which Rodin spoke. All flesh, and even that of the world, radiates beyond itself."[27] The emphasis would reside obviously not in the difference between photography and painting, but rather in the connection between painting, space, and movement from Altamira to Rodin and, indeed, in Mesoamerican paintings. What might at first sight seem an aberration in the picturing of the left arm as if protruding from the chest may be read against sketches with equal awkwardness by Leonardo da Vinci or Dürer experimenting on drawing movement. In fact, the *tlacuilo* could have derived the experimentation with movement from the multiple sketches by Dürer circulating in sixteenth-century Mexico. The missionaries' pedagogical effort introduced the Nahuas to images and technologies designed to instill three-dimensional perspective. Indeed, the use of the left hand suggests a comment on *camera obscura* as an optical device that produces inversions.

In reflecting on the depiction of the essential traits that define Franciscans and Dominicans, the *tlacuilo* could very well be seeking to protect herself and her community from the evil eye, from the destructive fury of the missionaries' will to objectify Nahua culture. Then again, the depiction of the two monastic orders might have fulfilled a taxonomic function, enabling the Nahuas to understand and place in *perspective* the two main lines of indoctrination. As argued by Marin, it is the case in all forms of representation, whether in the mode of the judicial sentence (e.g., this is a Dominican, this is a Franciscan) or that of the pictorial form, that a sense of empowerment is being exercised over the represented. We may further liken this practice to Michael Taussig's observation on Cuna figurines: "Yet the important point about what I call the magic of mimesis is the same—namely that 'in some way or another' the making and existence of the artifact that portrays something gives one power over that which is portrayed."[28]

PERSPECTIVE AS VIGILANCE

In this chapter I have argued that the *tlacuilo* invents a pictorial vocabulary for depicting colonial religious and secular institutions, as well as individuals and objects of which they are composed. The *tlacuilo* also alludes to spiritual economies of conversion. She records the sense of being observed by the colonial regime and offers a return of the gaze in which the observer is surprised by the *tlacuilo*'s lucid record of the colonial order. In this looking back, the *tlacuilo* reveals a self-conscious understanding of linear perspective; instead of representing the features of an individual friar, as in European portraits, she finds a way of encapsulating the privileged place of sacramental penance among the Franciscans. By portraying this characteristic of the Franciscan order, the *tlacuilo* would have made Dominican observers reflect on how Indians perceived the different orders, perhaps also prompting them to consider their failure to properly evangelize the Nahuas forty years after the introduction of Christianity. Having requested the codex, the missionaries found themselves portrayed by a subject who reminded them how fragile was the grounding of faith among the new Christians.

The penitentiary vigilance of the Franciscans responds to the eminent danger of apostasy at a time when missionaries from the different orders wondered whether the native neophytes were disguising their old beliefs under the semblance of Christian practices. Missionaries and lay authorities feared apostasy because of their hardened subjects' savvy negotiation of the inner workings of the colonial order. Not only had the narrative of ethnosuicide failed, but the *tlacuilo* makes manifest the clarity with which indigenous subjects drew the limits of empire. The *tlacuilo*'s juxtaposition of apostle and apostate, for example, is marked by the Mesoamerican glyph of water. This defines an *inside–inside out* topology of conquest, while at the same time denoting both a raging river and the real waters of baptism (as if the pictograph were an ironic allegory that stated one thing and meant another). The mental image of ladinos leading Indians into rebellion must have suddenly occurred vividly to the colonial viewer confronted by the *tlacuilo*'s sleight-of-hand mastery of European forms for purposes that didn't merely testify to effective religious indoctrination and aesthetic schooling.

In situating the production of Telleriano-Remensis within the history of objectivity, we have observed that the production of the album participated in a chiasmus between subject and object, identifiable with the Cartesian philosophy. Descartes and the grammarians of Port-Royal effectively formalized the epistemic mutations that emerged in the course of recording novel American natural and cultural phenomena. Given this epistemic chiasmus, the project of creating an album of Mesoamerican culture was conceived as a way of objectivizing the written modalities of religious and historical pictograms. The *tlacuilo* was thus caught up in a project that sought to neutralize the power of the pictograms by requesting that she picture her gods in an artificial setting meant for extirpation purposes. The *tlacuilo* of ancient times (having perhaps survived into the present) produced paintings of sacred forms for the use of healers and other spiritual leaders, whereas the missionaries placed her in a situation in which objectivization functioned like an evil eye trained upon ruining Mesoamerican life-forms. The missionaries' will to commit ethnocide had its match in the ethnosuicide they called forth via the *tlacuilo*'s participation in the project. The *tlacuilo*, however, knew well that the meaning and power of the pictograms exceeded the grasp of the missionaries, as manifest in their glosses. The pictographs were a means of producing knowledge of the differentiated missionary orders that provided Nahua spiritual leaders with the weapons to neutralize the friars' sphere of influence. The *tlacuilo*'s relativization of the monastic orders' preferences, however, echoes among her contemporaries.

Chapter 4

THE DISPUTE OF THE FRIARS

*Mira que los frayles y clérigos cada uno tienen su manera de
penitencia; mira que los frayles de San Francisco tienen una
manera de doctrina y una manera de vida y una manera de
vestido y una manera de oración; y los de San Agustín tienen
otra; y los de Santo Domingo tienen otra; y los clérigos otra . . .
y así mismo era entre los que guardaban a los dioses nuestros,
que los de México tenían una manera de vestido y una manera
de orar . . . y otros pueblos de otra; en cada pueblo tenían una
manera de sacrificios.* *

—DON CARLOS OMETOCHTZIN, 1539

According to one of the witnesses in the inquisitional trial of don Carlos
Ometochtzin, this cacique of Tezcoco laid out a plural worldview in
speeches to his town.[1] Ometochtzin's trial testifies to the limits of empire
in that he refused to participate in the narrative of ethnosuicide leading
to his execution. If there exist a variety of Catholic perspectives, Ometochtzin asks, why shouldn't they coexist with the multiple Mexican vari-
ants of the pre-Columbian period? This epistemological boldness led the
Holy Office to judge and execute Ometochtzin for being an *hereje dogma-
tizador*, a heretical dogmatizer. One of the greatest sources of confusion
among Indians in sixteenth-century Central Mexico, and perhaps also
one of the greatest impediments to a successful evangelization, were the
discrepancies in the approaches to evangelization of the religious orders,
differences that ultimately can be traced back to Scholastic philosophical
traditions under which—just to mention the two most important orders—
Franciscan and Dominican friars were trained. But these different philosophical conceptions of man and the world informed not only the missionaries' evangelical practices but also specific modes of conducting
ethnographic research. In the depiction of the Franciscan and Dominican
habitus, the *tlacuilo* of folio 46r would seem to participate in Ometochtzin's questioning of the missionaries' proprietary claims on spiritual life.

To my mind, the relativization on folio 46r could only have echoed the denunciation and execution of Ometochtzin in 1539. I have assumed that the interruption and intervention of Pedro de los Ríos in the production of Telleriano-Remensis was a consequence of the *tlacuilo*'s taxonomic brilliance. Although her censorship was not as extreme as the execution of Ometochtzin, it did lead to her removal from the project and subsequent marginalization.

As I have already pointed out in the "Overture" but should perhaps repeat, it is from the *tlacuilo* that I learned to conceptualize sixteenth-century debates among missionaries (the most well-known being, of course, between Motolinía and Las Casas), in terms of the philosophic-theological preferences of their orders that defined their ethnographic and evangelical practices. As far as I know, the question of the philosophical preferences between the orders and how they affected their conception of their tasks in Mexico has only been briefly discussed by Edmundo O'Gorman in *Fundamentos de la historia de América*: "Como miembro que fue el P. Las Casas de la Orden de los Predicadores, su formación es tomista; por eso se sustrae, en cuanto doctrina expresa, a la influencia directa de la escuela franciscana, representada en Escoto y Ockam" [As a member of the Order of the Preachers, the intellectual formation of Father Las Casas was Thomistic; this is the reason why he extracts himself from the direct influence of the Franciscan school, represented by Duns Scotus and Ockham].[2] O'Gorman goes on to offer a detailed discussion of Las Casas's Thomism and to argue that Las Casas should be read as an intermediate figure between the Scholastics and Descartes. O'Gorman, however, does not elaborate in what ways the evangelical and ethnographic styles of the Franciscans in Mexico reflected the teachings of Duns Scotus and Ockham. In Chapter 3 I examined the formal pictorial aspects of this page, which included the need to differentiate the concepts of depiction and representation. Of special interest in that chapter was the question of the symbolic uses of pictorial perspective for codifying Franciscan preferences for the sacrament of confession. Here I will examine in what ways the *tlacuilo* records the philosophic-theological differences between the two orders that defined the terms of the disputes over the sacraments in sixteenth-century Mexico and the ethnographic conceptualization of Indians as objects of study. In short, I attend to the specific discourses, philosophical doctrines, disputes, and ethnographic writings that a reader or commentator of folio 46r could bring forth in a verbal discussion of the philosophic-theological differences between Dominicans and Franciscans as manifest in the *tlacuilo*'s pictorial codification.

But before moving on, let me first add one more indigenous text that further documents how Indians perceived the two dominant orders. The passage comes from the Chalco historian Domingo Chimalpahin's *Séptima relación*, where he cites the testimony of don Feliciano de la Asunción Calmazacatzin, the *principal* from Tzacualtitlan Tenanco who died in 1611: "Y notlatzin don Juan de Sandoval Tecuanxayaca ca nel yancui christiano, amo quimati yn tleyn oquihtoco yn intechpatzinco teopixque San Francisco, ochicotlahtoco, oquito: 'Tleyque on yn iteopixcahuan notiachcauh don Thomás Quetzalmaçatl, tzotzomacuicuitlame omach xotetzatzayanque?; ma quinhuallita y noteopixcahua Sancto Domingo, mahuiztique, yn inmávito chipahuac amo tzatzayanqui, tlapachihui yn imicxi yca çapatos'" [My uncle don Juan de Sandoval Tecuanxayaca was a new Christian, and that is why he did not know what he said when he spoke about the Franciscans; he talked nonsense when he spoke thus: "What kind of religious people are those of my brother don Tomás Quetzalmazatl, with their dirty rags and cracked feet? See, in contrast, my Dominicans, how distinguished they are, with their clean and not torn habits, with their feet wearing shoes"].[3] Elsewhere in the *Séptima relación*, Chimalpahin mentions that the people of Amaquemecan paid no attention to the Franciscans, who eventually left Amaquemecan and were replaced by Dominican friars. Chimalpahin derives a certain delight in telling these anecdotes, especially the one about don Tomás Quetzalmazatl's description of the shredded habits of the Franciscans and the cleanliness of the Dominicans.

Chimalpahin's description of the habits of the two orders would seem to have in mind the depictions of the two orders on folio 46r. This folio demonstrates the new pictorial vocabularies the *tlacuilo* invented, building on pre-Columbian conventions, to capture the new realities of the horse, the colonial institutions, and differences among missionaries. With a parsimony enviable to a nominalist, the *tlacuilo* avoids essentializing Roman Catholicism by identifying the centrality of baptism among Dominicans (top left) and the emphasis on the sacrament of the penance among Franciscans (top right).

If the knotted cincture marks a Franciscan, the Indian bending over the baptismal font and the ceremonial white dress marks a Dominican. This identification of baptism with the Dominican order might seem arbitrary, especially when we consider the well-known Franciscan practice of mass baptisms where the multitudes, according to their accounts, reached up to fourteen thousand on one given day and 1.2 million for the period between 1524 and 1532.[4] The formal dress of the Dominican signals the debates with Franciscans over the administration of this sacrament in which the Dominicans emphasized following the liturgy strictly and providing a thorough indoctrination in contrast to the Franciscans' lax catechistic preparation and multitudinous baptisms. The debates over this issue raged in New Spain during the 1530s and early 1540s.

1541: APOSTLESHIP AND APOSTASY

In addition to the Franciscan and the Dominican, this folio includes images pertaining to the Mixtón War, a rebellion in Nueva Galicia that first started in 1541 and lasted at least until the end of the sixteenth century. (Some scholars have argued that the so-called pacification of the Chichimecas was never completed and that the rebellion of the Coras, Huicholes, Zacatecos, Tepehuanes, and others—i.e., their refusal to subject themselves to Spanish or Mexican rule—has lasted up to the present.) Tenamaztle, the Lord of Nochistlán (identified by the flowering cactus, the place-name of Nochistlán) figures prominently on top of the symbolic depiction of a mountainous stronghold. Viceroy Mendoza, who led the armies composed of Spaniards and Indians, appears on the other side of the cultural divide marked by the river, which separates the nativist magico-religious world of Tenamaztle from the Christian world of baptism and the Requerimiento that Viceroy Mendoza would have read to the rebels.[5]

The insert for 1541 could very well allude to an account by Las Casas in which he denounced the continued practice of baptizing without proper instruction and, adds Las Casas, "a veces medio forzado" [on occasions more or less forced].[6] As Helen Rand Parish has pointed out, this account gave place to an opinion by Francisco Vitoria, also from 1541, requiring proper indoctrination. In a letter of 1555, the Franciscan Motolinía openly acknowledges this practice when he asks Charles V to assume his eschatological vocation by hurrying to the ends of the earth doing all in his power to bring all Indians into the fold of the Church, even if by forcing them: "Porque dice el Señor: 'Sera predicado este Evangelio por todo el universo antes de la consumación del mundo'. Pues a vuestra merced conviene de oficio darse prisa que se predique el santo Evangelio por todas estas tierras, y los que no quisieren oír de grado el santo Evangelio de Jesucristo, sea por fuerza" [Because the Lord says: "The Gospel will be preached throughout the universe before the world ends." So Your Grace, in your capacity, should hurry that the holy Gospel be preached throughout these lands, and for those who do not willingly listen to the holy Gospel of Jesus

Christ, they must be forced].[7] Las Casas and Motolinía stand at opposite ends of temporality regarding a history and economy of salvation.

We can further pursue this line of association with respect to 1541 and bring to mind Las Casas's *De unico vocationis modo*, a treatise in which he argued that the only way to attract pagans to Christianity was through love and understanding. There is clearly a disjunction between the Indian bending over the baptismal font (I am always tempted to say jumping into the font) and the representation of the Mixtón War. In the next chapter, I examine the topology implicit in the interdependence between the apostle and the apostate that suggests the structure of a Möbius strip in which the two sides of the band (apostleship/apostasy) alternate being visible in the movement that inverts them while tying them together semantically. Here I place an emphasis on the tensions between the two orders and their evangelical preferences and the political implications.

The disjunction between apostle and apostate actually reproduces the three surviving chapters of *De unico modo*. For if chapter 5 of *De unico modo* establishes the ideal character and the disposition of Amerindians to receive the faith, and proposes love as the only way to attract them to Christianity, chapter 6 exposes the lack of precedents that would lend support to a method whereby Indians would first be politically subjected and then converted. Echoing the Requerimiento, Las Casas explains that to demand Indians to surrender their sovereignty would only lead to war: "Et quia nemo infidelium sua sponte velit se Christiani populi vel alicuius principis eius ditioni submittere, potissime infidelium reges, esset profecto necesse devenire ad bellum" [And since no infidels would willingly subject themselves to the dominion of a Christian people, or a Christian prince, especially the kings of the infidels, there would inevitably have to be war].[8] The real condition of Amerindians that results from the wars of conquests corresponds to what Frantz Fanon would diagnose as a colonial psychosis, so it would then not merely be a question of preaching love to ideally suited Amerindians, but one of spiritual and bodily healing and the restitution of goods, the subject of chapter 7. Las Casas first demonstrates that the war against Indians was unjust and then ponders how to go about compensating them for damages and restoring sovereignty to wronged Amerindians. One case taken to court was Tenamaztle's. After surrendering to the bishop of Guadalajara, Tenamaztle was exiled to Spain in 1552. With the assistance of Las Casas, in 1555 Tenamaztle presented at the court in Valladolid his *relación de agravios*, his account of damages, where he claimed rightful sovereignty and denounced the terror he and his people had been subjected to. Tenamaztle, however, as far as I know, disappeared from the public record after 1556. Implicit in Las Casas's treatise is the argument that war and imposed evangelization leads to apostasy. As such, the apostleship he promotes by grounding faith on understanding would have as its end the avoidance of apostasy.

1543: IMPLANTING THE MINIMALIST DOCTRINE

Under 1543 on folio 46r of Telleriano-Remensis one can mention the publication of Zumárraga's *Doctrina breve*, but as we have seen above, the agreement on establishing a common doctrine was hardly an identifying trait among the Franciscans. Other elements in the picture manifest the *tlacuilo*'s ethnographic acumen. The frontal representation of the Franciscan holding the doctrine and the rosary suggests the centrality of penance among Franciscans. There is only one other occasion in Telleriano-Remensis where the inquisitor and bishop Zumárraga looks back at us from a frontal position (see Figure 3). All Catholic missionaries in New Spain heard confessions, but it is no coincidence that the Franciscan missionaries in Mexico produced the majority of bilingual *confesionarios* in the sixteenth century and that they are known for their particularly methodical administration of this sacrament.[9] Whereas a thorough knowledge of the catechism was a requirement for baptism among Dominicans, the Franciscans enforced postbaptismal catechization by gathering those Indians who were scheduled to confess on a given Sunday. *Copia y relación del orden que los frailes desta Nueva España tienen en administrar á los indios todos los sanctos sacramentos de la iglesia* (ca. 1569) [Copy and account of the order the friars of this New Spain follow in the administration of the sacraments to the Indians] describes these sessions, which first tested their knowledge of the doctrine and were followed by talks concerning the necessity and efficacy of penance and, for the penitent, the contrition, confession, and satisfaction of the assigned prayers or deeds for the absolution of the sins.[10] This post-Tridentine account of the order followed by Franciscans in the administration of the sacraments claims that by the 1560s all Indians in Central Mexico had been baptized with the exception of a minority who eluded the vigilance of the friars in the early years or were hidden by parents to avoid receiving baptism. Only Chichimecas, *indios de guerra*, on the northern frontier remain outside the fold of the Church. Given this extreme situation, baptism would be imparted to the Chichimecas after the minimal preparation outlined in Juan de Zumárraga's manual from 1540.[11]

Clearly, from our historical vantage point, these preferences for one of these sacraments amount to different forms of evangelization. For the Indians, however, the existence of these two practices meant multiple understandings of Christianity, which led Ometochtzin and others to question why beliefs in their own gods and corresponding religious practices could not coexist with these conflicting Christian views. The ease and clarity with which the *tlacuilo* codes the Franciscan and Dominican orders must have been a source of annoyance and anxiety to missionaries and secular authorities, perhaps even one of the reasons why the production of Telleriano-Remensis falls apart a few pages after folio 46r when Pedro de los Ríos stops using color and his inscription of the dates lacks the care of the *tlacuiloque* (Figure 8). The embarrassment produced by the objectification of the evangelical programs was most likely exacerbated by the representation of the Mixtón War below the Dominican friar. This rebellion in Nueva Galicia was religiously motivated both in the articulation of its cause as well as in its display of nativist symbols. This event is not only painted in the traditional pictorial tradition but uses a magico-religious language to express its significance. Arguably, the feathers with pointed flints on the back of the otherwise naked Tenamaztle could be read as a citation of the accoutrements associated with Tezcatlipoca, as can be appreciated in the depiction of this god on folio 5r (see Figure 7). Numerous sources document the role the god Tezcatlipoca played as an inspiring force in the rebellion. José Francisco Román Gutiérrez and Guilhem Olivier have argued that we should approach the references to Tezcatlipoca in terms of the deities that ruled the different eras, or Suns.[12] Within the narrative of the Five Suns, Quetzalcoatl was defeated by Tezcatlipoca, which led to the end of the Fourth Sun. It is only "natural," Román Gutiérrez and Olivier argue, that the insurgents perceive the conquistadors as ancestors, indeed as returning nefarious forces, who had to be battled under the auspices of Tezcatlipoca.

By depicting the conflictive views on the evangelization in juxtaposition to the apostasy and insurgency in the northern frontier, the *tlacuilo* relativized the orders' philosophic-theological traditions and recorded the limits of empire in the Indian rebels that face off against Viceroy Antonio de Mendoza. She displays an uncanny ability to penetrate and expose the differences of the missionary orders while producing a trace of a world that escaped them. Whereas for the Scholastic philosophers informing sixteenth-century missionaries, the principle of noncontradiction was a most revered rule of reasoning, colonized and subaltern groups have historically faced the necessity of existing in multiple worlds. Along with

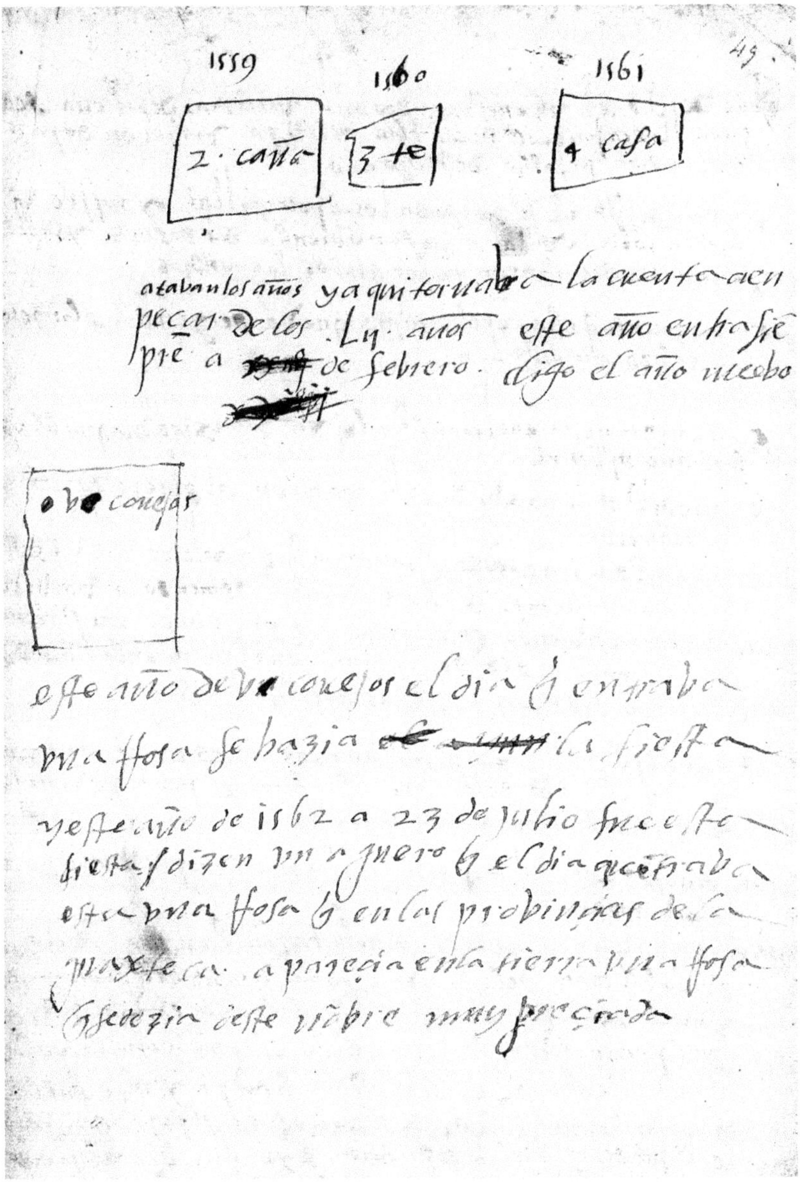

1559 1560 1561 49

2 · casa 3 te 4 casa

atauan los años ya qui tornado a la cuenta aen
pecar de los . Lij. años este año entrasie
pre a xxxx de febrero . digo el año nuebo

o be conejos

este año de be conejos el dia q̃ entraba
vna fiesta se hazia xxxx la fiesta
y este año de 1562 a 23 de Julio fue esta
fiesta/ dizen vn a ̃uero q̃ el dia que traba
este vna fiesta q̃ en las probinçias de la
mixteca . aparecia en la tierra vna fiesta
q̃ se dezia deste nõbre muy precinda

FIGURE 8   *Codex Telleriano-Remensis, fol. 49r. Courtesy of the Bibliothèque Nationale de France, Paris.*

the principle of noncontradiction, the missionaries also shared an essentialist view of the world. Scholastics were cognizant of the irreconcilable worldviews they contended for, but essentially agreed to contest each other's views to keep the specter of relativism at bay.

MEDIEVAL LEGACIES: BAPTISM, CATECHISM, AND LITURGY

One can single out at least three approaches to understanding the legacy of the Middle Ages on the missionaries: (1) Medieval texts provided rhetorical models, if not knowledge, for writing about the New World (Anthony Grafton, *New Worlds, Ancient Texts*); (2) Thomism is assumed to have been the dominant philosophy that missionaries followed in their interpretation of Amerindian religions (Sabine McCormack, *Religion in the Andes*); (3) Scholasticism was a system of thought that hindered empirical observations of Amerindian cultures (Serge Gruzinski, *De l'idolâtrie*). All these takes have made important contributions to our understanding of New World historiography. It is undeniable that in the new writing, one can trace, to borrow Anthony Grafton's term, "ancient texts," but one could make this observation about cultural artifacts in any period of Western culture if we soften what we mean by "ancient" and entertain the notion that all literature consists of a series of palimpsests. If, following Sabine McCormack, we restrict our study to Dominicans and Jesuits in the Andes, Thomism will certainly be the dominant philosophical mode of explaining religious phenomena, since the Dominicans as early as the fourteenth century had adopted it as the official philosophical doctrine of the Order, and it was the most influential Scholastic system among the Jesuits. Observations regarding the constraints of Scholasticism on some missionaries, namely Las Casas, have led Serge Gruzinski to underscore the empirical, hence modern, character of other missionaries like Diego Durán.

Of these three approaches, the third has the most affinities with my interest in ethnographic research, but Gruzinski's emphasis on discontinuity seems to take for granted an "empirical view" that has no connection to the Scholastic traditions in which the missionaries were trained. In pursuing medieval traces, we should, however, be wary of reproducing the biases that have determined the definition of the Renaissance vis-à-vis the Middle Ages, at least since Erasmus's penchant for drawing caricatures of schoolmen: "From the disputations he heard in the Sorbonne he brought back nothing but the habit of scoffing at doctors of theology, or as he always ironically calls them by their title of honour: *Magistri nostri.* Yawning, he sat among 'those holy Scotists' with their wrinkled brows, staring eyes, and puzzled faces."[13] Without denying the influence of Erasmus in sixteenth-century Spain, I propose reading colonial texts outside the paradigm that opposes the modern to the medieval. The result of applying, or better, of adopting the definition of the medieval in terms of the highly regarded Renaissance only leads to highly predictable commonplaces.[14] I limit myself to a mention of these questions of periodization here, since they merit chapters of their own. As I argue in Chapter 7, we have much to gain by approaching colonial texts in terms of an *elsewhere* that lacks the determinations of standard periodizations, which applies not only to "nonmodern" European texts (i.e., texts read outside the paradigm that opposes the modern and the medieval), but also to indigenous texts, about which it is abusive to speak in terms of early modern subjects when Indians dwelt in multiple spaces, which included the colonial order as well as Mesoamerican worlds defined by spatio-temporalities that cannot be reduced to European forms.

Pope Paul III's bull *Altitudo divini consilii* (1537) offers a benchmark for assessing the intensity of the debates between Franciscans and Dominicans when it outlines the criteria to be followed in evangelization, most particularly in preparing subjects for baptism: "Tradita tenore praesemntium: decernimus et declaramus: illos qui Indos ad fidem venientes non adhibitis ceremoniis et solemnitatibus ab ecclesia observatis in nomine tamen sanctissimae Trinitatis baptizaverunt non pecassee: cum consideratis tunc occurentibus sic illis bona ex causa putamos visum fuisse expedire" [In the course of the following, we discern and declare that those who brought the Indians to the faith in Christ did not apply the ceremonies and solemnities observed by the Church, and though they still baptized in the name of the Holy Trinity, did not sin; considering what they faced at that time, we reckon that they found it convenient for a good cause].[15] I will return to the bull. For now, note that as a result of this mandate by Paul III, Juan de Zumárraga, the first bishop of Mexico, drafted a brief manual in 1540. Over the next decade, several doctrines were published, including Juan de Zumárraga's *Doctrina cristiana breve para enseñanza de los indios: por manera de hystoria* (1543) and the *Doctrina breve muy provechosa de las cosas que pertenecen a la fe catholica y a nuestra cristiandad en estilo llano para comun inteligencia* (1544).

Indians seeing through the different philosophical traditions informing evangelical programs must have irritated the missionaries. As I have pointed out, Ometochtzin's intuition of a possible coexistence of and dwelling in several worlds led to his auto-da-fé in 1539 under the inquisitorial powers held by Zumárraga in his capacity as bishop of Mexico. Note that the Inquisition was not formally established until 1571. Of all the trials in the 1530s and 1540s, his punishment was the most severe. Only during the first years following the conquest do we find that resistance to Christianization and Spanish rule was punished by hanging at the scaffold or burning at the stake. Later *dogmatizadores* were subjected to expropriation; banishment to Spain; or more benign punishments like a public repentance, a whipping, or a brief time in jail—long enough to learn the Creed. As I have pointed out, Zumárraga also played a key role in the debates over the proper administration of the sacraments, especially of baptism and matrimony. There is a paradox in Zumárraga's efforts. On the one hand, Zumárraga had no qualms about executing Ometochtzin for polygamy, dogmatizing, and questioning the Christian dogma, while on the other, he promoted the formulation of uniform practices regarding the rites of baptism and the normalization of marriage. One cannot but sense, behind the rush to iron out evangelical differences, an embarrassment prompted by Ometochtzin's lucid assessment of the different worldviews among friars and clergy. His execution certainly caused a scandal that eventually led to the demise of Zumárraga as inquisitor.

In 1539, in the aftermath of Pope Paul III's 1537 bull *Altitudo divini consilii*, which was mainly concerned with establishing rituals that would leave no doubt regarding the differences between baptism and similar pagan rites (i.e., blessing the water, teaching the catechism, applying the chrism and the holy oil), Zumárraga gathered the bishops of New Spain to develop a cogent policy on the sacraments. Paul III's bull made allowance for exceptions to the strict rites of baptism in cases of "urgent necessity," leaving the definition of this to the conscience of the individual bestowing the sacrament. The bishops agreed to write a manual to prepare adults for baptism and explicitly excluded from "urgent necessity" the multitudes of Indians requesting it. Motolinía chronicles the debates and the differences, as well as the disobedience by Franciscan friars of Guacachula who baptized adults on demand:

> En un monasterio que está en un lugar de Coauhchula [Guacachula], los frailes se determinaron de bautizar a cuantos viniesen, no obstante lo mandado por los obispos; lo cual como fue sabido por toda aquella provincia, fue tanta la gente que vino, que si yo por mis propios ojos no lo viera no lo osara decir; mas verdaderamente era gran multitud de gente la que venía . . . que en cinco días que estuve en el monasterio, otro

sacerdote y yo bautizamos por cuenta catorce mil y doscientos y tantos poniendo a todos óleo y crisma, que no nos fue poco trabajo.[16]

[In a monastery located in Coauhchula (Guacachula), the friars determined to baptize all who came; when this became known throughout that province, so many people came, that if I had not seen it with my own eyes I would not dare to say it; indeed it was a great multitude that came . . . that in five days that I was at the monastery another priest and I baptized up to fourteen thousand two hundred and more, putting the holy oil and the chrism on all of them, not a light affair.]

As far as I can gather, Motolinía was not punished for his disobedience. Motolinía expresses the most radical view among the Franciscan millenarians who advocated the baptism of multitudes to prepare the way for the end of time. As I have noted above, Motolinía called on Charles V in 1555 to assume his role as emperor of the end of time and to hurry the conversion of all Indians, even by forced baptisms. We find a more measured view in Zumárraga's brief manual for adults published in Mexico in 1540 and in Juan de Focher's 1544 *Echiridion baptismi adultorum et matrimonii bapstissandorum* [Manual for the baptism of adults and the matrimony of the baptized], which defined a Franciscan position.[17] Although Focher deems multitudinous baptisms improper and prescribes teaching the doctrine prior to baptism, what constituted the minimal substance, length, and method of catechization continued to be a source of contention even when the different orders and secular priests had agreed on using a common *Doctrina*.

In addition to the call for a regulation of the minimal catechistical teachings and liturgy, there was a sense that the circulation of doctrinal materials also needed regulation, as expressed in an opinion by the Inquisition from 1575:

Con la ocasión de este libro [Maturino Gilberti, *Doctrina Cristiana*], se nos ofrece que consultar, acerca de mucha escritura sagrada impresa y de mano . . . que andan en lengua vulgar de los indios de que somos avisados por muchos religiosos que resultan inconvenientes para la doctrina de los indios, porque como raras veces concurre ser buena lengua y buen letrado, no se hace buena versión, sino falta y llena de impropiedades, y en los sermones que se hacen en lengua de los indios por hombres buenas lenguas y no letrados, hay las mismas impropiedades y errores, y estos inconvenientes nacen mayores en lo que los mesmos indios trasladan unos de otros.[18]

[On the occasion of this book [Maturino Gilberti, *Doctrina Cristiana*], the need to inquire about much sacred scripture in print and in manuscript . . . that circulates in the vulgar languages of the Indians became manifest; because a good interpreter [*lengua*] and a good scholar [*letrado*] rarely coincide, good versions are not produced, rather they are faulty and filled with improprieties. In the sermons done in the language of the Indians by men who are good interpreters but not scholars, one finds the same improprieties and errors. These inconveniences lead to greater ones in that the Indians themselves copy them.]

The Inquisition panel had been charged with the investigation of the orthodoxy of Maturino's *Doctrina*, published in 1559 but removed from circulation. The opinion offers a view on the wild or savage literacy among Indians who copied versions of sacred texts in their languages. *Letrado* refers to more than just the use of the Latin alphabet; it implies the authority of a learned scholar, hence the sense of a wild (i.e., grassroots) literacy among Indians outside the supervision of missionaries and bureaucrats. Indians write, translate, and produce copies that can hardly be controlled. Among the papers of the Chalco historian Domingo Chimalpahin we find one such instance of wild literacy in an *Exercicio quotidiano*, intended to prepare Indians for communion, that Bernardino de Sahagún felt the need to correct: "Este exercicio halle entre los yndios, no se quien le hizo ni quien se le dio tenia muchas faltas E incongruencias mas con verdad se puede dezir que se hizo de nueuo que no que se enmendo. Este año de 1574 fray Bernardino de Sahagun" [I found this exercise among the Indians. I don't know who produced it, nor who gave it to them. It had many errors and incongruities. But in truth it may be said that it was done anew rather than that it was corrected. In this year of 1574, Fray Bernardino de Sahagún].[19]

It doesn't escape irony that Chimalpahin's copy of Sahagún's copy of a doctrinal text in Nahuatl, which Indians held and perhaps had copied themselves from a text produced by a friar, comes down to us in the hand of another Indian. The incongruities mentioned by Sahagún may have had as much to do with the translation, a faulty *lengua*, as with the *letrado* source. Under analysis, we may trace Thomist theological principles (hence the influence of Las Casas) in the emphasis it places on developing an intellectual habitus that would prepare the soul for the sacrament of the Eucharist. I would argue that one can unequivocally trace a Dominican insistence on developing habits for the reception of grace rather than a mere insistence on accepting the articles of the faith, as was the case in Franciscan confessionals and doctrines. The subject of the *Exercicio* has been baptized and is reminded that he or she has made certain vows, which could hardly be the case with a subject who had been part of a multitudinous baptism. As a baptized subject, he or she is responsible for the doctrine, but the text goes beyond mere repetition by rote, the tendency in Franciscan evangelical instruments, and presupposes a subject who will meditate on the meaning of Christianity and keep vigilance over his or her spiritual health:

> These meditations, the acts of spiritually doing things with prudence, which are called an Exercise, which I set before you, and show you, are to be thought about each and every week, and each thought is to be thought about each and every day. . . . For if you accustom yourself to them, your soul will consider them a great satisfaction, great good fortune. A Great light, a torch, a great brilliance will proceed with it; it will guide you; it will go before you; it will show you the way that goes direct to Heaven.[20]

The fact that Chimalpahin was most likely educated by Dominicans in Chalco might explain why he chose to copy it. Including Sahagún's warning would have protected him from charges of possessing illicit doctrinal texts.

All evidence suggests that Sahagún not only participated in the inquisitional investigation of Maturino, but that he also confiscated other samples of wild literacy and participated in the definition of the policy. The ample circulation and call for control reflects similar policies with respect to sacred texts circulating in Spanish in Spain, but gives further evidence that the friars in 1575 had hardly resolved their opinions regarding a common doctrine: "Convernia que todo fuese una doctrina general por unas mesmas palabras, sin diferencia alguna, y no que haya muchas doctrinas y que cada fraile haga la suya diferente, y que los indios según la orden de San Francisco, Sancto Domingo, y San Agustin, por quien son doctrinados se apliquen a ella como a secta diferente" [It would be convenient that all were a general doctrine with the same words, without any difference, and not that there were many doctrines and that each friar makes his own differently, and that Indians according to the Order of Saint Francis, Saint Dominique, and Saint Augustine, by whom they are indoctrinated, apply themselves as if to a different sect].[21] This passage exemplifies the malaise provoked by the relativization of Christianity I have traced in Chimalpahin, Ometochtzin, and the *tlacuilo* of folio 46r.

In spite of hasty solutions to the scandal, antithetic differences remained between the intellectualism of the Dominican Bartolomé de Las Casas's *De unico vocationis modo* (ca. 1537), which discusses at length the limits of explaining and conveying the mysteries of the Christian faith by rational means, and the pragmatics of Zumárraga's *Doctrina breve cristiana: en que en suma se contiene todo lo principal y necessario que el cristiano debe saber y obrar. Y es verdadero cathecismo para adultos que se han de bautizar; y para los nuevos baptizados necessario y saludable documento: y lo que mas conviene predicar y dar a entender a los indios: sin otras cosas que no tienen necesidad de saber* (ca. 1545), which, as the lengthy titles indicates, is less concerned with providing the specifics of the doctrine than with a theoretical justification of its minimalist tenets, "sin otras cosas que no tienen necesidad de saber" [without other things they have no need of knowing]. Whereas conversion for Las Casas would entail inculcating an intellectual habitus, for Zumárraga catechization consists of using the *Doctrina* to lead Indians to "stutter" the articles of faith: "y los indios . . . comienzen a tartamudear en ella." This treatise is mainly concerned with less educated Indians and Blacks, "los indios menos entendidos y mas rudos y negros" (100), but the reasoning that compares Indians and Blacks to children entails a counter-argument to the Dominicans' insistence on a thorough catechization before baptisms. The art of Franciscan sermonizing—as developed theoretically by Juan Focher's *Itinerarium Catholicum proficiscentium ad infideles convertendos* [Catholic itinerary of the missionaries that set out to convert the infidels] (Seville, 1574) and Diego Valadés's *Rhetorica Christiana* (Perugia, 1579), and practically by Bernardino de Sahagún's *Psalmodia Christiana* [Christian Psalmody] (Mexico City, 1583) and Juan Bautista's *Sermonario* [Sermons] (Mexico City, 1606)—conceived its task as conveying the truths of revealed religion in a rhetorical and poetic mode that would lead Indians to love God, a key tenet in the Franciscan preference for affective and contemplative theology. In passing, note that Sahagún's *Psalmodia* was authorized to circulate in manuscript as early as 1564. Given the policies to control wild literacy, of which Sahagún was part, copies of the *Psalmodia* must have been among those texts the Inquisition sought to confiscate.

Even when Aquinas defines theology as a theoretical science, the process of indoctrination would include, as Las Casas puts it in *De unico vocationis modo*, an appeal to the emotions: "Ergo modus docendi homines fidem religionemque Christianam est vel esse debet intellectus persuasivus et voluntatis allectivus et excitativus" [Then the mode to teach men the Christian faith and religion is, or should be, a persuasive mode with respect to the intellect, and an attractive and compelling mode with respect to the will].[22] Whereas for the Franciscans, the missionaries would communicate revealed truths (the tenets of the faith) that Indians were expected to accept, love, and desire, for the Dominicans, the missionaries would work on developing an intellectual habitus that would lead to the reception of grace: "Nam secundum S. Thomas praedicatores se habent exterius tanquam disponentes ad fidem et removentes prohibens. Et item est de gracia et charitate et aliis dones, scilicet, movendo, instruendo, exhortando, corripiendo, vel huiuscemodi ministerium ahibendo ordinatum ad fidei vel gratiae susceptionem. Et sic cooperantur ad hoc, [ut] gratia alicui detur vel data non perdatur" [According to Saint Thomas, preachers so to speak are those who by their exterior action dispose faith and remove impediments. Likewise they proceed with respect to grace, charity, and the other gifts: namely, by instructing, exhorting, correcting, or employing any other similar labor ordered for the undertaking of faith and grace. And in this way work together for grace to be given to someone, or, if already received, not lost].[23] Las Casas finds an analogy between the attraction of men to religion and the mode of attracting them to science. Both science and the instruction of the faith build on knowledge first apprehended by the senses, "ad hoc quod ex his intellectus agens accipiat formas sive intelligibiles et describat sive depingat eas intellecto possibili" [so that the agent intellect receives the forms or intelligible species and records them and impresses them on the possible intellect]. Indeed, the missionary must work against fear, sadness, pain, ire, and other passions by adopting the methods of induction, persuasion, and softness; otherwise "impossibile est intellectum asentire ailcut propositini, nisi prius quiete persuadeatur et tranquille manuducatur mod praetacto" [it is impossible that the intellect assents to any proposition, if before it is not persuaded with quietness and is taken with tranquility to the desired end].[24] As an example of this dialogical method, we may mention Las Casas's fellow Dominican Domingo de la Anunciación's *Doctrina cristiana breve y compendiosa por via de dialogo entre un maestro y un discipulo, sacada en lengua castellana y mexicana y compuesta por el muy reverendo padre, fray Domingo de la Anunciación, vicario que al presente es de Coyoacan, de la orden del bienaventurado padre Santo Domingo* (Mexico City, 1565). In Domingo de la Anunciación's *Doctrina*, even though the dialogue feels staged, persuasive arguments and detailed explanations pursue the creation of an intellectual habitus.

Although Las Casas promotes the globalization of Christianity, we should not underestimate the differences between Las Casas's universalism and the Requerimiento's ultimatum, or for that matter Motolinía's call for forced conversions. We should emphasize instead Las Casas's call for a slowing down of the temporality of Christianization: "Manifestum est potissimus requiri omnia, quae circa credituros agenda sunt, esse debere voluntati placida, grata, suavia, delectabilia, amabilia et desirabilia et huiusmodi, quemadmodum sunt quies, tranquillitas, explicatio morosa, non onerosa, ordo suavis, processus lentissimus" [It is clear, then, that above everything it is required that what is done among the future believers must be pleasant to the will, gratifying, soft, delectable, kind, and desirable, and in the manner of a peaceful, tranquil, thorough explanation, not onerous, but in an agreeable order, a very slow process].[25] The slowing down of the conversion contradicts Motolinía's apocalyptic hurrying of Charles V to assume his responsibility.

This *processus lentissimus*, which presupposes appealing to the will and the assumption that the understanding approach is the only way to attract people to Christianity, entails the creation of a habitus, a familiarity that can only arise out of familiarity: "Illud enim, quod est consuetum, est nobis magis notum. Cuius ratio est quia consuetudo veritur in naturam, unde et habitus ex consuetudine generatur, qui inclinat per modum naturae" [Since what is familiar is better known by us. The reason is that custom turns into nature; and from this custom a habit is engendered that produces an inclination in the mode of nature].[26] Inasmuch as Las Casas must assume that infidels have an intellect with a habitus, he faces the following aporia: either to bring about the wholesale replacement of one intellectual habitus by another, which would entail the negation of the habitus of those he sought to convert, or to find a language that mediates between the two habitus without assuming the dominance of one intellectual habitus over the other.

De unico modo offers examples drawn from Cicero of "savages" developing their intellect from scratch, which, as it wouldn't apply to the Americas, functions as a theoretical postulate. In fact, Las Casas suggests examples from the Americas that open the possibility of dialogical processes of learning that can be further documented with passages from the *Apologética historia sumaria*, his philosophical anthropology. In *De unico vocationis modo*, Las Casas states in a speculative mode (in the spirit of countering those who negated the ability of Amerindians to rule themselves): "Cum re vera quamplurimi eorum vel vita monastica vel economica vel etiam politica possint nos regere atque ad bonos mores deducere, quinimmo nos cum naturali rationi dominari" [But the truth is that many of those men could rule us in monastic life, in the economic, and still in the political, and take us to the good customs; indeed, they could rule us with natural reason],[27] and in the *Apologética*, he explicitly states that Europeans could learn much from Amerindians about conducting the monastic, economic, and political orders: "Dejemos agora todos estos reinos, dentro de los cuales si penetrásemos veríamos que en más cosas en sus policías y tal orden que pudiésemos más con razón aprender dellos para perficionar las nuestras que improperárselas" [Let us now leave behind these kingdoms, within which, if we went deeper, we would see more things in their political institutions and order that we would have more to learn from them to perfect our own than to revile them].[28] In the end, the call for understanding as the *only way* involves the need to recognize the existence of at least two forms of understanding and an endless process of translation. Otherwise the appeal to the understanding would wind up in the imposition of a form of reasoning that would be deaf to the voice of the interlocutor. This is a cerebral process that involves the coexistence of two habitus and the possibility that one must accept that revealed truth may be understood in more than one intellectual habitus. But then how is the preacher going to develop the required habitus that would enable the reception—the recognition of faith, hope, and charity as states of grace?

This understanding of the theological virtues is the direct opposite of the truths conveyed by the Requerimiento, which even when its principles were understood, would merely communicate the historical fact that Indians were obligated to subject themselves to the Crown and to listen to the missionaries expounding the catechism. In fact, the political obligation to recognize the sovereignty of the Spanish Crown builds on the assumption of a *revealed truth*—the universal authority of the Roman Catholic Church and the right of the pope to grant Spain the responsibility for the evangelization of the Amerindians. It functions on the assumption that the *truths* are self-evident and that the mere communication of them suffices for requiring their acceptance. Clearly, Las Casas does not recognize the Requerimiento as conveying *revealed truth*, let alone the call to violence. Nor does he accept the injunction that infidels must allow Christian preachers into the territories or face war, as stated by Francisco Vitoria in Spain and Alonso de la Vera Cruz in Mexico. Las Casas couldn't be more unequivocal when he cites Matthew 10:14: "If anyone will not welcome or listen to your words, shake off the dust from your feet as you leave that house." He goes on to comment on this passage: "Non dixit: resistire illis et, velint nolit, praedicate aut, si pertinaciter in repellendo vos perseveraverint, penis humanis punire non differte" [He didn't say: contend against them and, whether they want it or not, preach to them, and if they obstinately persevere in expelling you, do not hesitate to punish them with human penalties].[29]

Las Casas goes on to argue that the effects of war hinder evangelization, since violence damages the senses and the intellect, thus corroding the possibility of forming the habitus necessary for understanding and accepting the tenets of Christianity. For Las Casas, missionaries would be obligated to engage Indians in a dialogical exchange in which the end would not simply consist in developing a predetermined intellectual habitus but to have an interaction between different understandings that would include not only the transformation of the habitus of the Indians but also the one the missionaries would bring forth. And who is to say what is the most appropriate habitus for understanding *revealed truths*, indeed, for the reception of infused faith as a state of grace?

If in their *Psalmodia* and *Sermonario*, Sahagún and Juan Bautista communicate revealed truths by inciting the will with precious metaphors, Franciscan *doctrinas* place an emphasis on instilling fear by denouncing the gods and the sacrifices as Satanic inventions. Even when the Franciscans emphasized the preeminence of will, cognition of the object precedes its love: once the Nahuas were informed about the truths of revelation, they were obligated to accept the Creed. If revealed truth cannot be proven by rational arguments, one can certainly rationally explain the desirability of accepting revealed truth on the basis of biblical origin, the clarifications by the Fathers of the Church, and the authority of the Church. Because wise theologians had laid out the doctrine, one was obligated to lend it credence.

In this respect, Sahagún's *Psalmodia Christiana* offers examples of conveying the basic articles of the faith in Nahuatl psalms; these psalms adopt the metaphors and rhetorical inflections of the chants that the Nahuas had in ancient times directed to their deities but that his sixteenth-century Nahua collegians had refurbished with Christian motifs.[30] These psalms operate under different principles than the aggressive litany against the ancient gods that one may find in other evangelical instruments by Sahagún, such as the doctrine at the end of *Colloquios y doctrina cristiana* (1564) or in the declarations and confutations at the end of Book I (dedicated to the gods) in the *Historia general de las cosas de la Nueva España* (Florentine Codex).

Take the following as a taste of the terror Sahagún warns of for the errors of idolatry: "Los idolatras en el infierno son atormentados con mayores tormentos que todos los otros pecadores; su lloro y sus lastimeras palabras, sus lamentaciones y dolor no remediable, en la Sagrada Escritura está escrito" [The idolaters in hell are tormented with greater torments than any other sinners; their cries and sighing words, their lamentations and pain are not redeemable; it is written in the sacred Scripture]. These words follow the explanation that after the first evangelization, God inflicted suffering because some among them continued to be idolaters. In the economy of salvation, these sorts of statements were intended to lead those preparing for baptism into attrition for the lives they and their ancestors had lived and to accept Christianity out of fear of eternal damnation. In the context of multitudinous baptisms, attrition couldn't play a significant function, but could come into play in the preparation for confession and penitence. Moreover, the sacrament of penance offers sinners the possibility of converting to God through attrition and contrition. All sinners convert (again and again) by the sacrament of penance. This is not the place to examine in detail the debates over attrition and contrition, but note that the difference between these two states of mind is that the former builds on fear of eternal punishment whereas the latter leads to the love of God. The Council of Trent ended up defining attrition as sufficient for the granting of absolution on the assumption that the love of God resulting from contrition would be granted by God's infusion of grace. Among the Franciscan Scholastics, Duns Scotus made the distinction between the state of grace that results from contrition as *ex opere operantis* (that is, as a consequence of the process of repentance and turning toward God), and the infusion of grace by God as *ex opere operato* (that is, as an effect of the absolution). Protestants will mock the purported infusion of grace that results from the sacrament as magical thinking; the Franciscans in Mexico were particularly immune to this accusation, as were those who met at the Council of Trent.[31] Now, for the Franciscans practicing multitudinous baptisms on demand, the power of granting grace in baptism did not need the state of attrition, since it would come as a result of the mere reception of the sacrament and the corresponding infusion by God. As we have seen above, Las Casas, and in general those ascribing to a Thomist position on the role of the intellectual habitus in the reception of grace, would insist on the need for thorough instruction.

The *Psalmodia* deploys a rhetoric that places the emphasis on color, brilliance, and affection, underscoring the desirability of theological virtues or the beauty of the heavenly afterlife. The *Psalmodia* exemplifies the Franciscan preference for affective theology. Contrary to Aquinas's view that theology is a theoretical science—"It [sacred doctrine] is more theoretical than practical, since it is mainly concerned with divine things which are, rather than with things human beings do"—Franciscans tended to view theology as affective or contemplative. Furthermore, Duns Scotus emphasizes the practical nature of theology at the expense of theory: "The intellect perfected by the habit of theology apprehends God as one who should be loved, and according to rules from which praxis can be elicited. Therefore, the habit of theology is practical."[32] As if citing Duns Scotus's emphasis on praxis derived from affect (theology as bearing action-directed force), Sahagún writes a psalm dedicated to the *Matlactetl teunaoatilli* [The Ten Commandments of God]: "Titeuiutica titecpilli, in titlaçopilli, in timaquiztli, in tichalchiuitl in titeuxiuitl, in tiChristiano: xicmati, xiquiximati, auh xicmauiço in teuiutica motlaçotilma, in anemiuhqui, in mauiztic, in tlaçotli, in teucuitlaquetzaltonatiuhio, in vel tonameio, in tlamumuxoltic, in ie iehoatl matlactetl teunaoatilli" [Spiritual noble lord, beloved son, bracelet, precious jade, turquoise, Christian: know, recognize, and pay honor to your spiritual precious cape, incomparable, marvelous, precious with quetzal suns [glinting with] gold, with real rays of light, with intricate designs: the Ten Commandments of God]. Sahagún uses the verb *neci* in a causative form with a reverential applicative, *quimonestilili*, to convey the meaning of revelation: "Vel iehoatzi, vel inomatcatzinco in totecuio Dios, tepeticpac quimmonestilili in itlaneltocacaoa, in vmpa Sinay" [Our Lord God Himself revealed them to His faithful ones on a mountaintop in Sinai].[33]

This is just one instance of Sahagún's use of Nahuatl poetics to convey the truths of revelation by working with a theology of affect that aspires to have action-directed force as articulated by Duns Scotus's understanding of theology as a practical science. As Richard Cross puts it, "[Duns Scotus] reasons that every item in the science of theology is, or can be, action-directing, because the more we know about theology, the more we might be disposed to love God."[34] Here again we find the primacy of the will, which even though it presupposes cognition of revealed truths, in the end acts on affect, that is, by inculcating the desire to love God. This desire, of course, does not exclude conveying the sinful nature of the previous life, the promotion of fear, and the affliction and contrition that would prepare the soul for the reception of baptism and God's infusion of faith as a state of grace. The psalm dedicated to the *Chicuntetl Sacramentos* [The Seven Sacraments] calls for humility and abjection (but also celebration) in the face of our Lord God for the gifts he has given us: "In izquitlamantli y, in omito, ma ic ximotlamachti, auh ma ic xicmotlacamachiti, in motlaçoteouh, ma muchi ica moiollo, xicmotlaçotili" [For all these things that have been told of, may you rejoice, and may you obey your beloved God; may you love Him with all your heart].[35]

Given these scientific and rhetorical differences between the two orders, Ometochtzin's statement and the *tlacuilo*'s juxtaposition of the two orders on folio 46r capture the irreconcilable worldviews informing the debates. Ometochtzin's execution confirms the anxiety provoked among the religious orders when they realized that Indians were seeing through their incompatible differences. The abandonment of the project at the end of Telleriano-Remensis also suggests unease in the face of the *tlacuilo*'s return of the gaze. The inquisitor and the ethnographic missionary sought to objectify Nahuatl culture but found themselves observed in the process. In their debates in the 1530s and 1540s, the orders sought to arrive at a consensus on the basic articles of faith and the baptismal rites, but not on the philosophical styles of understanding the process and meaning of conversion. Deep-seated differences regarding affective and theoretical theology continued to define the perspectives of the two orders.

SCHOLASTIC ANTHROPOLOGY

Rather than seeing Indians and their cultures as readily available for observation, my aim is to understand how different Scholastic philosophical traditions informed the production of the missionaries' object of ethnographic inquiry. This shift on emphasis also allows me to consider how the missionaries' philosophical orientation understood differently the subjects of conversion. Observe, however, that the object of ethnography and the subject of conversion inform each other. If in the previous section I placed the emphasis on theoretical and affective theology and the rhetoric and methods of indoctrination, here I examine the philosophical backgrounds that underlie their recording of systems of belief, resistance to Christianity, and the production of new syncretic life-forms. Scholasticism should not be reduced to a series of dogmas, however dogmatic some versions or aspects of a particular philosopher might be, but understood as a series of concepts of the soul, epistemologies, ontologies, and theories of language, very often in conflict between the different orders and even within them. As we have already seen in the section dedicated to theology and rhetoric, differences comprise deep-seated beliefs and forms of reasoning that ultimately entail contending philosophical anthropologies and worldviews.

In what, for lack of space, can only be done in very schematic terms,

I outline below some of the basic tenets of Thomism, the official doctrine of the Dominicans, and the philosophies of Duns Scotus and William of Ockham, two dominant thinkers among the Franciscans. In addition to these Franciscan thinkers, Franciscan theologians and rhetoricians in Mexico often cite the late-fifteenth-century nominalist Scholastic Gabriel Biel, who, even though he was not a member of the Franciscan order, held philosophical and theological views that coincided with those dear to the Franciscan order.[36] Differences regarding the concept of *habitus*, the place of the senses in the acquisition of knowledge, and the relationship between mind and language not only underlie Dominican and Franciscan approaches to evangelization but also inform the production of Indians as anthropological objects of study. Ethical and epistemological but also theological positions entail a concept of man or human nature that serves as a conceptual framework that defines the ethnographic tasks of reading Nahua everyday life—that is, identifying superstition, idolatry, or, more generally, pagan beliefs in feasts, dances, clothing, and language. I am not interested in the epistemology (how they defined truth) of the missionaries' research, or the ethical positions (how they justified their place in the conquest), but in tracing how epistemological and ethical beliefs underlie their understanding, thinking, and recording of Nahua culture as an instance of human nature.

Let us assume that both Diego Durán and Bernardino de Sahagún's ethnographic methods are empirical, that they base their knowledge on the direct observation of phenomena; then their specific approaches, topics, obsessions, and ethnographic styles correspond to differences in how they constitute, construct, and map reality. As I have pointed out, in the frontal representation of the Franciscan on folio 46r, one can trace the gaze of the *tlacuilo* looking back at the missionaries, relativizing their worldview and thereby raising the specter of a failed conversion. The burden of relativization consists in the multiple versions of Christianity, often in conflict, the Nahuas could draw from and reproduce in terms of a *habitus* that the missionaries could not comprehend. I must insist that the question of an authentic conversion remains outside the purview of what we contemporary scholars can know about the intimate soul of sixteenth-century Nahuas. The specter of a failed conversion is the background of the ethnographic work of both Sahagún and Durán.

Central concepts in Aquinas for understanding Durán are: (1) the Aristotelian principle that the human mind understands nothing that was not first in the senses, *nihil in intellectu quod prius non fuerit in sensu*, and its corollary that the soul never thinks without a phantasm, *nisi convertendo se ad phantasma*; and (2) the centrality of habits not only with respect to moral and theological virtues but to knowledge and science. Following Aristotle, Aquinas explains the uniformity of our experience of the world based on common sense, the faculty that sorts out sensoria according to specific senses. Hence the implantation of sense data in the mind would be uniform to all humans. There is no room for differences in cognition at the level of the phantasm outside of mental deficiencies or distortions caused by the devil. Moreover, the emphasis Aquinas places on the senses entails an understanding of the union of body and soul that, in leaving no room for thought originating independently of the senses, would make the task of this life to develop habits that further spiritual perfection.[37] By inform-ing the body, the soul completes human nature. Even when all Scholastics drew a clear distinction between what can be known by natural reason and revealed truth, their philosophical preferences inflect their understanding of theological science. Since the ends of man exceed what can be known by natural reason, habits leading to perfect happiness would ultimately depend on knowledge of revealed truths. In this respect, Aquinas and the Franciscan thinkers would agree that in addition to accepting the Creed, that is, accepting the dogma, the *habitus* of faith as a state of grace would ultimately be infused by God. However, Aquinas would emphasize the development of intellectual *habitus* that enable the understanding of the science that clarifies the meaning of revelation and leads to contemplation as a step in preparing the soul for the gift of faith. Spiritual deficiencies would consist of misguided or underdeveloped habits, pertaining to both natural reasoning and the supernatural gifts of the theological virtues.[38] For Aquinas, the sacraments are instrumental, efficient causes of grace whose efficacy depends on the right intellectual habits, hence the Indian bending over the baptismal font would be fully prepared for the reception of the holy waters. As Las Casas would insist, there is more to conversion, to the supernatural gift of faith, than knowing and "stuttering" the Creed.

Franciscan thinkers generally share an Augustinian-inspired emphasis on intuition as an active component in cognition. Intuition conveys an epistemology wherein the intellect and external objects interact in the for-mation of sense impressions. If Duns Scotus, like the majority of Scholas-tics (from Bonaventure to Ockham), felt pressed to draw from Aristotle to build a systematic theology, in particular the epistemic principles that con-strue concepts and abstractions from sense impressions, Duns Scotus and Ockham also find the need to supplement Aristotle with an understanding of intuition that enables the mind to grasp objects in their immediacy: in the present as given (perfect intuition/proximate objects), in the past as remembered (imperfect intuition/remote objects), and in the future as anticipation. Duns Scotus provides the example of the experience and recollection of having perceived a white object as an instance of the remote and the proximate, of pertaining to the sense and to the intellect, "[when] the intellect intuitively recognized that I see something white and afterwards retains this knowledge and remembers I saw something white. And here is a case where both proximate and remote objects are a matter of intellective remembrance." But what are the implications of supplementing Aristotle's epistemology with intuition? Duns Scotus offers an answer when he underscores that many proximate objects need not be matters of sense remembrance such as past intellections or volitions: "Otherwise we could not repent of our bad will, make sense of past intellectual experience in the future, or from the fact that we had thought about such matters, set out to explore other consequences thereof."[39] Among the subjects (themes and subjectivities) of ethnography, Franciscans would seek to understand the mind of the Nahuas in order to discipline their memory in confessional practices (i.e., sin must be intuited as such to be remembered). Moreover, the Franciscans held the belief that the Nahuas should readily intuit the necessity of recognizing and accepting revealed truths (i.e., the divine nature of the source and the authority of the Fathers).

Intuition also enables Franciscans to develop a theory of the will and man's natural desire to love God that eschews the necessity of an intellectual habit or even supernatural intervention. Although, as Allan Wolter has pointed out, several Scholastic thinkers, notably Peter Lombard and Hugh of St. Victor, had espoused "the notion that God reveals himself in nature as well as through the Scriptures," there are two consequences to the centrality of the will in Duns Scotus's interpretation of natural law and natural reason.[40] First, the emphasis Duns Scotus placed on freedom of the will invested a personal as well as historical dimension to the otherwise impersonal understanding of natural law in Augustine's and the Stoics' *lex aeterna*. For Duns Scotus, reason, properly speaking, belongs to the will and not to the intellect. He bases this on the freedom of choice of "acting and not acting (liberty of contradiction) or acting now in this way, now that (liberty of contrariety)."[41] Thus Duns Scotus writes: "If rational means to act with reason, then it is the will that is properly rational and it is concerned with alternatives both as regards its own actions and the actions of the powers it controls, but the alternative it selects is not determined by its nature (as is the case of the intellect, which could not determine itself to act otherwise), but acts freely."[42] Humans create laws and act on them with reason, with the will. This point opens the possibility of comparative studies of laws and moral systems that Wolter phrases in the following unequivocal terms (though, I am afraid, without taking full stock of the implications): "Though [Duns Scotus] stated the principle of the evolutionary development *Deus ordinate agens procedit de imperfecto ad perfectum* in reference to God's supernaturally revealed law, there seems no reason why it cannot be extended to his promulgation of the law of nature as well, viz. to a gradual growth in moral awareness, protracted over periods of centuries or even millennia if you will. *In processu generationis humanae, semper crevit notitia veritatis.*"[43] Beyond law, this *processu generationis humanae* implies a development of the will's desire for truth, that is, different states of human nature that Duns Scotus understood in temporal terms, but that the participants in the discovery and conquest of America translated to geographic categories that included the historical difference of Amerindian peoples living in isolation from the rest of humanity. In this regard, we can trace a radical difference between the historicity of revelation and the theological anthropology it presupposes, as a component of Christian economy of salvation espoused by all Scholastics, and the philosophical anthropology that would place different peoples in different relationships to truth in general.

Before moving to Franciscan and Dominican empirical anthropologies, let me briefly summarize two key notions in Ockham's (but also in Gabriel Biel's) philosophy of language that played a central role in Franciscans like Bernardino de Sahagún, Alonso de Molina, and Diego Valadés. For Ockham, oral and written languages were arbitrary systems that had to be differentiated from mental concepts; one must underscore that Ockham did not understand writing as mere image of speech, but a specific linguistic practice. In its most basic formulation, Ockham would argue that if the names "*flor*" and "*xochitl*" in Spanish and Nahuatl differ, the mental name would be the same for subjects speaking these languages.[44] The notion of mental concepts entails a realist epistemology. Languages can thus be categorized and evaluated in terms of their capacity not to convey the mental concept but to utter sound statements. Latin (and by extension Greek and Arabic) would be a more appropriate language than the vernaculars for science, logic, and grammar. Scientific habits entail forms of cognition that would be determined by linguistic differences. Though Ockham, as far I have been able to grasp, did not pursue the sort of understanding of language as worldview that we have come to associate with Benjamin Whorf,[45] the work of Sahagún not only investigated the different names given to things in Nahuatl but their metaphorical meaning and mental associations. Indian languages would be studied not solely to preach, confess, and translate doctrines, but as windows to the intellect and will of the people that spoke them.

DOCUMENTING HABITUS AND DECEPTION

Both Sahagún and Durán viewed the lucidity I have traced in Ometochtzin and the *tlacuilo* of the *Telleriano-Remensis* as an indication that the faith was superficially implanted in Mexico and that Indians were concealing their ancient ceremonies in Christian rituals, everyday practices, or feasts purporting to have no religious significance. For both Sahagún and Durán, Indians were liars, and the task of their ethnographic research was to learn to decipher their veiled, inscribed bodies—that is, their dress, religious paraphernalia, dances, and languages. Their understanding of the lying subjects, however, is radically different and cuts across the philosophical traditions of their orders.

Durán attributes the Indians' superficial faith to an inborn wretchedness, a poverty of spirit and gloomy temperament—a consequence of the social conditions in which they lived both before and after the conquest.[46] He compares the Nahuas to Spanish peasants who could also have weak intellects, but whose faith would nevertheless be solidly implanted, "creyendo firmemente aquello que les enseñaron sus padres, y lo que tiene y cree la Santa Madre Iglesia" [believing firmly what their parents taught them and what is believed and sustained by our Holy Mother Church].[47] Contrary to Spanish peasants who would simply respond to questions regarding the faith by saying "why not?" or "that is the way it is," Indians, like Ometochtzin and the *tlacuilo* of Telleriano-Remensis, would press them to answer why there is only one god or one set of beliefs rather than a plurality of truths that could include their own. Actually, by the time Durán writes in the 1570s, this sort of defiance had gone underground—hence his explanation of lying as timidity, wretchedness, and so on. Ultimately, for Durán, the underlying reason for the Indians' travails and afflictions "es tener la imaginativa tan lastimada y enflaquecida, con tanto miedo, que todas las cosas que no tienen muy tratadas y conocidas las aprenden como dañosas y temerosas: así como las fieras cuando son acosadas, que todo les amedrenta y hace huir" [is that their spirit has been so hurt, so crippled, that they live in fear. They look upon everything unfamiliar or unknown as harmful and fearful to them. They are like wild animals that when hunted, are intimidated by everything and forced to flight].[48] Horcasitas and Hayden's translation of *imaginativa lastimada* as "hurt spirit" fails to capture the Thomist terminology and understanding of the imagination as a faculty belonging to the interior senses. The *imagi-nativa lastimada* entails lacking proper habits and dispositions, which precludes Indians from receiving the sacraments properly. As an example of the *imaginativa lastimada*, Durán mentions the Indians' practice of wearing earrings (on the recommendation of healers) that would keep them from dying during epidemics, giving more credence to the healers than to the Holy Trinity: "para quitarles de aquella ironía es menester especial favor del Espiritu Santo" [to remove them from that incongruity it would be necessary to receive a special favor from the Holy Spirit].[49] Here the discourse of natural science—the incongruity that earrings would keep them from dying, an instance of the *imaginativa lastimada*—resonates with questions of theological faith. Clearly, Durán's Nahuas are no longer the ideal Amerindians of chapter 5 of Las Casas's *De unico vocationis modo*, but subjects in need of healing and remedies to compensate the injustices committed against them. Durán defines his ethnographic objects of study as wounded subjects, but he lacks the moral outrage of Las Casas, who called for the restitution of goods and restoration of sovereignty.

If the identification of pre-Columbian beliefs and the variations Indians have invented in their practices since the conquest are central to Durán's ethnography, he is at least equally concerned with the proliferation of new superstitions. Their habitus (a combination of Mesoamerican cultural continuities and the *imaginativa lastimada* by the wars of conquest) leads Indians not only to fear the new, but also to generate new superstitions. As long as the ancient habitus remained, Indians were condemned to be irremediable idolaters and fabricators of superstition: "Poniendo y fingiendo superstición en las cosas que de suyo no tienen mal; hasta en horadar las orejas y poner sarcillos en las niñas y mujeres han introducido superstición" [Making up and inventing superstition in things which in themselves are not evil. They have even introduced superstitious beliefs in perforating and placing of earrings in girls and women].[50] But there is perhaps no place more indicative of age-old habit barring a solid implantation of the faith than in the often-quoted passage in which Durán questions an Indian as to why he collected a great amount of money only to offer a fiesta and spend it all, to which the Indian answered: "Padre, no te espantes, pues todavía estamos *nepantla*" [Father, do not be astonished; we are still *nepantla*].[51] In response to queries about what he meant by *nepantla*, the Indian explained to Durán that "como no estaban aún bien arraigados en la fe, que no me espantase; de manera que aún estaban neutros, que ni bien acudían a una ley, ni a la otra, o por mejor decir, que creían en Dios y que juntamente acudían a sus costumbres antiguas y ritos comunes" [since the people were not well rooted in the faith yet, I should not marvel that they were neuter, that they neither followed one religion nor the other. Or better said, they believed in God and also followed their ancient customs and common rites].⁵²

What for Durán means a weak standing in the faith, for the Indians signifies the compatibility of both worlds: "que creían en Dios y que juntamente acudían a sus costumbres antiguas y ritos comunes" [they believed in God and also followed their ancient customs and common rites]. This compatibility, not unlike the discourse of Ometochtzin that exposed the inconsistency in the Christian call for exclusivity, suggests an agile subject who can travel between worlds, hardly a torn double consciousness. I would emphasize that Durán's phrasing (the Indian's voicing of *nepantla*) entails dwelling in two discrete worlds rather than a mestizo consciousness. And yet Durán at one point seems to accept the inevitability of Indians mixing the two religions as he joins a procession where instead of candles they were carrying flowers, introducing an old practice into a Christian feast: "Véolo y callo, porque veo pasar a todos por ello, y también tomo mi báculo de rosas, como los demás" [I see these things and I am silent, since I realize that everyone feigns ignorance. So I pick up my staff of flowers like the rest].⁵³ Even when Durán identifies the old gods, his method places greater emphasis on the new modes of celebrating than on accuracy, as can be perceived in the representation of Quetzalcoatl (Figure 9) in his book, which marks a radical departure from the traditional style of depicting deities in Telleriano-Remensis (see Figures 6 and 7). The naturalistic depiction of a god in the mode of a human should not be read as misrepresentation but as an image that would fulfill the function of serving to identify Indians dressed as the god in real feasts, "es de saber que aquellos representan dioses y a éstos iban haciendo la fiesta y baile, interior y exteriormente" [be aware that these men represent Gods, that the feast is for them, both inwardly and outwardly].⁵⁴

Like all missionaries, at least partly because of demands by the Crown, Durán insisted that the friars must learn Indian languages to be able to preach and confess Indians effectively. But unlike Franciscans like Sahagún and Molina, he did not see language as a key to understanding and assessing the mentality of the Nahuas. The end point in Durán's research is the beginning for his Franciscan counterparts: "Estos conjuros andan escritos y los he tenido en mi poder y pudiéralos poner aquí, si fuera cosa que importara. Pero, además de no ser necesario en nuestra lengua, vueltos, son disparates" [These incantations have been written down, and I have had them in my hands, and I could set them down here if they

FIGURE 9 *Diego Durán*, Historia de las Indias de la Nueva España e islas de tierra firme, *fol. 251v. Courtesy of the Biblioteca Nacional de España.*

were important. Aside from their not being necessary, however, once they have been translated into our Spanish language, they become nonsensical].⁵⁵ Sahagún's project takes on the issue of the obscurity of Nahuatl. For him, as for his fellow Franciscan Molina (1571), the study of Nahuatl was plagued with difficulties that created impediments to communication, though Molina seems more certain of overcoming them.

In his "Prólogo al lector," Molina lists three difficulties he faced in producing his *Vocabulario en lengua castellana y mexicana* (1571): (1) the first difficulty arises from the fact that Nahuatl is not his native tongue, "por no auer mamado esta lengua con la leche" [for not have suckled this tongue with the milk], which created difficulties when he aspired to "descubrir los secretos que ay en la lengua, la cual es tan copiosa, tan elegante, y de tanto artificio y primor en sus metaphoras y maneras de dezir, quanto conoceran los que en ella se exercitaren" [discover the secrets of the tongue, which is so rich, so elegant, with so much art in its metaphors and manners of speech, which will be known by those who practice it]; (2) the second difficulty has to do with the variety of words used in different provinces that "solo el que ouiese biuidio en todas ellas las podria dar a entender" [only someone who had lived in all of them would be able to convey]; (3) the third inconvenience is the result of "tener muchas cosas que ellos no conocian, ni alcançauan: y para estas no tenian no tienen vocablos propios: y por el contrario, las cosas que ellos tenian de que nosotros careciamos, en nuestra lengua, no se pueden dar bien a entender, por vocablos preciosos y particulares: y por esto asi para entender sus vocablos como para declararlos nuestros, son menester algunas vezes largos circunloquios y rodeos" [having many things that they did not know, or reached; and for these they lacked their own words; and on the contrary, the things that they had and we lacked, in our tongue, they cannot be conveyed well by means of precious and particular words: consequently to understand their words and to declare ours, one needs long circumlocutions and roundabouts].[56] Molina's optimism suggests an ecclesiastical positivism in which the implantation of faith would consist of finding the appropriate words—as it were, *le mot juste*—for the communication of revealed truth.[57] From a nominalist position, the right words should convey the mental words common to the terms in both languages. As I have pointed out, for the Franciscans, cognition of revealed truth must precede love of God.

Sahagún generally agrees with Molina's praise of Nahuatl, but he also foregrounds the obscurity of the language with an understanding that goes beyond the nonsensical or childishness of Durán's assessment. Sahagún's views on the lack of transparency in language would seem to build also on Ockham's distinction between mental names and the arbitrary nature of vocal and written terms. But in clearing up the obscurity of language, Sahagún aspires to access mental discourse to unmask liars, to confess, but also to understand conceptual subtleties in Nahuatl metaphysics and mappings of the body.[58]

If Durán's paintings were mainly concerned with documenting the apparel of the ancient gods that would enable missionaries to identify individuals performing rites in feasts, Sahagún's inclusion of paintings forms part of the project to collect samples of Nahuatl speech. Although the painting of what the gods ate in *Primeros memoriales* (Figure 10),[59] as in the work of Durán, could serve to identify ancient ceremonies still practiced,

FIGURE 10   *Bernardino de Sahagún,* Primeros memoriales. *Códice Matritense del Palacio de Madrid, fol. 254r. Courtesy of the Real Biblioteca and Patrimonio Nacional.*

or individuals bearing the attributes of gods, say, of Quetzalcoatl, painting as a form of writing partakes of the same impulse that constituted the study of language as an investigation into the mind of the Nahuas: "Todas las cosas que conferimos, me las dieron por pinturas, que aquella era la escriptura, que ellos antiguamente vsauan; y los gramaticos las declararon en su lengua, escrjujendo la declaration al pie de la pintura: tengo aun agora estos originales" [They gave all the matters we discussed in pictures, for that was the writing they employed in ancient times. And the grammarians declared them in their language, writing the declaration at the bottom of the painting. I still have these originals].[60] The sense of *declarar* carries a judicial dimension that links the inquiries to inquisitorial investigations and has a bearing on making manifest what is occult, obscure, and not understood.

The grammarians were Indians who had been trained in grammar, natural science, and logic at the College of Santa Cruz de Tlatelolco, and spoke Nahuatl, Spanish, and Latin. It is not clear, however, whether it was the grammarians who elaborated the discourses or whether they limited themselves to recording by means of Latin script what the informant said. My inclination is for the second option, given that Sahagún also mentions the gathering of elders to request their paintings and verbal statements. This mention of the method in the prologue to Book II of the *Historia general de las cosas de Nueva España* (ca. 1579) refers to the materials collected in *Primeros memoriales*, the result of the first ethnographic inquiries in Tepepulco. The project in Telleriano-Remensis resembles the recording of pictorial-writing forms in *Primeros memoriales* in that the former also has the objective of recording forms of writing, of creating an album; however, it lacks the systematic linguistic dimension of Sahagún. Moreover, in Sahagún we don't find the glosses that "translate" the paintings in Telleriano-Remensis, but a parallel collection of speech forms that though thematically related to the pictorial do not pretend to exhaust the meaning of the painting. Verbal and pictorial records convey meanings that cannot be reduced to each other. The research process would go from painting to oral text to alphabetical writing; each of these forms, in turn, beyond serving to identify veiled practices, provided keys to understand and evaluate how the Nahuas perceived and articulated the objective world—their *quilates*, their "carats," in Sahagún's lingo. For the most part, Sahagún's assessment of the intellect of the Nahuas is positive; he is less enthusiastic about their will.

Although in other places Sahagún speaks of the Nahuas as lacking writing, these are incidental comments that hardly reflect some sort of ideological negation of or blindness toward writing practices among the Nahuas. He is clearly more interested in using paintings/writings to understand the mentality of the Nahuas than in casting them as intellectual inferiors because they lacked a phonetic alphabet. Sahagún ascribes the failed conversion to moral weakness. In terms of Duns Scotus's view of historical evolution, Sahagún considered the Nahuas to have a very undeveloped will: "aviendo visto por experiencia la dureça de la gente" [having seen from experience the hardness of the heart of this people]. The *dureça de la gente* led Sahagún to speculate that the Nahuas would completely revert to paganism within fifty years if the Spaniards abandoned the New World.[61] Rather than seeing this disposition in terms of damaged intellectual faculties that resulted from the wars of conquest, epidemics, and labor exploitation, as we have observed in Durán, Sahagún finds a conspiracy to deceive the Spaniards from the start. The Nahuas willfully deceived the missionaries when they were first asked at the beginning of the evangelization if they accepted the Christian tenets. Central to this submission to the new church was the required belief in one god and the wholesale repudiation of their world. It is not a question of not fully understanding the doctrine of one god but of refusing to accept it and lying.

To Ometochtzin and the *tlacuilo* of the Telleriano-Remensis, the missionaries espoused different worlds that they felt could coexist with an equally plural set of indigenous worldviews. This capacity to dwell in or at least to conceive the coexistence of a plurality of equally valid worlds was unacceptable to the missionaries, even though they understood that Nahuatl culture consisted of deep-seated habits that could not be shed overnight (Durán) or of languages that held the secrets to forms of conceiving the world (Sahagún). They saw the multiplicity but could only accept one world in spite of the irreducible differences in the philosophical traditions of Franciscans and Dominicans. Sixteenth-century Nahuas, on the other hand, seem to have grasped the value of accepting the notion of a plurality of worlds that cannot be simply subsumed into one another by a process of translation or by inclusion in terms of degrees of complexity.[62]

Although the texts of Ometochtzin and the *tlacuilo* partake of a fabric of rebellion, resistance, and subversion, the concept of plural-world dwelling liberates us from the moral economy that exclusively values cultural artifacts in which one can find acts of resistance. *Telleriano-Remensis* exemplifies the capacity to create a discursive space that does not react to, but instead adopts elements from Western codes to communicate the specificity of a plurality of worlds. We never find the *tlacuilo* situating herself in opposition to alphabetical writing or Renaissance pictorial perspective. The frontal image of the Franciscan captures the individualism enforced by the confession, but beyond the inquisitorial vigilance, we ought to imagine the *tlacuilo* looking back at us from the past with an ironic smile that brags of her ability to codify in her own pictorial language a Western cultural modality by means of a symbolic use of perspective. We witness the delineation of borders and a plurality of worlds but not a transitional existence nor a demand for recognition. Secular and religious authorities *recognized* all too well the *tlacuilo*'s as well as Ometochtzin's historical and epistemological lucidity—but it blinded them. Colonial discourse, moreover, aspires to create intermediary subjects, states of *nepantla* according to the Nahuatl expression, subjects working on becoming purer Christians, and persecutes those who like Ometochtzin refused to think of themselves within a master-slave dialectic. However, the concept of *nepantla*, neither here nor there, neither in the ancient order nor in the Christian, can also be understood in terms of *a-not-being-really-convinced-of-the-necessity-of-dwelling-in-only-one-world*. The exteriority and incommensurability of the subaltern world engenders fear of insurrection (the war of the Mixtón or the Zapatista uprising today), as well as anxiety in the face of epistemological lucidity that captures the relativity of Western forms of life, not by denying their truth but by inhabiting them and acting on them without abdicating one's own.

In earlier chapters, I examined in detail the vocabulary the *tlacuilo* invented for classifying the two main religious orders in Mexico. We found that her taxonomy entailed a distinction between the Dominicans and the Franciscans that highlighted the main differences in their evangelical practices and ethnographic styles. The *tlacuilo* captures the irreconcilable differences with an economy of language that, in avoiding essentializing Catholicism—that is, reducing all missionaries to a single ideology—would be enviable to a nominalist. It is also important to note that her taxonomy does not presuppose a binary; she simply places them on the page as two distinct entities. In fact, the *tlacuilo* could have included on folio 46r a figure that would record the evangelical and ethnographic practices of the Augustinians, the other major order active in Central Mexico. Consider, for instance, the *tlacuilo* capturing the Augustinian form by means of a depiction that would draw its inspiration from a painting of Alonso de la Vera Cruz dictating theology in Latin to a captive Antonio Huitzimengari, a son of the "Indian king of Michoacan," as the legend in the upper left-hand corner on the painting puts it (Figure 11). The *tlacuilo* could have painted a friar clad in black, with a pointed finger indicating a subtle move in his argumentation, and an Indian student taking notes assiduously. Vera Cruz, as such, would be emblematic of the philosophic-theological contributions of the Augustinians. My mention of Vera Cruz is not incidental. As we will see later on in this chapter, Vera Cruz's discourse on apostasy in *De dominio infidelium et justo bello* (1553–1554) offers a discourse on apostasy that departs from the positions espoused by Franciscans and Dominicans.

On folio 46r, we find another instance of brilliant taxonomy in the topology of conquest and conversion the *tlacuilo* devises in juxtaposing the Dominican imparting baptism with Viceroy Mendoza battling the insurgent Tenamaztle (see Figure 1). The *tlacuilo* introduces into the missionaries' experience of language and space a dimension they couldn't quite understand, given the absence of prior topological referents in their se-

FIGURE II *Portrait of Alonso de la Vera Cruz lecturing at the Colegio de Tiripetio, Michoacán, Mexico. Courtesy of Laurence Cuelenaere.*

mantic and semiotic horizon. In fact, the *tlacuilo*, once again, looks at them from an *elsewhere* that circumscribes them with a logic that exposed how the apostle and the apostate mirrored each other. Here again the *tlacuilo* does not produce a taxonomy ruled by a binary, but rather reveals the inseparability of the terms *apostle* and *apostate* by means of a topological register that reminds us of the nonorientable surface of a Möbius strip. I will return to the implications of a Möbius-like mirroring surface; for now, allow me to sum up my findings from another article that draws the historical and epistemological limits of writing an account of apostasy or, for that matter, of the failed narrative of ethnosuicide.

In "*Without* History?: Apostasy as a Historical Category," I have shown how the *tlacuilo*'s topology of conquest illustrates the concept of "*without* history."[1] There I argued that the term *without* entails an amphibology: it at once signifies absence and outside. The concept of history itself presupposes an absence and an outside in positing an origin or beginning that either assumes a nothing, that is, an outside that cannot be taken as a source and ground of history (out of nothing, its nonfoundation, ex-nihilo), or posits an origin in mythical expressions, that is, a prehistory that contains the seeds of history proper (in a progression, a lack to be supplemented, teleology). As an amphibology, which only works in English but not in Spanish or Latin, the concept of *without* lends itself to constructive equivocation. These observations on the limits of history and its *without* entail the need to recognize the forgotten lost experience of the depicted events while at the same time underscoring that the events remain unforgettable. In addressing the paradox of the forgotten as unforgettable, we may cite Agamben's maxim that emphasizes the need to resist institutionalizing histories: "To respond to this exigency is the only historical responsibility I feel capable of assuming fully."[2] The concept of *elsewhere* underscores a space of indeterminacy that must remain unforgettable in the forgotten experience of the *tlacuilo* and her world. She offers a mask of death, of an unsurpassable dislocation that bears witness to the impossibility of speech. It testifies to the failed narrative of ethnosuicide. Agamben's maxim also proves pertinent for sorting out the pretence of memorializing apostasy instead of retaining its status as *without* history.

In "*Without* History?" I also analyzed a wide variety of documents that have sought to historicize the figure of Tenamaztle. These texts included Spanish histories, indigenous narratives and pictorial texts, opinions on the legality and justness of wars of extermination, letters drafted by Tenamaztle in collaboration with Bartolomé de Las Casas, celebrations of the Indian rebel as the first *guerrillero* of the Americas and first expositor of human rights doctrines, and monuments in the central plaza of Nochistlán, Zacatecas. The objective there was not to exhaust all the documentation on the wars against the Chichimecas in the sixteenth century, but rather to delineate the limits of history in accessing the figure of the apostate. The *tlacuilo* warns us that the discourses we elaborate might end up reproducing the mirroring that binds the apostle and the apostate.

Whereas the apostate (from Greek *apostates*, literally "rebel," from *aphistanai*, "cause to revolt," apo- = away from + *histanai* = to cause to stand) takes flight from history, the apostle (from the Greek *apostolos*, literally "messenger," from *apostellein*, "to send away," apo- + *stellien* = to send) is one whose calling is to incorporate new peoples into the sweep of history, in this instance, the friar administering baptism who has traveled to the New World in pursuit of an ever-expanding historical mission. This topology of conquest and conversion should make us wary of apologetics (another *apo*- word, this time one that links to *logos*, "word" or "reason," denoting a defense from) that underscore the historicity of indigenous peoples, whether in the mode that describes precolonial history as partaking of the Judeo-Christian teleology, a mode much favored by Mesoamerican and Andean historians like Guaman Poma, Garcilaso de la Vega, Tezozomoc, Chimalpahin, or Ixtlixochitl, or in the mode that defines historicality as a trait of humanity, a mode much favored by modern historians. Again we should retain the paradox of the *forgotten-that-remains-unforgettable*. There is little commemoration in the *tlacuilo*'s depiction of Tenamaztle. To some extent, she forms part of the same archival fog that prevents us from accessing the apostate, that is, the insurgent, on and in his own terms. There is a difference, however, between the *tlacuilo*'s depiction of a topology of conquest and the historians (as well as the modern apologists) who cite Tenamaztle's voice as if it were immediately available in the archives and narrate the events as if the forgotten—inevitably lost—memory of the events were not obscured by the colonial discourses that recorded them. Without concern for the silenced subject of apostasy, historians and apologists repeat the violence that circumscribed the apostate either by naturalizing the semblance of the apostate in terms of an inversion and violation of the ideals of the Christian evangelization or by domesticating the insurgency in terms of our contemporary ideals of human rights discourses. If the *tlacuilo*'s picture lends itself to telling these stories, it also reveals the structure that binds the discourses of the apostate to those of the apostle.

In the scenes depicted in folio 46r, we find this dual sense of *without*. In the top left-hand corner, we find the baptismal event, where the stream of water signifies the entry of a willing subject to the Roman Catholic Church, and thus a passage from an absence of history to history. In addition to the metaphorical sense of baptism as "door of the church," we must note that the liturgy actually called for the introduction of subjects to be baptized into the actual architectural structure of the church. For this purpose, a baptistery in the exterior of the church or a railed-off baptismal font located in one of the main entrances provided a liminal space for the full spiritual and physical incorporation. Thus there is both a symbolic and a material topology of conversion. The *tlacuilo* has devised a Mesoamerican-inspired pictogram composed of shells and drops for marking the administration of the holy water but also for symbolically inscribing the threshold of baptism as a gate of the church. The *tlacuilo* also marks the Dominican's compliance with the strictures of the liturgy by depicting him wearing highly stylized pantaloons tied around his calves. This is a clear example of the *tlacuilo*'s invention of a pictorial language for codifying the Dominican order. There is no exterior referent of Dominicans wearing pantaloons that the *tlacuilo* could draw from.

Below, the same precolonial pictogram for water marks the boundary between the space of those who bolt out of the political, religious, and economic structures of the Spanish spiritual and secular dominion to place themselves *without* history, outside it, as apostates, and the space of Viceroy Mendoza's rule. The naked Caxcan leader stands next to the pictogram for the town of Nochistlán (the place of the flowery cactus) sending arrows across the river. The nakedness resonates with accounts by his contemporaries that describe the rebels as going into battle naked. Though we should also note that the feathered shield on his back recalls the accoutrement of the ubiquitous god Tezcatlipoca, a central deity among the Mexicas who was known for practicing sorcery (see Figure 7). This reference clearly defines the rebellion as nativist, as a return to pagan forms of life. Observe that the Latin term most commonly used for apostatizing is *retrocedere*, "to go back." The placement of the rebel on top of a crag, a *peñol*, does not merely allude to the mountaintop from which they battled the Spaniards but also to taking refuge in the mountains after abandoning the *reducciones* to which they had been confined for their evangelization and the instillment of civilized ways.

The topology implicit in the semantic interdependence between the apostle and the apostate suggests the structure of a Möbius strip in which the two sides of the band (apostleship/apostasy) would alternate being visible in the movement that inverts them. Consider the following definition by Dylan Evans:

[The Möbius strip] is a three-dimensional figure that can be formed by taking a long rectangle of paper and twisting it once before joining its ends together. The result is a figure which subverts our normal (Euclidian) way of representing space, for it seems to have two sides but in fact has only one edge. Two sides can be distinguished, but when the whole strip is traversed it becomes clear that they are continuous. The two sides are only distinguished by the dimension of time, the time it takes to traverse the whole strip.[3]

I am not suggesting that one can find the Möbius strip in the painting. The circumscription of the Nahua by the baptismal water and that of Tenamaztle by the river form a continuum with inverted values that are semantically bound. It is the same band, defined by the baptismal water and the river, which includes both forms as they would in the unfolding of the Möbius strip. In doing so, it breaks from the mirroring of opposites that would naturalize them in a binary opposition. Thus the *tlacuilo* exposes how the inside/outside of the universal history of church and empire are not discrete entities but continuous with each other. In this regard, we may say in Lacanian terms that the *tlacuilo* traverses the fantasy of the discourse on apostasy.[4] For there is a comic element (which would explain the impact of the *tlacuilo*'s revelation on the missionaries who see the truth but are also blinded) in her not-so-innocent pairing of the jocular pantaloon-clad Dominican who brings the Nahua inside the Church and Viceroy Mendoza who battles the feather-attired naked Tenamaztle outside the empire. The fact that Pedro de Alvarado, Tonatiuh, dies in the assault on the *peñol* of Nochistlán, after referring to the rebels as "cuatro indios gatillo," four Indian punks, would have provoked roaring laughter at his haughtiness.

One could certainly write the history of the rebellion by following Ranajit Guha's proposal that in reading the documents of counterinsurgency, we ought to provide reading in reverse, that is, read the narratives against their grain to offer a semantic transvaluation of the terms; when the colonial historian writes rebellion, we should read self-defense; when criminal theft, legitimate expropriation.[5] This method was already articulated in the case presented by Francisco Tenamaztle in collaboration with Bartolomé de Las Casas that called for the restitution of goods and the restoration of sovereignty to the Caxcan peoples. The Las Casas–Tenamaztle dossier collected by Miguel León-Portilla[6] includes two letters in which Tenamaztle denounces the atrocities committed against his people and explains that he had been arrested and exiled to Spain by Viceroy Luis de Velasco after he surrendered to the bishop of Guadalajara, who died shortly after. Although the documents are prepared in the language of law expected by the Council of the Indies, and the legal discourse that structures these documents makes it practically impossible to identify a voice that would correspond to Tenamaztle, we should attend to their (Las Casas's and Tenamaztle's) ability to remove themselves from the mirroring discourses of apostleship and apostasy. We should be cautious, however, about attributing authorship to Tenamaztle. Although these documents present his case, Tenamaztle disappears, leaving no paper trace of what happened to him after presenting his case to the Council of the Indies in Valladolid in 1556.

At any rate, let's observe how, in collaboration with Las Casas, Tenamaztle develops a language that questions the semantics of conquest. Tenamaztle writes: "Este huir, y esta natural defensa, muy poderosos señores, llaman y han llamado siempre los españoles, usando mal de la propiedad de los vocablos, en todas las Indias, contra el Rey levantarse" [This taking flight, and this natural defense, most powerful lords, is called and has always been called by the Spaniards, making bad use of the propriety of words, in all of the Indies, to rise against the king].[7] Tenamaztle makes this statement right after giving an account of the oppression of Nuño de Guzmán, Juan de Oñate, and Miguel Ibarra. These Spaniards had subjected the Caxcanes to torture, persecution, murder, rape, and the hanging of their leaders, atrocities that forced them to flee to the sierras of Xuchipila and make strongholds in the *peñoles*, the crags, of Nochistlán and the Mixtón. Tenamaztle underscores that these abuses countered all principles of natural law and the law of nations (*ius gentium*): "El principio y medio de estos daños y agravios recibidos fue un Nuño de Guzmán que primero vino a mis tierras, siendo yo señor dellas, no recognociendo a otro señor en mundo alguno por superior, como hoste público de mi señorío y república, violento opresor mío y de mis súbditos contra derecho natural y de las gentes" [The beginning and middle of all these received damages and offenses was the so-called Nuño de Guzmán, who first came to these lands, while I was lord over them, not recognizing any other lord as superior, as public enemy of my dominion and republic, violent oppressor of mine and of my subjects against natural law and the law of peoples].[8] This brilliant denunciation of the semantics of conquest also carries an apologetic discourse that offers the semblance of Caxcanes living in peace when they were attacked as if they were enemies of the Spanish people or king, or as if they had offended the Church, *la universal iglesia*. Tenamaztle argues that these abuses entitle his people to "justamente [impugnar] a

mano armada y resistille" [justly (challenge) with arms and resist him].⁹
Given that fleeing and resisting were for Tenamaztle more than a question
of survival but legitimate responses to the violence of conquest, he puts the
king in a situation in which he would have to examine his conscience:

> Juzgue Vuestra Alteza, como espero que juzgará justa y católicamente,
> como jueces rectísimos, quién de las naciones aunque carezcan de Fe de
> Christo, ni de otra ley divina ni humana, sino enseñada por sola razón
> natural y qué especie de bestias hobiera entre las criaturas irracionales
> a quien no fuera lícito y justísimo el tal huir, y la tal defensa, y el levan-
> tamiento como ellos lo quieren llamar.

> [May Your Highness pass judgment, since I expect that you will judge
> justly and in a Catholic manner, in the manner of most just judges of
> nations even if lacking the Faith of Christ, or of any other human or
> divine law, but by means of natural reason alone and what species of
> beast among irrational creatures for whom it would not be licit and just
> to flee, and such a defense, and uprising as they like to call it].¹⁰

The exposure of the semantics of conquest should warn us about writing
a history in which the terms would assume a positive turn for characterizing apostasy or insurgency for that matter. The celebration of Tenamaztle
as an early human rights advocate would tread on a thin road that would
subordinate him to the Spanish legal codes at the expense of the discourse
that has been irremediably silenced and lost.

We also risk naturalizing a docile Tenamaztle who commits himself
to bringing "naciones que están bravas" into the fold and service of the
Crown. He commits to conducting this service by peaceful means only,
"sin lanzas ni espadas" [without lances or swords], on the condition that
they never be removed from the protection of the Crown nor given in *encomienda*: "jamás serán de ella sacados, ni encomendados a españoles ni
particulares, ni dados en feudo, ni por otra vía alguna que pueda ser pen-
sada."¹¹ The consideration that he would attract the rebels by peaceful
means resonates with Las Casas's *De unico vocationis modo*, though we
should also consider that after the Nuevas Leyes of 1542, the Crown stipu-
lates that only love and peaceful means should be used in the pacification
of Indians. *Pacificación* replaces *conquista* in this legal tract that responded
to Las Casas's denunciations and exposure of the illegality of the slavery
and the *encomiendas*. Here we find Las Casas, through the voice of Tenamaztle, articulating a case for limiting Spain's claims to dominion and sovereignty. Obviously no form of slavery would be justified, nor war for that

matter, but neither would there be *encomiendas*, or fiefs, or any form of subordination to Spaniards. Tenamaztle's suzerainty is immediately subordinated to the suzerainty of the king of Spain. Thus, we may speak of it as an autonomous state within an empire claiming universality but also the peaceful coexistence of its autonomous kingdoms. Other conditions include: "Y que los caciques y señores queden y sean en sus estados y señoríos sustentados y confirmados, y sucedan en ellos sus herederos conformemente a sus leyes y costumbres justas que tuvieren, recognosciendo siempre por supremos y soberanos señores y reyes a los reyes de Castilla universales" [And that the caciques and lords be sustained and confirmed in their estates and dominions, and be succeeded by their inheritors according to their just laws and customs, always recognizing as supreme and suzerain lords and kings the universal lords and kings of Castile]. Tenamaztle adds that in recognition of this universal rule they will give "cierto tributo ellos y los que les sucedieren en los dichos estados" [a certain tribute they and those who followed them in the said estates].[12]

I have translated *soberanos* as "suzerain" and not as "sovereign" to underscore that the gist of this passage is the formulation of the existence of autonomous states within the Crown rather than their subjection under the dominion of Spain. Let me briefly define semantic differences in the terms *suzerainty* and *sovereignty*. Although the distinction between *sovereignty* and *suzerainty* is recent, dating back in English to medieval scholars in the nineteenth century, these terms were used interchangeably in French as early as the thirteenth century. Nineteenth-century scholars speak of suzerainty when addressing the relationship between the fief and king. According to Guizot, the king in the "feudal" regime was the suzerain of the suzerains, the lord of the lords. He outlines a chain that links different subjects under the obligation of recognizing suzerainty that begins with the king: "qu'en appellant autor de lui [the king] ses vassaux, puis les vassaux de ses vaussaux, et ainsi de suite, il appelait tout le peuple et se montrait vraiment roi."[13] The most common terms in *Siete Partidas* are *señorío/señor* and *vasallo*; in the documents on the Americas by the Reyes Católicos, the preferred term is *súbditos*, which we may translate as "subjects." By using *súbdito* to speak of Indians under Spanish rule, the Reyes Católicos placed them on equal ground before the law, even when they draft special legislation, inspired in the *Siete Partidas*. This is the same legal status of Indians who have been summoned by the Requerimiento: "Sus Altezas los recibieron alegre e benignamnte, y ansi los mandó tratar como a los otros sus súbditos y basallos" [Your Highnesses received them joyfully and kindly, and thus ordered that they should be treated like the others of his subjects and vassals].[14] Either as *súbditos* or as *vasallos*, the status of Indians would correspond to that of any other subject of the Crown's *señorío*. Tenamaztle willingly subordinates his *señorío* to the Crown's and its chain of suzerainty. In offering his obedience and willingness as a *señor* to pay tribute to the king, he also explicitly excludes the possibility that he could be subjected to the *encomienda* regime.[15]

If the Requerimiento could be viewed as conveying the natural suzerainty of the Spanish Crown over Indians, in compliance with the papal donation, by denouncing the absurdity of the demand to surrender political authority to the king of Spain, Las Casas emphasizes the imperial bond based on domination. Although the distinction between these categories is recent, they may be used fruitfully to identify two modes of colonial authority. Whereas "vassal and suzerain are bound to each other by a reciprocal oath of allegiance and assistance," writes Jean-Luc Nancy, "in the case of the sovereign, on the contrary, it is power that founds and forms the bond."[16] The Requerimiento's claim to present the Spanish Crown as natural lords would ultimately reveal its illegitimacy when it constitutes its dominion by means of war and slavery if the authority of the Spanish Crown is not recognized. There is no semblance of natural vassalage when claiming sovereignty from the outside. Las Casas exposes the absurdity of the Requerimiento when he denounces its method to first subject infidels to Spanish rule and then preach them Christianity in chapter 6 of *De unico vocationis modo*: "Et quia nemo infidelium sua sponte velit se Christiani populi vel alicuius principis eius ditioni submittere, potissime infidelium reges, esset profecto necesse devenire ad bellum" [Because no infidel will willfully subject to the dominion of the Spanish people or to one of its princes, especially infidel kings, it will without doubt be necessary to arrive at war].[17] The key word in this passage is *ditione*, from *dicio*, meaning "dominion, sovereignty, authority."

We may thus trace in Las Casas's assessment of the Requerimiento a diagnosis of the emergent structure of imperial power, perhaps a "first" instance of globalization, of *mondialisation*, to adopt Jean-Luc Nancy's French term that includes not only the worldwide circulation of goods but the formation of a world through and through inflected by Christian creationism. But by placing the emphasis on surrendering to dominion (*ditione submittere*)—the demand to recognize us or face war and enslavement—Las Casas goes beyond the supposition that the Requerimiento constitutes sovereignty that emerges from nowhere (as in the Christian ex nihilo) and in its constituted form involves a corresponding subject with the right of contestation (Indians with rights as subjects of the Spanish

Crown). But because Las Casas uses the *unico vocationis modo* to introduce Indians to Christianity, his evangelical program forms part of the globalization (as in Nancy's *mondialisation*) that the Requerimiento seeks to impose by force. Note that if Las Casas denounces the political subjection of Indians, he acknowledges that the Requerimiento predicates evangelization by peaceful means. The problem for Las Casas resides in the demand to recognize political subordination to the Crown and the inevitability that war would result from this mandate. Although the Franciscan position on multitudinous baptisms justified forced conversion in Motolinía's letter to Charles V, this position was clearly in the minority among missionaries in Mexico.

Beyond Las Casas, we find a brilliant articulation of the need for thorough evangelization to preclude apostasy in Alonso de la Vera Cruz's *De dominio infidelium et justo bello*, which consists of a series of lectures he dictated during the inaugural year of the University of Mexico in 1553–1554. Note that Gregorio López's compilation of laws in the *Ordenanzas reales de la Casa de la Contratación de Sevilla y para otras cosas de las Indias y de la navegación y contratación de ellas* was written in 1543 but not published until 1552. The years that go from 1551 to 1555 correspond to debates on the proper authority of the Crown in the Indies. I have listed Motolinía's letter to Charles V summoning him to assume his obligations as emperor of the end of time, the presentation of the Las Casas–Tenamaztle dossier, the publication of Las Casas's *Brevísima*, the publication of Lopez's *Ordenanzas*, the edition of the *Siete Partidas* with Gregorio López's glosses in 1555, and the debates between Juan Ginés de Sepúlveda and Las Casas in Valladolid. Vera Cruz's *De dominio* corresponds to this exceptional moment in the theorization of imperial rule.

According to natural law as presented by Alonso de la Vera Cruz, who in this regard follows Francisco Vitoria, all nations have the right to travel through the territories of others, to extract metals from unclaimed mines, to appropriate wastelands, to participate in commercial exchanges, and to preach Christianity. This implies that the Chichimecas had the obligation to adopt Spanish forms of settlement, participate in commercial ventures, accept preachers, in sum, the obligation to incorporate themselves into the empire and universal history. To be just, the state was obligated to promote the common good. The task of the missionaries would be to teach Indians the most effective means of acting within the state. In the end, there is only one choice, because even though Vera Cruz insists that one cannot force Indians to convert and underscores that missionaries were to instruct them by the best means (he specifies that syllogisms will not do, perhaps an aside on Las Casas's insistence on the use of reason as the only valid means of converting, "with reasons and adequate information, not arranged in syllogistic form since such could not be done"[18]), there is a point when, in good faith, one could say that they have been preached to sufficiently and that delaying their conversion would be in bad faith. But even then, Vera Cruz leaves room for those who have heard the word, have understood it, and choose not to abide by it: "If unbelievers of the New World received the missionaries and allowed them to evangelize freely, and then did not wish to believe [et si credere nolint], they should not for that reason be deprived of their dominion," and just in case this was not clear enough, Vera Cruz highlights the intended meaning: "What I want to say in this conclusion is that, supposing that these unbelievers admitted the first missionaries and allowed them to preach the faith publicly and privately, but then did not wish to accept the belief in the true God, they should not for this reason be attacked nor should they be deprived of their otherwise just dominion."[19]

In following Vera Cruz's train of thought, one wonders what would be the difference between ladino Indians, *españolizados*, who in apostatizing would be worse than in their original state, and Indians who would arguably be exposed to Spanish and Christian mores in sufficient depth for them to reason their choice for not accepting Christianity. I gather that the difference would reside in that the apostate rebels against the Crown, whereas the latter would live in peace and in conversation with the Spaniards. One may choose to remain *without* history in Vera Cruz's tract. But wouldn't this choice lead, in the long run, because of the exchanges with Spaniards, to the incorporation into history in that Indians would have to recognize and live by Spanish mores? Isn't this the whole logic behind the creation of peaceful settlements that would induce Indians into the Spanish fold? Would avoiding apostasy by all means be a form of exemplary patience? Is this what Vera Cruz meant when he wrote, "It is no less a calamity to apostatize from the faith than not to accept it; in fact, it is a more enormous sin"?[20] Why did the policy of peaceful settlements fail and lead to the extermination of peoples who dwelled on the northern frontier? Antonio Tello records devastated demography in the mid-seventeenth century. Ultimately, Vera Cruz's discourse on apostasy and his inability to understand nomadic peoples creates one more shroud of silence. Moreover, if apostasy were the consequence of insufficient indoctrination, the blame would fall on the responsible friars. We could hear here a critique of the Franciscan insistence on multitudinous baptisms. Indeed, narratives of Tenamaztle's insurgency bind the apostate to inversions of apostleship.

In fact, we find Tenamaztle recognizing not only the vassalage and tribute he owes to the Spanish king but also the willingness to mediate with "rebels" by the exclusive means of peacefully summoning them into the fold of the Crown. The Crown's suzerainty over Tenamaztle's suzerainty, which arguably would retain an autonomous existence with respect to the colonial authority that could claim power to subject them to *encomiendas*, would correspond to the *tlacuilo*'s Dominican, who in thoroughly evangelizing the Nahuas would lead them to accept baptism and the consequent incorporation into the Church and universal history. But then again, if the Las Casas–Tenamaztle discourse necessitates stepping out of the mirroring logic that would link apostle to apostate, the *tlacuilo*'s juxtaposition suggests that apostasy is the consequence of a failed evangelization, perhaps a forced conversion. Indeed, the *tlacuilo* suggests that the insurgency, the rising against the oppressors, hence against the illegitimate rule of the conquistadors, ends up reduced to the inversion of the apostleship in the stories missionaries and lay officials tell of the rebellion in the northern frontier, the Mixtón War.

In Las Casas–Tenamaztle's discourse there is no room for apostasy, given that Tenamaztle claims the right to define self-defense. As a result, the tone, the ends, and the spirit of the insurgency remain lost in the fantasies of the Spanish historians or the celebrations of projected idealization by our contemporary apologists. There is thus a link between the discussion of the semantics of conquest by Las Casas–Tenamaztle and the topology of conquest and conversion by the *tlacuilo*: both cross the limits of fantasy. What should we say when considering the *tlacuilo*'s and Las Casas–Tenamaztle's stand outside the mirroring that binds the discourse on apostasy to fantasy?

In closing this chapter, I briefly consider the significance of Las Casas–Tenamaztle's and the *tlacuilo*'s traversing fantasy in light of work in psychoanalysis and ethnology. Let's consider the following statement on fantasy by Lacan: "The world is symmetrical to the subject—the world or what I last time called thought is the equivalent, the mirror image, of thought. That is why there was nothing but fantasy regarding knowledge until the advent of the most modern science."[21] What does Lacan mean by the "most modern" science? What about the long history of ethnographic fantasies that haunt the "most modern" discourses in anthropology? Would it prove useful to clarify the question of science by drawing a distinction between what Lévi-Strauss calls the neolithic revolution, that is, primitive science vis-à-vis the (relatively) recent emergence of modern science?

If the *tlacuilo* and the missionary-ethnographer manifest instances of objectivity in the production of an album of Mesoamerican writing systems that avoid the mediation of religious fantasies (the belief that the terms *superstition*, *idolatry*, or even *apostasy* are mere designations), wouldn't they exemplify a "most modern" attitude? Clearly, we need to differentiate the picturing by the *tlacuilo*, and even the request by the missionary, from the fantasies expressed in the glosses, most prominently, from those that record the authoritative voice of Pedro de los Ríos. To what extent do the co-authors of the Las Casas–Tenamaztle texts, in which Las Casas actually removes himself from the position of author, participate in attitudes we have identified as postmodern and postcolonial? Does this mean that the "most modern science" of Lacan amounts to one more fantasy in the history of Western hubris? Can we complicate this narrative by conceptualizing the *tlacuilo*'s invention of a pictorial language for the depiction of the colonial world as a revelation of the fantasy of the missionaries in terms of what Lévi-Strauss defined as the science of the concrete in *The Savage Mind*, where he compares the neolithic revolution and modern science and asserts, "There is only one solution to the paradox [the lapse between the neolithic revolution and modern science], namely, that there are two distinct modes of scientific thought"?[22]

The differences and similarities Lévi-Strauss draws between mythical thought and science prove useful for dismantling historical teleology, but inasmuch as they constitute a binary built on analogy, we risk repeating utterances predetermined by the paradigm. Should we consider whether Lévi-Strauss's recuperation of "primitive" thought as scientific amounts to a form of charitable thinking often found in scholars of the last half century who have felt the urgency to recognize non-Western life-forms as literature, art, history, and science? What is lost in assuming transparency in the descriptive power of these terms?

For Lévi-Strauss, these modes of science are certainly not a function of different stages in the development of the human mind, but rather two strategic levels at which nature is accessible to scientific enquiry: "one roughly adapted to that of perception and the imagination: the other at a remove from it." Lévi-Strauss further develops this analogy by juxtaposing the ways of the engineer and the "bricoleur," where the first works with concepts that attempt to make reality transparent, and the second works with signs that demand noting how the human component is incorporated into reality. "Both scientist and 'bricoleur' might therefore be said to be constantly on the look out for 'messages'. Those which the 'bricoleur' collects are, however, ones which have to some extent been transmitted in advance. . . . The scientist, on the other hand, whether he is an engineer or a physicist, is always on the look out for *that other message* which might be wrested from an interlocutor in spite of his reticence in pronouncing on questions whose answers have not been rehearsed."[23] The difference is of degrees, and the analogy Lévi-Strauss draws about mythical thought in the end enables him to generalize scientific thought. However, by underscoring that the *bricoleur* and, by analogy, mythical thought collect pretransmitted messages, we find a limitation for understanding the topology of the *tlacuilo* in that she does not merely collect transmitted messages but actually produces a vocabulary for wresting the message from the new realities she chooses to depict and classify; or, if you will, she is "on the look out for *that other message* which might be wrested from an interlocutor."[24] The topology of conquest goes one step further in that it reveals the fantasies of the missionaries—a gesture that approximates the *tlacuilo*'s intervention in what Lacan characterizes as the "most modern science": "there was nothing but fantasy regarding knowledge until the advent of the most modern science."[25] Was not the call to internalize this epistemological break one of the main modalities of implementing ethnosuicide? For requesting the telling of the story of one's conquest involved leading Nahua subjects to the articulation of the failure of magic, that is, of their epistemic regime.

Chapter 6

"TELL ME THE STORY OF HOW I CONQUERED YOU"

In the prefatory remarks to *Book XII: De la conquista mexicana* (ca. 1569) of the *Historia general de las cosas de Nueva España*, which provides a Nahuatl version of the conquest of Mexico, Bernardino de Sahagún gives two reasons for writing this history. First: "quanto por poner el lenguaje de las cosas de la guerra, y de las armas que en ella vsan los naturales: para que de alli se puedan sacar vocablos y maneras de dezir propias, para hablar en lengua mexicana cerca desta materia" [to record the language of warfare and the weapons which the natives use in it, in order that the terms and proper modes of expression for speaking on this subject in the Mexican language can be derived therefrom]; second: "allegase tambien a esto que los que fueron conquistados, supieron y dieron relacion de muchas cosas, que passaron entre ellos durante la guerra: las cuales ignorarō, los que los conquistarō" [To this may be added that those who were conquered knew and gave an account of many things that transpired among them during the war of which those who conquered them were unaware]. Sahagún closes his remarks by stating that the history was written "en tiempo que eran vivos, los que se hallaron en la mjsma conquista: y ellos dieron esta relacion personas principales, y de buen juizio y que se tiene por cierto, que dixeron toda verdad" [those who took part of the very conquest were alive. . . . And those who gave this account [were] principal people of good judgment, and it is believed that they told all the truth].[1] This extraordinary text that solicits a version of the conquest from the conquered enables us to further explore the questions we have been asking, taking folio 46r of Codex Telleriano-Remensis as a point of departure, regarding how Indians perceived and depicted the colonial order. I first reflect on the theoretical implications of telling the story of one's ruin but will return to folio 46r later.

To think about Europe in Indian categories or to respond to the demand to tell the story of how one was conquered occasions cross-cultural intersubjectivity. The demand seeks to understand the Indian mind, but the response inevitably conveys the destruction of a world as well as the anguish, if not resentment and grief, for a lost worldview. Anguish, resentment, grief, and loss reveal the violence of the conquest, but the query also sought to provoke an internalization of the defeat in terms of an epistemological and moral debacle. The request to tell the story of how one was conquered had the unexpected effect of soliciting the gaze of the indigenous subjects—a brilliant instance of the observer observed. The return of the gaze defines the limits of the project that sought to objectivize Nahua culture in close collaboration with indigenous subjects charged with the tasks of creating verbal and pictorial records of their own culture. The subjectivity responding to the demands to "tell the story of how they were conquered" alternated between melancholic expressions of loss and lucid depictions of colonial institutions. Both types of responses manifest the incorporation of European systems of representation (Latin script and three-dimensional perspective) into Nahuatl linguistic and pictorial artifacts grounded in a Mesoamerican habitus.

OF MELANCHOLIA AND MANIA

To appeal to Freud's classic essay "Mourning and Melancholia" has become common in studies of trauma and oppression. Freud's view of the healing process involved in mourning and the pathological clinging to the past in melancholy has been the subject of debate. Already in Freud, there is an opening to an understanding of melancholia as leading to self-knowledge, but even more interesting for colonial and postcolonial studies is his statement, "Melancholic . . . reaction . . . proceeds from a mental constellation of revolt, which has then, by a certain process, passed over into the crushed state of melancholia."[2] Both Homi Bhabha and Judith Butler have noted this passage. A brief discussion of their readings enables me to gauge the limits of the concepts of mourning and melancholia when the existence of *elsewheres* is taken into account. In Bhabha's view of postcolonial melancholy, the concept of ambivalence suggests a hybrid "in-betweenness," a third space beyond the colonizer/colonized binary. Bhabha underscores the "crushed state of revolt" when he writes: "All these bits and pieces in which my history is fragmented, my culture piecemeal, my identifications fantasmatic and displaced; these splittings of wounds of my body are also a form of revolt. And they speak a terrible truth. In their ellipses and silences they dismantle your authority. . . ."[3] This third space where grief and ambivalence dismantle authority involves going beyond the colonizer and the colonized, but insofar as Bhabha reinscribes the revolt in terms of one more version of Western discourse, in which Bhabha's *self* stands for *his* oppressed peoples, he ends up erasing the possibility of conceiving a space that is altogether different from the Freudian-derived discourse that Bhabha elaborates in English. There is no room in Bhabha's proposal for an *elsewhere* to Greco-Abrahamic tradition from which the colonial order is observed.[4] In passing, I should note that the dispute between friars I examined in the last chapter should make it obvious that I do not conceive the Greco-Abrahamic tradition as a homogeneous entity, but as a space of strife. For Butler, the "crushed state of melancholia" can lead to mania, rage, and ambivalence as psychic states that enable an active form of melancholia, an affirmation of life that demands the restitution of sovereignty, reparations for damages, and social transformation. Indians thinking Europe in indigenous categories and the responses to the demand to tell the story of how one was conquered run through this gamut of possibilities. As in Bhabha, these stories speak a terrible tale, and there is certainly a dismantling of authority, but as in Butler, the passage to rage conveys a state in which rebellion follows the crushed state of melancholia. Butler also does not contemplate the possibility of an *elsewhere* to Greco-Abrahamic tradition. In telling the story of how one was conquered from an *elsewhere*, melancholia in its interplay with mourning would convey the refusal to recognize that something has been lost, a refusal to internalize a law that demands self-deprecation and conceives of melancholia as a form of sin. Because of the nature of the demand to tell the story of conquest, the passage from mourning to melancholia is never completed, and the possibility of mania haunts the observers' (i.e., Spanish lay and religious authorities') certainty about the expected story of victory and defeat.

In reading the Nahua versions of the conquest, the Freudian concepts of melancholia, mourning, rage, and ambivalence serve as heuristic categories that we must at some point abandon and whose limitations we must expose. If appealing to these Freudian categories certainly makes sense from our present Western interpretative modes, we should also keep in mind that in projecting psychoanalytical categories on Nahuatl expressions of grief and mania, we may be universalizing our own provincial schemas and modes of understanding affect. This has less to do with the dangers of anachronism, since I would argue with Willard Van Orman Quine that there is no outside to these provincial schemas, only a wide range of acceptable possible translations: "Wanton translation can make natives sound as queer as one pleases. Better translation imposes our logic upon them, and would beg the question of prelogicality if there were a question to beg."[5] Even if I were to concur with Quine that the development of better dictionaries and other linguistic tools might soften the indeterminacy of radical translation (one with no previous linguistic contact with native speakers)—though I am not certain that we have advanced much from what Sahagún, Molina, and Carochi knew of what we term Classical Nahuatl—our modern production of commentary using letters remains blind to the visual communication of iconic script, in spite of our disparagement of the early colonial written glosses in the codices. The preference for better translations and the imposition of our logic over wanton translation—frolicsome, gay, playful, and so on—is not self-evident. In fact, the queer may turn out to be *queer*.[6] Quine does not entertain a world in which his *Word and Object*, or, for that matter, Butler's and Bhabha's psychoanalytical discourse, would be translated into Nahuatl (or other indigenous language) categories.[7] Although today a Nahuatl understanding of Quine, of Western discourse in general, seems unlikely (and I wonder if this isn't so because of ethnocentrism), Sahagún and other missionaries actually asked sixteenth-century Nahuas to make sense of the Spanish world in their own provincial modes of thought. If it is pointless to speculate on terms sixteenth-century Nahuas might have used to speak of psychoanalytical understandings of melancholia, mourning, and mania in Nahuatl, we may legitimately trace early modern understandings of melancholy in these Nahuatl texts. We must insist that there was a time when melancholy was not yet melancholia. Even if Freud (by this proper name Freud, I include the particular interpretations by Bhabha, Fanon, Lacan, and Butler, just to mention the most prominent) informs our discourse on melancholy, we may trace phrases, expressions, and forms of mourning and grieving that cannot, *must not*, be subjected to "better" translations but allowed to retain their queerness. We may also find the incorporation of typical figures of melancholy, such as the melancholic Renaissance prince, in particular, when afflicted with the "acedia" that Walter Benjamin has written about in *The Origin of German Tragic Drama*.

Let us first examine the semblance of a pathological Moteuczoma, the most commonly cited example of melancholia in Indian accounts of the conquest, and then move on to visual and verbal texts in which we find instances of mourning, melancholy, and mania that cannot be reduced to Freud's or to Benjamin's understanding of these terms. The best-known melancholic Moteuczoma appears in chapter 9 of Sahagún's *Book XII*. (I am citing from the Nahuatl version, not from Sahagún's translation to Spanish, for the obvious reason that my intention is to trace Nahuatl expressions of melancholy.) Although the heading speaks of the whole population of Tenochtitlan as awestruck—"Ninth Chapter, in which it is told how Moteucçoma wept, and how the Mexicans wept, when they knew that the Spaniards were very powerful"—the chapter emphasizes the fear, melancholy, and paralysis of Moteuczoma: "And when Moteucçoma had thus heard that he was much inquired about, that he was much sought, that the gods wished to look upon his face, it was as if his heart was afflicted; he was afflicted. He would hide himself; he wished to flee." A few lines farther down, the translation reads: "No longer had he strength; no longer was there any use; no longer had he energy."[8] This semblance of an afflicted Moteuczoma echoes the Renaissance commonplace of the melancholic prince suffering from acedia. It should not surprise us that the Tlatelolcas—better, that the collegians whom Sahagún had trained in Latin, Nahuatl, and Spanish—knew this figure and deployed it. It forms part of a whole set of European forms—namely, perspective, omens, horses, guns, chairs, terms, letters, Christian motifs—that the collegians used to imprint symbolic meaning in their verbal and pictorial versions of the conquest.[9] The story of Moteuczoma's melancholy does not exhaust the Tlatelolca account, since it can be read as an expression of mania that derives pleasure from its perverse rendition of the Tenochca ruler's infamous character in terms that would have been readily recognized as Spanish.[10] This melancholic Moteuczoma is a commonplace in Spanish accounts of the conquest, but Nahuatl verbal and visual texts do not depict a paralyzed, indecisive Moteuczoma. This melancholic Moteuczoma suffering from acedia differs from other instances in *Book XII* in which the informants mourn and grieve for a lost Nahua world. In the melancholic telling of the story of loss and destruction resides the survival of the Nahua life-forms. The story of the loss constitutes an act of rebellion that displaces the military victory to a spiritual and epistemological terrain in which Spanish and Indian forms coexist yet do not suppose a third space of in-betweenness; instead there is a retention and reinscription of differences in which Western forms are quoted and fulfill a symbolic function within a Nahuatl semantic space. This last point is crucial for understanding the phenomenon of the observer-observed in Indian texts, since they conduct the observation in Indian categories.

Codex Telleriano-Remensis (ca. 1562) and *Book XII: De la conquista mexicana* (ca. 1569) answer the command, "Tell me the story of how I conquered you," a primordial demand in the narrative of ethnosuicide. They provide a narrative of moral and epistemological disintegration; we can also trace a return of the gaze. In addition to texts that respond to Spanish demand, there are others that were written—in both iconic script and alphabetical writing—outside the supervision of secular and religious authorities, such as the alphabetized *Historia de Tlatelolco desde los tiempos más remotos* (in *Anales de Tlatelolco*), the pictorial and alphabetical Codex Aubin, and the pictorial Codex Mexicanus and Codex of Tlatelolco.

DOMESTICATED GLYPH, SAVAGE LITERACY

The resistant, subversive, or collaborative nature of texts produced outside the supervision of missionaries or lay authorities cannot be simply an issue of European alphabet vs. Indian painting. Paraphrasing Jack Goody's *Domestication of the Savage Mind*, a study on the consequences of literacy, we can make a distinction between *savage literacies* (alphabetic texts produced using Latin script with no supervision by the missionaries) and *domesticated glyphs* (pictorial texts produced to document collaboration in the imposition and perpetuation of a colonial order). Goody's parody intends to undermine the absolute separation between literacy, orality, and painting. As instances of indigenous textualities, these texts undo any appeal to writing-versus-orality binaries, whether produced to undermine indigenous cultures or to recuperate a suppressed oral text. Contrary to the commonplace that presumes that the opposition between orality and writing is transhistorical, I would not only argue that it assumes different values in different historical moments and cultures, but also insist that this binary was hardly central to sixteenth-century Spaniards.[11] There are, of course, instances of Spaniards claiming superiority on the basis of possessing a phonetic alphabet, such as in Joseph de Acosta's *Historia natural y moral de las Indias*, Juan Ginés de Sepúlveda's *Democrates alter*, and Juan de Torquemada's *Monarquía Indiana*, the texts that are most commonly cited to buttress arguments that generalize the opposition of oral and writing cultures. Paradoxically, critics and historians bent on recuperating the orality of indigenous peoples in the Americas—the assumption being that these are oral cultures!—contribute to the same prejudice against non-alphabetical writing forms.[12] The proliferation of texts using iconic script from the colonial period to the present suggests not only that Spanish colonial authorities viewed pictorial texts as holding documentary evidence but also that Indians valued and retained their forms of writing, often in juxtaposition to alphabetized records of verbal performances.

The concept of indigenous textualities enables us to conceptualize a fluidity between a broad array of writing forms—textile, glyph, landscape, inscription on gourds and other durable materials, tattoos, and alphabetical writing—and speech forms that might underlie the production of written texts or might further elaborate the recorded stories. This fluidity ne-

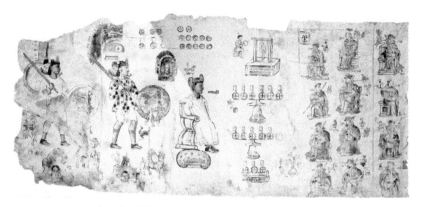

FIGURE 12   *Codex Tlatelolco. Courtesy of the Biblioteca de Antropología e Historia, Mexico City.*

cessitates an understanding of reading as performance rather than as the silent, private activity we tend to associate with the bourgeois reader in the solitude of the sunrooms of the nineteenth century. Recent studies in the ethnography of reading enable us to modify the terms of the debate.[13] Not only Goody but also other scholars who follow him, like the early Serge Gruzinski and Walter Mignolo, ignore the fact that people read in historically and culturally defined ways. Sixteenth- and seventeenth-century Mesoamerican texts were primarily read and performed in public rather than read in private. This is still a practice in Native American communities where *lienzos*, *títulos*, *tiras*, and *mapas* provide scripts for ritual. Indeed, there is plenty of internal evidence that texts were written collectively and hence reveal a multiple sense of authorship. The use of the alphabet did not exclude the practice of performing and producing texts in collective settings, nor did it exclude improvisation and expansion in verbal renditions of written texts using the Latin alphabet.

Whereas the *Historia de Tlatelolco*, which forms part of the collection known as the *Anales de Tlatelolco*, actualizes savage literacy in that it records Nahuatl oral performances of pictorial histories that condemn the conquest in absolute terms, the Codex of Tlatelolco exemplifies domesticated glyphs in that it represents Tlatelolca leaders negotiating a privileged position from within the colonial order (Figure 12).[14] To all appearances, the pictorial Codex of Tlatelolco was produced with a Spanish audience in mind, and the *Historia de Tlatelolco* was produced for a performance within the community of Tlatelolco. The apparent subordination to the Spanish authorities in Codex of Tlatelolco demands the recognition (as in knowing again) of an iconic articulation of the role Tlatelolco played in the Mixtón War. As for the *Historia de Tlatelolco*, take as exemplary of the denunciation of the conquest the following descriptions of the massacre of the Templo Mayor and the devastation of Tlatelolco: "While dancing they went bare [of weapons], with only their net cloaks, their turquoise [ornaments], their lip plugs, their necklaces, their forked heron-feather ornaments, their deer's hooves. The old men who beat the cylindrical drums had their tobacco pots and their rattles. It was them they first attacked; they struck off their hands and lips. Then all who were dancing, and all who were looking on, died there." A view of Tlatelolco in ruins offers a most terrifying description of war: "And on the roads lay the shattered bones and scattered bones and scattered hair, the houses were unroofed, red [with blood]; worms crawled in and out of the noses of cadavers; and the walls of the houses were slippery with brains."[15] Note that this graphic—indeed, photographic—image could only be conveyed verbally and by the mimetic faculty of alphabetic writing that, allow me to insist again, does not stand in place of the pictorial version, but rather reproduces speech, a verbal performance of a pictorial history that in using precolonial conventions excluded the depiction of such gruesome details. This is savage or wild literacy at its most resistant countercolonial mode. This is clearly an instance of resistance preceding power[16] in that the Spanish religious and lay authorities could never anticipate Indian understandings of writing and reading for invoking the dead; moreover, their attempt to suppress the calling forth of ghosts would entail the destruction of writing itself.

My connection to photography is not arbitrary or fortuitous. Writing, like photography, inscribes the dead for their invocation as ghosts, as revenants that reading and performance bring about. In his commentary on Walter Benjamin and photography, Eduardo Cadava draws parallelisms between the mimetic faculty of writing and photography that would suggest that the written descriptions of graphic visual details are in fact possible because of the concept of photography that preexists the development of the technology. As it were, writing and, even before that, language and the interpretation of the stars anticipate photography: "To say that the history of photography begins in the interpretation of the stars is to say that it begins with death."[17] The connection between writing and death and the return of ghosts through the performance of the recorded voice could not have escaped the Tlatelolcan *tlacuilo*'s adoption of the new mimetic technology.[18]

The condemnation of the conquest in the *Historia de Tlatelolco* leaves no room for a narrative of collaboration or an apology for the colonial order. The internal date of the *Historia* is 1528: "This book, as it is written, was done here in Tlatelolco in the ancient times, in the year 1528."[19] James Lockhart holds that this text could not have been written before the 1550s. This latter date would suggest disparate views between those who wrote and those who painted history in Tlatelolco, especially when we compare the unequivocal denunciation of conquest in the alphabetical *Historia de Tlatelolco* to the narrative of collaboration and accommodation within the colonial order in the pictorial Codex of Tlatelolco, which bears 1565 as its last date. The melancholic remembrance of the destruction of Tlatelolco and Tenochtitlan, still alive during the years of the Mixtón War, would seem not to have affected the decision of the Nahuas from Central Mexico to participate in the war against the Caxcanes, another Nahuatl-speaking group in the so-called Chichimeca, in what is today the state of Zacatecas. Even if this disparity would suggest that the internal date of 1528 is correct, we would still have to account for the place the performances of the *Historia de Tlatelolco* and Codex of Tlatelolco occupied in the imagined community of Tlatelolco. Can we assume that *Historia de Tlatelolco* was a text to be performed within the community, whereas Codex of Tlatelolco was to be performed for the colonial authorities? If so, why use alphabetical writing in a text for internal performance and pictorial writing in a text for external performance? Perhaps the pictorial texts carried a rhetorical force that authenticated their representation of the community in front of Spanish authorities. And perhaps the alphabetical record of a verbal performance entails a magical understanding of writing: it certifies the death of words as it embalms them but also ensures their continuance as ghosts to be brought to life. One may also speculate on the possibility that the verbal performance of Codex of Tlatelolco could have been recorded with the alphabet. Even though Codex of Tlatelolco seeks accommodation within the colonial order, it exceeds a mere subordination. In its surrender lies a countercolonial gesture that enables Tlatelolco to retain its own memory.

Note in this section from Codex of Tlatelolco (see Figure 12) the miniature renditions of the Spanish soldiers underneath the two gigantic representations of a Tenochca and a Tlatelolca warrior who went to Nochistlán (glyph: flowery cactus) in the 1541 Mixtón War to suppress the rebellion of the Caxcanes.[20] The severed head under the glyph indicates that this was a war of conquest. We are missing the first part of the *tira* in which most likely there was a Texcocan or a Tlacopan warrior behind the last Spanish horseman on the far left. The Tenochca and Tlatelolca wear a mixture of Spanish and Indian dress. Of the two, the Tlatelolca's dress is the more elaborate: note the sword, the socks, the short pants, and the *jubón* (doublet) made out of jaguar skin. In front of these figures, we see the cacique of Tlatelolco, Don Diego de Mendoza Huitznahuatlailotlac, sitting on a Spanish chair, the new symbol of authority that has replaced the indigenous mat. Below him, we find the glyph of Tlatelolco, and he appears to be recounting to the eight Spaniards the exploits of the Tlatelolcas during the Mixtón War in the year 10 Tochtli (Rabbit), 1554. The box adorned with quetzal feathers contains a chalice and host, symbols of the Eucharist. The hanged man stands for the two Tlatelolcas who refused to pay tribute when the system of *alcaldes* was instituted in 1549. We read in Codex Aubin that "it was in the year of 1549 when it was imposed and ordered to elect *alcaldes* and it was then that tribute was first charged, and because two caciques resisted that Natives paid tribute, they were hanged."[21] The minor place the hanged man occupies in the pictorial narrative suggests that a reading would mention the event but only to further buttress the loyalty and subordination of the current Tlatelolca leadership to the Spaniards.

This detached citation of a hanging in Codex of Tlatelolco contrasts with the melancholic reminiscences of atrocities committed against Tlatelolcas and other Nahuas from the Valley of Mexico in the *Historia de Tlatelolco*: "There they hanged the ruler of Huitzilopochco, Macuilxochitzin, as well as the ruler of Culhuacan, Pitzotzin. They also hanged the Tlacateccatl of Quauhtitlan, and they had the Tlillancalqui eaten by dogs. And they had some Tezcoca, one of whom was Ecamaxtlatzin, eaten by dogs. They just came to stay. No one accompanied them, they just brought their painted books [*ymamatlacuilollo*]."[22] Observe that the statement "they only brought with them their painted books" lacks any doubt as to the status of writing. We ignore the reasons why they brought the books or why the writers felt the need to mention them, but we do know that this is one of many mentions of painted books in the *Historia de Tlatelolco*, suggesting their centrality in native life. It is also worth mentioning that the *Historia de Tlatelolco* closes with a statement on events that followed the fall of Tenochtitlan: "Then the Captain proclaimed war against Oaxaca. They went to Acolhuacan. Then to Mextitlan. Then to Michuacan. Then to Ueymollan y Quauhtemallan and Tehuantepec."[23] Does this passage express solidarity with the peoples of Oaxaca, Guatemala, and Michoacan? It certainly places them as foes of a common enemy. The *Historia de Tlatelolco* closes with an enigmatic reflexive statement: "With this this book ends in which it was told how it was made" [Ca zan oncan tlami ynic omopouh ynin amatla yn iuhqui omochiuh].[24] Spaniards could not but appreciate the importance of writing and their documentary value in native culture. For the Spaniards, both the form and content held authority. The Codex of Tlatelolco continues this pictorial tradition and testifies to its adaptability within the colonial power struggles.

Although these texts were not produced to respond to the demand "Tell me the story of how I conquered you," they certainly are instances of "thinking Europe in Indian categories." There is no suggestion of an attempt to reproduce a European historical model to gain recognition. In the Codex of Tlatelolco, recognition is sought for the deeds, not for the mastery of European historiography and painting. These are Tlatelolca deeds told in a Tlatelolca style.

TELL ME THE STORY

As we turn our attention to the response to the demand "Tell me the story of how I conquered you," in folio 46r of Telleriano-Remensis (see Figure 1), we find that the *tlacuilo*'s return of the gaze must have annoyed the missionaries, in particular Pedro de los Ríos, who took over the production of the codex four folios later (see Figure 8). As I have already pointed out, Ríos soon abandoned the replacement of indigenous codes, color, and style with shoddy writing. He must have realized the futility of continuing a project that, in the first place, had the finality of recording native ways of writing—not scribbling mere facts. Telleriano-Remensis, however, lacks the alphabetical version of a native oral text telling the stories of the depicted colonial events. The verbal texts telling the story of conquest—for instance, of Tenamaztle's nativist rebellion (even when told from the *tlacuilo*'s Central Mexican perspective)—are found in Spanish sources or Nahuatl accounts by Indians from Central Mexico who participated in the Mixtón War. Reading these accounts of the Mixtón War, we realize that they constitute an archival fog that covers the story of the Caxcan insurgency by inevitably binding the story of apostasy to the discourse of apostleship (see Chapter 5). The apostate/apostle binary brilliantly laid out in the *tlacuilo*'s topology of conquest and the missionary differences brilliantly codified in the symbolic use of perspective (see Chapter 3) manifest the *exappropriation* of normalizing pedagogic ends of teaching pictorial perspective and the Latin alphabet.[25] In asking the *tlacuilo* to depict colonial events and institutions, the missionaries encouraged the development of a pictorial vocabulary that made manifest the fact that the observer had turned into the observed. For the *tlacuilo*, the task consisted in saying *without* saying, in keeping at bay the reduction of sense in reappropriation. The missionaries could *sense*—could be touched by—the *tlacuilo*'s eyes observing them, but the *sense* of the code—by means of which she *exappropriates* their signifying systems—eludes them, though it punctures their assurance of control.

Even when, in some instances, the glosses on folio 46r cite Nahua voices in translation (e.g., at the bottom of folio 3v, Ríos cites in very simplistic terms what was said when praying to Tezcatlipoca: "dezian: 'O señor cuyos siervos somos concedenos esto'"), the glosses for the most part limit themselves to identifying the depicted objects or events, and correcting the information written by others, but they do not elaborate a narrative nor can we find an indigenous account. Nevertheless, we know that missionaries and indigenous historians wrote alphabetical histories in which we can trace the kinds of oral stories elders told based on pictorial accounts like Telleriano-Remensis. The request for the story of the colonial past, that is, of the story of how the Nahuas had been colonized, conveys a playful use of key European forms that make manifest the limits of the normalization process.

The *Historia general de las cosas de Nueva España* (Florentine Codex) takes a radically different approach in that it reproduces the verbal accounts given by elders subjected to ethnographic inquiries. One can sense puzzlement in the request to provide a record of how they had been conquered—as well as exhilaration at the opportunity to record a version that preserved their memory of the events. Paradoxically, the response in *Book XII* must communicate the destruction of a world and its corresponding anguish using the same terms of the banishing worldview. Thus, the telling of destruction preserves the object that was supposed to have been destroyed. Sahagún wrote a revision in 1585. He explains his motivation in a parenthetical remark: "(En el Libro nono, donde se trata esta conquista, se hicieron ciertos defectos: y, fué, que algunas cosas se pusieron en la Narracion de esta Conquista, que fueron mal puestas: y otras se callaron, que fueron mal calladas. Por esta causa, este año de mil quinientos ochenta y cinco, enmende este libro)" [In this book nine, in which the conquest is treated, some mistakes were made: and it was that some things were put in the narration of the Conquest that were badly put: and others were silenced, that were badly silenced. For this reason, in this year of fifteen eighty-five, I corrected this book].[26] The earlier text consisted of a Nahuatl version derived from testimonies by elders who witnessed the conquest, a Spanish version whose language and syntax bear no resemblance to the original Nahuatl and often chooses to paraphrase or elide whole passages, and a visual version that should be read as a text of its own and not merely as an illustration (Figure 13). If the visual component in other books in Sahagún's *Historia general* functions as illustrations, this is mainly due to the lack of antecedent in pre-Columbian texts for painting daily life or natural history. And even in the illustrations of natural history one would have to evaluate each individual case. Images in these books also function as albums of illustrations to which the alphabetical texts provide commentary or supplement. Sahagún's earlier texts, the *Primeros memoriales* (ca. 1558–1560), best exemplify this approach.

The visual text of *Book XII*, however, can be read on its own terms. Indeed, one can read the Nahuatl narrative as an oral rendition of a pictorial version.[27] Because Sahagún apparently did not include a pictorial version in 1585, scholars have limited their speculations on the above comments to Sahagún's need to revise the Nahuatl verbal text and the paraphrased translation to Spanish. I say speculations because the Nahuatl version is lost. It seems that Sahagún was concerned with both the contents of the narrative and with the style, the *cosas mal puestas* [things badly put] pertaining to the Nahuatl diction. The 1585 version included three columns: "La primera es, el lenguaje indiano, asi tosco como ellos lo pronunciaron, y se escribió en los otros libros: la segunda columna, es enmienda de la primera, asi en vocablos como en sentencias: La tercera columna esta en romance sacado segun las enmiendas de la segunda columna" [The first is in Indian language, thus coarse as they pronounce it, and was written in the other books: the second is an emendation of the first, in the words and sentences: the third column is in romance drawn according to the emendations of the second column].[28] The *mal puestas* refers to a specifically Nahuatl conceptualization of the events that Sahagún might have considered subversive, but he also underscores that he is including the original Nahuatl version so that it be known that the faults emended in the second column were not done on purpose ("para que todos entiendan que nos se erró adrede").[29] To my mind, it remains a mystery how the inclusion of the original Nahuatl would lay to rest the suspicion that the faults were not committed *adrede*, "on purpose." Sahagún clearly does not censure the original Nahuatl, but leaves it there for comparison with the emended version. These revisions suggest at least two different readers: on the one hand, bilingual Nahuatl-Spanish readers, most likely but not exclusively missionaries, would benefit from the emendations in their use of the Nahuatl language of war in their sermons; on the other, Spanish readers would get a less offensive version. The absence of a visual text could be read as a suppression of the story told by the elders; a story that depicts the atrocities committed provides visual information regarding

teca, cempoalteca, injc qujmo
ichteca tlatlanjque: conjtvque
ca amoie. ichoatl tvtecujtoane.
Inin tzioac popocatzin. q.ujnj
xiptlatica in. Notecuçomatzin:
qujshujque. cujx iete intiMo
tecuçoma: Conjtv. Canehoatl
jnnamotechiuh caieh in njMo
tecucoma. Auh njman qujlhuj,
que. Nopaxiaul, tloica inti
techiztlacavvia, actitechmati,
amo vel titechiztlacavviz, amo
vel tica timocaiaoaz, amo vel
titech quamanaz, amo vel ti
techix mamatiliz, amo vel ti
techich chioaz. amo vel titechix
cuepaz, amo vel titechixpa
tiliz, amo vel titech tlacuepi
liz, amo vel titechixpopoloz,
amo vel titechix mjmjctiz, a
mo vel titechix coqujviz, amo
vel titechix coqujmatvcaz, a
motehoatl canvca in Mote
cuçoma, amo vel technetla
tiliz, amo vel mjnaiaz cam
pniaz, aujx totvll, cujxpa
tlaniz, cujnoço tlallan quj
quebaz yiovi, cujx canaca
tepetl coionquj yitic calaquiz

iz5

Ni Motecuçoma se nos podra asconder
por mucho que haga, aunque sea ave
y aunque se meta debaxo de tierra
nose nos podra asconder de verle
avemos yde oyr avemos loque
nos dira. Y luego con asienta em
biaron aquel principal yatodos

warriors' insignia and other symbols infused with magical powers and juxtaposes, hence confronts, European and native systems of writing and painting. But since Sahagún says nothing about the visual text in the preface to the 1585 revisions, this amounts to pure speculation.

Whatever the changes of the Nahuatl version might have been, the *enmiendas* we read in the 1585 Spanish version are for the most part additions, corrections, and suppressions that could not have been part of a revised Nahuatl account, whose main purpose was linguistic. Clearly, extrapolations by Sahagún could not have been part of a new Nahuatl text. Other changes in the Spanish column merely further the softening of language already in place in the Spanish translations in the Florentine Codex. Take, for instance, the encounter of the Spaniards near Popocatepetl. The Nahuatl text reads, "And when they had given the things [golden banners, banners of precious feathers, and golden necklaces], they seemed to smile, to rejoice and be very happy. Like monkeys they grabbed the gold. It was as though their hearts were put to rest, brightened, freshened. For Gold was what they greatly thirsted for; they were gluttons for it, starved for it, piggishly wanting it." The Spanish version of the Florentine Codex translates: "alli los recibieron y presentaron el presente de oro que lleuauan, y segun que a los indios les parecio por las señales exteriores que vieron en los españoles, holgaronse y regozijaronse mucho con el oro mostrando que lo tenian en mucho" [There they received them and gave them the present of gold that they brought, and according to the external signs that the Indians saw in the Spaniards, it seemed to them that they were pleased and greatly rejoiced over the gold, for they held it in great esteem].[30] The 1585 Spanish emendation reduces the passage to: "presentaron su presente al capitan ordenándolo á sus pies: lo cual él y todos recibieron con gran gozo" [they gave the Captain their gifts, placing them on the ground: all received them with great joy].[31] These Spanish stories of the encounter in Popocatepetl censor the Nahuatl in different degrees, but we need to ask ourselves what Sahagún meant when he characterizes the language of the first column as a "lenguaje Indiano, asi tosco como ellos lo pronuncian" [Indian language, coarse as they speak it], and adds that the second column "es enmienda de la primera, asi en vocablos, como en sentencias" [is an emendation of the first, both in the words and in the opinions].[32]

Is the speech *tosco*, "coarse," because it lacks the civilizing effect of the style and rhetoric of proper historiography as exemplified in the Spanish version, or is it coarse because it denounces the Spaniards in unequivocal terms? I would go for the second explanation, given Sahagún's praise of the rhetorical complexity and beauty of Nahuatl in the *Historia general* and other writings. It seems that Sahagún is treating the deficiencies of the Nahuatl version and the Spanish translation as independent cases. One may thus speak of the Nahuatl version in the Florentine Codex (unfortunately we do not have the 1585 version) as an instance of savage literacy. As Sahagún points out, the errors were not *adrede*. Even if the Nahuatl version was produced at the request and under the supervision of Sahagún and his *colegiales*, who arguably just produced an alphabetical transcription of the speech event, we cannot trace their influence, even less the imposition of a grammatical ideal of logical and narrative refinement ("tosco como ellos lo pronuncian").[33] The Nahuatl version (and there are plenty of others we can draw from in the Florentine Codex, the *Historia de Tlatelolco*, and other Nahuatl texts) suggests that the alphabet could remain neutral, that is, merely function as a mimetic technology that records speech.[34] The neutrality of the alphabet would consist in the capacity to record speech events, to set down the informant's declarations as linguistic instances of Nahuatl. Again, the point is not that Sahagún's are authentic records of pre-Columbian forms of address but of multiple voices responding to Sahagún's queries. In these responses, in the neutrality of their alphabetical recording, one can hear—as Sahagún came to hear—mockery, melancholy, and multiple voices interacting with each other. These voices would reflect the multiple informants participating in the collective declarations of the pictorial texts they produced in response to Sahagún's queries, but they would also reflect the interventions by the collegians that transcribed them into Latin script. The task of drawing echographies of voice in Nahuatl alphabetical texts remains a project, however.[35] The presence of savage literacy in a text that was solicited and supervised by Sahagún corroborates the fact that the Spaniards never held a monopoly over the uses of alphabetical writing, and that reading and writing was a two-way street in New Spain.

TWO COROLLARIES

For the first corollary, based on the analysis of the *Historia de Tlatelolco* and Sahagún's *Historia general*, we can state that the concept of "tyranny of the alphabet" would miss its target by assigning power to the technology rather than to a certain definition of grammaticality. As a mimetic device, the alphabet has the purpose of recording speech, not taking the place of painting; the writing and not only the reading of alphabetical texts entails a performative act that cannot be appropriated by the historiography of missionaries and lay Spanish or even mestizo historians.

Grammars such as Horacio Carochi's *Arte de la lengua mexicana* (1645), one of the finest examples of seventeenth-century Jesuit linguistic studies, speak of Nahuatl as lacking syntax. Syntax is thus presumed to pertain to Latin and, by derivation, to Spanish, but in his *Arte*, Carochi suggests that Nahuatl morphology fulfills an analogous function: "En el quarto, en lugar de sintaxis (que esta lengua no la tiene) se pone el modo con que vnos vocablos se componen con otros" [In the fourth, in place of syntax, which this language lacks, I give the manner in which some words are compounded with others].[36] Shouldn't we be scandalized and point out that this denial of syntax betrays an ethnocentric prejudice that assumes that all languages should have a syntax? No. The last thing Carochi or Sahagún had in mind was to produce an *arte de la lengua* that would impose syntax or any other linguistic form purportedly lacking in Nahuatl.

There is an effort to control indigenous languages by developing grammars, but at least in the case of Nahuatl, which developed a phonetic system with the intent of recording speech, written Nahuatl should not be seen as an artificial language, as might be the case with doctrinal Quechua and Maya, which often were so divorced from the spoken languages that Indians had difficulties understanding priests. In the course of time, indigenous writers adopted these written forms of Quechua and Maya with highly standardized orthographies.[37] In the case of Nahuatl, however, writing was intimately bound to the phonetic recording of speech reflecting regional variations and accents. Perhaps in time, under the influence of Spanish, Nahuatl developed similar patterns, but that is mere speculation with little use for someone learning to speak and to write Nahuatl in the sixteenth and seventeenth centuries.[38] And there is no indication that Carochi would have entertained such an objective. If anything, Sahagún and Carochi deplored the Hispanization of Nahuatl. The end is to understand Nahuatl in order to speak it and write it correctly—that is, make sense in it—which means be understood by Nahuatl-speaking listeners. A form of Classical Nahuatl was certainly embalmed in the grammars, and one can identify the emergence of literate forms of Nahuatl no longer bound to speech in missionary writings of *doctrinas*, *confesionarios*, and *sermones*, which often imitated the rhetoric of songs that from all appearances recorded performances and recitations. We also find a literate Nahuatl (namely, without an immediate connection to a speech event) in Domingo Chimalpahin's *Diario*, which records his observations of daily events.[39] But there is no reason to assume that a Nahuatl grammar would be more or less effective in controlling change and innovation in speech and writing than a Spanish counterpart.

Grammars ultimately are instruments of power insofar as they seek to control and regulate the language of the elite, of those charged with governing. The governability reinforced by Spanish and Nahuatl grammars perpetuates the structures of power through the education of criollos and the native elite, much in the same way that Antonio de Nebrija spoke of grammar and empire as going hand in hand, not because of the need to regulate the language of the populus or because he sought to impose Spanish over all the territories (the multiple languages spoken in the Peninsula and the endurance of indigenous languages in the Americas would indicate a monumental failure), but because Spanish would become the language of empire, of the bureaucratic machinery. And this would be true even within the Morisco community, where, on the eve of the second Alpujarras rebellion in 1568, very few spoke, as J. H. Elliot has pointed out, "any language but Arabic."[40] Even though the *cartillas* (primers) designed to teach reading and writing promoted Spanish, they were trilingual manuals for learning the phonetics of Spanish, Latin, and Nahuatl; in the context of the Peninsula, one finds bilingual *cartillas* that include an Arabic version in Latin script. Learning Spanish, as promoted by the Crown as early as 1534, had the objective of training a native elite who could function in Spanish governmental and ecclesiastic institutions.[41] On the other hand, we find numerous *ordenanzas* that insist on the missionaries learning indigenous languages for their proper indoctrination.

Second corollary: The Codex of Tlatelolco and the *Historia de Tlatelolco*, as instances of *domesticated glyph* and *savage literacy*, lead me to assert that sixteenth-century Spaniards were not particularly given to privileging data derived from alphabetical writing over data taken from iconic script.[42] The history of the production of Sahagún's *Historia general*, but also of Codex Telleriano-Remensis, also suggests that Spanish authorities were prone to trust the expertise of a *tlacuilo*, a *letrado* in his own tradition, over an alphabetical text produced by a suspect Spanish or Indian source. Often, iconic script carried more force in court than an alphabetically recorded oral testimony. The most convincing texts, however, included both iconic and alphabetical scripts that complemented the information each writing form communicated. Writing conveys the weight of tradition, which in both Spanish and Nahuatl contexts was defined by the status and trustworthiness of the source. We must not assume a priori that pictorial texts would be more resistant to colonial power than an alphabetical rendition of a verbal performance. Numerous pictorial texts seek the recognition of compliance to the evangelization and of participation in the military conquest. But this same heterogeneity, which should keep us from inventing a homogeneous Indian culture, furthered the exercise of power by fostering conflict among the different ethnic groups. As such, pictorial texts reinforced the identity of the ethnic groups that claimed a right to privileges. Thus, we find in the Codex of Tlatelolco a record of the Mixtón War (1541) in which the Tlatelolca leaders figure prominently in comparison with the miniaturized Spanish soldiers riding their horses. Certainly, this text preserves a pictorial tradition and worldview in its representation of the colonial order. On the one hand, a verbal performance telling the accomplishments of the Tlatelolcas would articulate a magic-religious understanding of time and space; on the other, the performance of the codex in front of the Spanish authorities would then require switching codes and articulating a discourse clad in Spanish legal terms. Spanish authorities invited versatility in languages and worldviews by recognizing pictorial texts throughout the colonial period.

IN THE MODE OF A CONCLUSION

Telling this story of how one was conquered is not unlike the story of one's personal conversion to Christianity, given that it involves telling the story of resistance to the missionaries' revelations of the idolatrous nature of their beliefs. If the Nahuas continued to paint histories *that sought the recognition of their rights and desires as ethnic groups or individual litigants* (pictorial texts whose categories and narrative styles retain their authority in Spanish courts as well as for Spanish historians), then the solicited story of how one was conquered would *seek to implant in the Nahuas the recognition of a lost world by prompting an account of how the gods, the magic of warriors and sorcerers, and the system of mores had failed them.* It is a story in which the gods anticipate the end of their life-forms, the Spaniards ridicule the magic of the sorcerers, and the magical force of the warrior's ensigns and accoutrements proves ineffectual. And yet the melancholic rendition refuses to recognize the Spanish Conquest as liberation from magic, superstition, and Satan. It is much like a confession in which one fails to recognize conversion as a turning point in one's life, instead indulging in a sweet melancholy that postpones indefinitely the realization of living in a state of sin, of that loss symbolized by original sin. Indeed, the narrative of ethnosuicide, whether in the mode of the confession or of the epistemic privileging of European science, faces its limits in the ability to use the language that would have assured the authorities of its success. It is less a question of not telling the expected stories (they would be told and retold endlessly) or using the expected terms (*Dios, gracia,* and *la Vir-*

gen are always on their lips) than of not internalizing the narrative of their transformation. The Tlatelolcas' stories are also stories of resistance inasmuch as they denigrate and mock the Spaniards' desire for gold, denounce the terror of the massacres, and, in telling the story in their own categories, retain an indigenous memory of the end of their world, which in fact testifies to its survival. Telling the story of how magic and the warriors' insignia failed to impart fear in the Spaniards retains a memory of magic and, paradoxically, enables Indian warriors to continue to wear their accoutrements. Magic may thus continue to exist within the new order. As we saw in the Codex of Tlatelolco, the Tlatelolcas wore their traditional, though hybrid, dress when they fought at the Mixtón, and the representation of the *tlatohuani* (in Nahuatl, "he who speaks well") who solicited the recognition of the Tlatelolcas' role in the Mixtón War follows pre-Columbian conventions. As such, the Spanish order assumes a particular value in the pictorial text. The specific meaning of the Spaniards within this textual mesh would demand knowledge of Nahuatl and, of course, of the stories told regarding the event.

One can only wonder what would have happened if the Tlatelolcas had identified themselves with the Caxcan uprising and joined forces to expel the Spaniards from their lands. It is in these instances where the heterogeneity of Indians works in tandem with the perpetuation of the colonial order. One explanation for the Tlatelolcas' failure to support and participate in the rebellion could be the lack of a common culture with the peoples from the North, but heterogeneity also worked against peoples who shared language and culture in the immediate vicinity. Witness the splintering of opposing forces and alliances with the Spaniards that enabled the conquest of Tenochtitlan. Joining forces with the Caxcanes, the Zacatecos, the Huicholes, and other groups in the Chichimeca would not have necessarily implied abandoning one's ethnic identity in the pursuit of some sort of common ideology, but rather joining forces in the constitution of a multitude fighting a common enemy.

We may also wonder why the pages pertaining to the early years of the conquest were removed from Telleriano-Remensis. And why the Dominican Pedro de los Ríos felt pressed to take over the production of the text rather than incorporate a *tlacuilo* more to his liking. The depiction of the Dominican friar baptizing an Indian; the Franciscan holding the confessional; Mendoza enforcing the language of history, love, and war of the Requerimiento; and the figure of Tenamaztle imbued with magic-religious symbolism captures four independent worlds. The inclusion and relativization of these worlds reminded the friar of the fragility of the colonial order. Perhaps, it was not Ríos who resented the fragmentation of the world but another Dominican. Perhaps Ríos, as a Dominican, was in full agreement with Las Casas's condemnation of the conquest and justification of the rebellion in terms of the right the Indians had to erase the Spaniards from the face of the earth. Perhaps, Ríos truly believed that he was continuing the project with his scribbling of dates. The question would then be, why destroy the physical integrity of the codex with scratches, blobs, and crude writings if Ríos supported the Indian world in the Lascasian mode of an unconditional acceptance that would have justified sacrifice and anthropophagy as instances of the religiosity of the Nahuas? There is also the possibility that there was a rush to finish the codex, something we find in the case of the hurried translation of *Book XII* and the incomplete paintings of the Florentine Codex, and the famous note at the end of Codex Mendoza wherein the commentator complains of the short notice to write the glosses: "Diez dias antes de la partida de la flota se dio al ynterpretador esta ystoria el cual descuido fue de los yndios que se acordaron tarde y como cosa de corrida no se tuvo punto en el estilo que convenia interpretarse" [The Interpreter was given this history ten days prior to the departure of the fleet, and he interpreted carelessly because the Indians came to an agreement late; and so it was done in haste and he did not improve the style suitable for an interpretation, nor did he take time to polish the words and grammar or make a clean copy].[43] This observation conveys the perplexity of a specialist in native things ("como es el ynterpretador dellas buena lengua mexicana") who fails to furnish an adequate alphabetical interpretation of a native pictorial history.[44] It is as if the letter could not match the complexity of iconic script, even when he blames his poor interpretation on the Indians who came to agree too late. This comment provides further evidence of the collective authorship in native historical writing. No internal evidence in Codex Telleriano-Remensis points to a time pressure, and we can only speculate on the reason for the shoddy writing and the interruption of its production.

We also lack any clues regarding the removal (perhaps just a loss) of pages corresponding to the early years of the conquest. There is a similar text in the Vatican, Codex Vaticanus A, also known as Codex Ríos, which includes some of the pages pertaining to the early years of the conquest. Codex Ríos was produced in Rome (most likely) by an Italian hand that used a native text as a prototype. There has been speculation on a third text that served as a model for both Telleriano-Remensis and Codex Ríos. Others speculate that it was Telleriano-Remensis itself that served as a model for Codex Ríos and that the painter chose not to include the dates scribbled by Ríos at the end of Telleriano-Remensis.[45] But then, what was the source for the early years in Codex Ríos? These early years are bloody and apparently were not offensive to those in Rome (Figure 14). Codex Ríos and Telleriano-Remensis must have functioned as a defense of Native American cultures at the Vatican by Dominicans seeking an indictment of the conquest. One thing that differentiates Telleriano-Remensis from the Florentine Codex is that the latter provides both a pictorial and a verbal rendition. Does this have to do with the importance Sahagún gave to language as a key to the mentality of the Nahuas? Why would the Dominicans, if this is an apologetic text, cut the tongue of the *tlacuilo*, reducing all speech in the codex to the glosses written by Indian and mestizo scribes, which for the most part merely name and describe the painted objects, and the lengthier, interventionist glosses by Ríos and other missionaries? Or is it that we have failed to identify some of the glosses, obviously not the ones that destroy the beauty of the text with scratches and scribbles, as products of the *tlacuilo*, as if she could not have learned to use Latin script? Whatever answers we provide to these questions, they will inevitably further complicate the apparent opposition between "people with writing, history, and so on vs. people without these forms."

The texts we have examined suggest that the demand "Tell me the story of how I conquered you" and the more generalized instance of texts in which we can observe how Europe was thought of and represented in Indian categories entail cross-cultural communication in which alphabetical script coexists with iconic script. We find Indians partaking of the modernity of the colonial order, in fact as active participants in its creation, while also dwelling in an enchanted world that contrasts with the rationalization of life that the missionaries sought to implant. Clearly, the missionaries partook of a world of magic of their own, but they also set out to extirpate what they perceived as superstition and idolatry in native beliefs and objects they felt lacked logical and rational grounds. Magic and pre-Columbian life-forms in general were targets for destruction by the missionaries. In fact, the enchanted nature of Mesoamerica results from the privileging of (Christian) rationality over magic, a gesture we can trace to the early Fathers of the Church, for example, in Origen's *Contra Celsum*, if not to the condemnations of idolatry in the Old Testament. Disenchantment is an integral component of the Greco-Abrahamic tradition, of what Nancy and Derrida refer to as "globalatinization," after the French term *mondialatinisation*.[46] Obviously, Mesoamericans didn't think of themselves in terms of the binary enchantment vs. disenchantment. The demand to tell the story of conquest sought the internalization of how

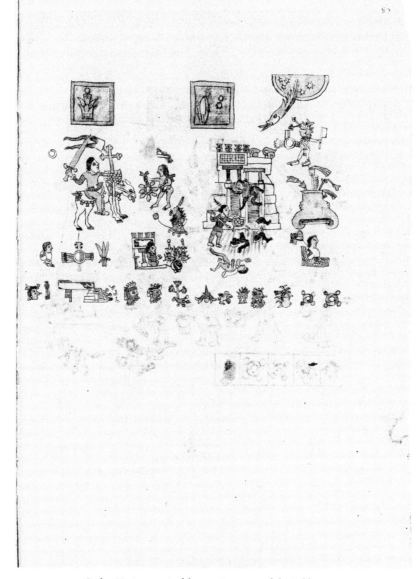

FIGURE 14   *Codex Vaticanus A, fol. 89r. Courtesy of the Biblioteca Apostolica Vaticana, the Vatican.*

magic failed, but, paradoxically, the missionaries solicited stories that would only make sense in terms of a world infused by a sense of magic. In soliciting a representation of the colonial order, they encountered a gaze that relativized their world by showing the multiple ways of worldmaking that operated in Spanish institutions, texts, and practices. The return of the gaze, the actual looking back of the *tlacuiloque*, made evident the fragility and tenuousness of colonial power. Beyond an understanding of melancholy as crushed rebellion, I find in folio 46r a sweet melancholy that gives place to mania, to the exhilaration, if not happiness, of crossing languages and forms of life. In tracing the participation of the *tlacuilo* in the production of modernity, we must also keep in mind that the modern divide does not encompass, that is, exhaust the significance and experience of the European invasion, which retains its own terms for drawing a periodicity. The globalization (*mondialisation*) of Christianity depends on the success of the narrative of ethnosuicide, which, paradoxically, would coincide with the stories we tell of imperial power and the rise of (colonial) modernity.

Chapter 7

THE ENTRAILS OF
PERIODIZATION

We cannot not periodize.

—FREDERIC JAMESON

Auch cuij ie teonantin, toconitlacozque in veve tlamanjtiliztli? *

—BERNARDINO DE SAHAGÚN

The exigency of the lost does not entail being remembered and commemorated; rather, it entails remaining in us and with us as forgotten, and in this way and only in this way, remaining unforgettable.

—GIORGIO AGAMBEN

In reconsidering the Medieval/Renaissance periodization—the slash that both separates and unites the Middle Ages and the Renaissance—we find ourselves in the terrain of relativism and the violence of producing global statements about time.[1] Periodizing the rise of modernity is hardly an innocent practice. It constitutes an exercise in the exclusion of life-forms deemed undesirable. This is perhaps nowhere more detrimental than in considering the historical temporality of subjects under colonial rule. If colonialism, in particular the events we may date beginning in 1492, is an instance of modernity, this exercise in periodization would further expose native subjects to the historical iron-fisted rule of modernity. The destructive force that first becomes manifest in the European invasion of the Americas—arguably distinct from previous forms of conquest by Romans, Arabs, Turks, the Crusades, or even the Reconquista—gave place to a history that has affected the totality of the globe.[2]

The modern, however, is not merely a descriptive category arising out of nothing, as it were, ex nihilo. The paradigm and the limited set of statements to be derived from the medieval/modern binary not only make its universal applicability suspect but keep us from reading "medieval" texts on their own terms. In this chapter, I first critically examine the universality of the modern divide, and then move to a discussion of Spanish and indigenous texts that have much to gain from their disentanglement from the medieval/modern paradigm.

THE COLONIAL DIVIDE

What is to be gained by being conceptualized as modern when the concept of modernity has a built-in teleology that defines transitions in terms of an internalization of undesirable traits? Among these, we find the technologies of conversion and conquest that sought to lead the Nahuas to ethnosuicide by means of confessional practices, the internalization of epistemic regimes, and the participation in the wars of conquest as allies of the Spaniards. In the *tlacuilo*'s depiction of the colonial world we may intuit a self who observes and records these destructive technologies from a distance even when she has been recruited to bring about the destruction of her own culture. She is asked to ruin her own culture, but does she? To what extent does she subvert the demand that she objectify her own culture? The *tlacuilo* thus reminds us that the colonial divide is experienced from radically different temporalities. Indeed, the colonial divide must be seen as one more story that seeks to implant the narrative of ethnosuicide.

As we examine folio 46r of the Codex Telleriano-Remensis (see Figure 1), we cannot fail to notice that this pictorial depiction of the colonial order was produced from an *elsewhere* that, while it includes European objects, institutions, and people, must not be reduced or read through the Medieval/Renaissance/Modern divide or continuum. In what ways does this *elsewhere* complicate periodization? Does folio 46r remind us that the experiences of the *tlacuilo* or those of Francisco Tenamaztle—the Caxcan rebel fighting off Viceroy Antonio de Mendoza—have been lost? These experiences fall outside the criteria that define Medieval, Renaissance, or Modern terms. We can no longer cross the divide that separates the native world from the Spanish, not simply because these events happened a long time ago or their worlds have been destroyed: we are barred from accessing them in terms of the European languages and categories we are bound to use. In Chapter 5, I have argued with Giorgio Agamben that the experience and the dwelling place of the *elsewhere* from which and against which the *tlacuilo* and the rebel made sense of the world remains nevertheless unforgettable. In Agamben's paradoxical phrasing, the *tlacuilo*'s depiction leads us to recognize not only that these worlds have been forgotten but also that they are unforgettable. Should we resist the impulse to commemorate, archive, and monumentalize the pictorial languages of Codex

Telleriano-Remensis? If we cannot do without the body of knowledge that has accumulated over the centuries in the glosses, historical accounts, and archaeological studies, we can certainly interrupt and interrogate the tendency to celebrate these figures by turning them into confirmations of our "modern" values. Agamben underscores most lucidly the need to resist institutionalizing histories when he states: "To respond to this exigency is the only historical responsibility I feel capable of assuming fully."[3]

Frederic Jameson's maxim "We cannot not periodize" provides a point of entry into the limits of periodization, limits that I find in his concept of a *singular modernity*.[4] At once we face the task of thinking the *singular modernity* as a single structural event with global implications and the task of understanding singularity as a "particular," always local event that, though it has global repercussions, lacks totalizing effects. My objective in this chapter, then, is to problematize the understanding of periodization—even if I agree with Jameson about the questionable notion of *alternative modernities*—that would assume that historical breaks in European culture have global implications. We face the exigency to imagine *elsewheres* from the modern, not necessarily as antimodern, countermodern, or even postmodern, but just as nonmodern.

Jameson's maxim conveys his conviction that we must narrate, that we cannot do otherwise than elaborate narratives that make sense of history and its breaks. Thus, Jameson reminds us that the period we know as the Middle Ages emerges as a result of the stories we have been telling about the Renaissance over the last two hundred years, narratives that marked out a period after Antiquity. But if this seems like a truism that Medieval and Renaissance scholars have in recent years sought to undo or at least rigorously question, in thinking about processes of colonization in the Americas we face the emergence of *other* antiquities, though now paradoxically *living*, coexistent with a modernity that confines them to a past/present that no longer *can* continue to exist. Indeed, as expressed by Indian leaders in the "dialogue" with the first twelve Franciscans who arrived in Mexico in 1524, and who supposedly shortly after held the *coloquios*, Indians were asked to perform the unforgettable act of *ruining* their own ancient wisdom. In the demand to commit ethnosuicide, the Nahuas were asked to destroy the ancient wisdom, to reduce to ruins not only temples and effigies of the gods but also their beliefs and practices. For the fragmented debris lying on the grounds of the city, used for building the new Spanish cities, there is a corresponding effect in the fragments we identified in the album of Mesoamerican writing samples collected in Telleriano-Remensis and in missionary ethnographies generally. Indeed, the fragments of Nahuatl speech in ethnographic inquiries (Sahagún's *Historia general*, the *Cantares Mexicanos*) and linguistic artifacts (*artes, vocabularios*) are used to construct evangelical instruments (psalmodies, catechisms, confession manuals). These are vestiges of a world that disappeared in the span of a decade, turning the world of the Nahuas into a living antiquity. Those who give testimony of the destruction or participate in the creation of albums reside in an *elsewhere* that cannot be reduced to the positive knowledge missionaries or modern scholars have drawn from the fragments.

The epigraph above drawn from Sahagún's *Colloquios y doctrina christiana* captures the story missionaries sought to instill in native colonial subjects (to their dismay, bewilderment, and confusion).[5] I speak of astonishment, dismay, and bewilderment rather than some form of more active oppositional consciousness, because I find forms of resistance in this seemingly passive suspension of belief, an attitude Nahua spiritual leaders tragically expressed in their response to the missionaries' claim that their God is the only valid divinity. The apparent resignation to commit ethnosuicide turns into one more instrument designed to lead the Nahuas to recognize the inevitability of accepting the Christian doctrine. We cannot ascertain whether Sahagún's reporting of the Nahuas' response was faithful to the exact words of the native leaders participating in the colloquium, but certainly Sahagún's language sought verisimilitude if the performance of the *colloquios* were to have credible impact for indoctrinating the Nahuas of the second half of the sixteenth century. Although we can place Sahagún, and even the collegians with whom he wrote the *Colloquios y doctrina christiana*, within the grid that separates the medieval from the modern, it is clear that those subjects who experienced the call to ruin their cultures cannot be subsumed under this periodization. It is one thing to participate in the production of a (medieval/modern) text intended to lead Nahuas to attrition and contrition—that is, conversion—for their pagan beliefs and subjection to the devil, another to experience this call to ruin, to ethnosuicide. Here again we should also draw a difference between the terms we may use to periodize the main representatives of the Franciscan and the Dominican orders.

In his *Fundamentos de la historia de América*, Edmundo O'Gorman draws from Las Casas a parallelism between the arts of conversion and of science that enables him to place Las Casas's *De unico vocationis modo* as a transitional text between Scholasticism and Descartes. Furthermore, O'Gorman likens the period of "learning" in which infidels turn into believers to the provisional morality Descartes assumed in the *Meditations* while doubting the existence of self and world. In drawing this parallel, O'Gorman underscores a paradox, if not a contradiction, in Las Casas. But I would add that this "suspension" is hardly paradoxical in Las Casas, given that Indians would continue to conduct their daily life according to their own life-forms until properly indoctrinated and fully conscious of the implications and significance—political as well as spiritual—of baptism, and even then they would have the option of not accepting Christianity. But is this recognition of the right of infidels to remain in their infidelity a modern "thing," an invention of the Renaissance, or, for that matter, a medieval attitude? What would our understanding of colonial Indian subjects gain from this exercise in periodization? After all, it only concerns European subjects. But these same European subjects working with indigenous informants suggest forms of thought that enable us to critique standard forms of periodizing modernity.

If at least two subjects with distinct habitus participated in the production of Codex Telleriano-Remensis, one must assume that they shared a common ground enabling them to communicate. This would suggest that the *tlacuilo* participated in the production of information while observing the epistemic regime of the missionaries conducting ethnographic inquiries. Telleriano-Remensis is but one instance of the systematic inquiries into Mesoamerican culture. In other projects, notably in Bernardino de Sahagún's prologues to his multivolume *Historia general de las cosas de Nueva España*, we find unambiguous instances of what Niklas Luhmann calls second-degree observers.[6] Luhmann argues that the emergence of these observers entails a capacity for differentiation and self-reflexivity that defines the beginning of modernity. Fredric Jameson, in his exercise in periodization, *A Singular Modernity*, derives his argument for a structural modernity with global repercussions from Luhmann. O'Gorman's reading of Las Casas would challenge this clear, periodizing break. Indeed, for O'Gorman, after the discovery and conquest of America, Europe could not be anything but Euro-American in its intellectual and scientific background. In the end, wouldn't the *tlacuilo* also reveal herself as a second-degree observer, though grounded in a habitus distinct from the emergent modern subject of Luhmann?

It might be pertinent to extend here the argument that the invention of the Renaissance produced the Middle Ages, and ask ourselves how it makes sense to speak of a Renaissance (and for that matter of a medieval) colonial America. Our friars might be seen as lacking the humanist values characteristic of the Renaissance, but then again they might actually embody humanism more intensively than anywhere else in Europe during this period. In the end, these breaks make sense only from within a narrative of Euro-America, but we must retain the *elsewhere* from which and against which the colonial (indigenous) subject makes sense of the world. According to O'Gorman, the emergence of Euro-American thought depends on the incorporation of America into European consciousness. This incorporation clearly affects subjects on both sides of the Atlantic, but we must also understand the ways in which Europe was incorporated into Mesoamerican thought and culture.[7] This sense of a two-way road in the traffic of goods, ideas, peoples, and technologies suggests that the culture that emerges in Mesoamerica after the European invasion clearly carries a break, indeed, one in which its past is constituted by Europeans as a form of antiquity. Clearly, the *tlacuilo* invents a pictorial vocabulary for depicting European objects, hence she participates in Euro-American institutions; however, it is my main contention in this chapter and book that the Mesoamerican *elsewhere* from which she makes sense must remain irreducible to the statements the missionaries and modern scholars produce. The incorporation of Mesoamerica into European thought does not merely involve the appropriation of indigenous artistic and intellectual findings but rather a process of *exappropriation* in which Indian intellectuals challenge European ethnographic projects.

I prefer the term *exappropriation* to *appropriation* or *expropriation*, of which periodization and narrativization are but one manifestation. In this I follow Derrida and quote him generously:

> As always, the choice is not *between* mastery and nonmastery, any more than it is *between* writing and nonwriting in the everyday sense. . . . The choice does not choose between control and noncontrol, mastery and nonmastery, property or expropriation. What is at stake here, and it obeys another "logic," is rather a "choice" between multiple configurations of mastery without mastery (what I have proposed to call *exappropriation*). But it also takes the phenomenal form of a war, a conflictual tension between multiple forces of appropriation, between multiple strategies of control. Even if no one can ever control everything, it is a question of knowing whom you want to restrict, by what and by whom you don't want what you say or what you do to be immediately and totally reappropriated.[8]

Paraphrasing Derrida, I would add that in "rethinking periodization," one does not have a choice between *periodization* and *nonperiodization*. We may also cite Jameson's maxim "We cannot not periodize," though not with the gusto he derived from the double negative that determines the obligation *to* periodize. We would then work with multiple configurations of periodization in what has been a temporal war or a war of temporalities since Spain invaded the Americas. In this "since" we find ourselves framed within the maxim "We cannot not periodize," but fully in the terrain of the epistemic violence that underscored the narrative that constituted an insuperable break between the before and the after of the conquest, as if this break had the same meaning for all the actors involved in the events. This break is most dramatically expressed in the second epigraph to this chapter: "Auch cuij ie teonantin, toconitlacozque in veve tlamanjtiliztli?" [And now we, ourselves, will destroy the ancient wisdom?]. Needless to say, the response of the missionaries was in the affirmative.

The events on folio 46r are organized in terms of three dates, 1541, 1542, 1543, which according to the Mesoamerican calendar would correspond to the years 10 House, 11 Rabbit, and 12 Reed. The Judeo-Christian dates on top of the glyphs offer a translation (that is, a mere transparent equivalence) into a homogeneous temporality (years-are-just-years-for-dating-all-past-present-and-future-events) that undermines the significance of Mesoamerican dates within the Tonalamatl (the 260-day count of the days), its connection to the 360-day count of the agricultural year, and the 52-year cycles that synchronize the two counts. One reading of this page would emphasize the similarities with the European genre of the annals, which would lead us to think of the depicted events as discrete fragments of events in a given year.[9] Although these fragments would ultimately be meaningful according to the European calendrical system of anno Domini, these possible meanings remain extraneous to the Mesoamerican count. The significance of 10 House remains invisible when one ignores the Mesoamerican spatio-temporal habitus that cannot be reduced to its "transparent" equivalence of 1542. If the equation of 12 House and 1542 is significant with respect to the Spanish colonial order, the reconfiguration of Mesoamerican counts imposes a grid (anno Domini) that circumscribes the events in the Ancient times in terms of the Judeo-Christian calendar.

The story of how anno Domini became prevalent escapes the scope of this study. My point here is not to generalize the use of anno Domini among all (late) Medieval and Renaissance historians but to signal the specific use of what has become a standard procedure. As alternatives to the use of anno Domini, consider the following chronology in the *Siete Partidas*:

E este libro fue começado a fazer e a componer, vispera de S. Iuan Baptista, a quatro año e.xxiij.dias andados del comienço del nnro

reynado, q começo quando andaua la AEra de Adam en cinco mill e
veynte vn años Hebraycos, e dozientos e ochenta e siete dias. E la AEra
del diluuio, en quatro mill e trezientos e cinquenta e tres años Romanos,
e ciento e cinco dias mas. E la AEra de Nabucodonosor en mill e noue-
cientos e nouenta e ocho años Romanos, e nouenta dias mas. E la AEra
de Felipo el grand rey de Grecia, en mill e quinientos e sesenta e quatro
años Romanos, e veynte y dos dias mas. E la AEra de Cesar en mill e dozientos ochenta e nueue años Romanos, e ciento e cinquenta dias mas.
E la AEra de la Encarnacion en mill e dozientos e cinquenta e vn años
Romanos, e ciento e cincuenta e dos dias mas. E la AEra de los Arauigos
en sycientos e veynte nueue años Romanos, e trezientos e vn dias mas.
E fue acabado deesde que fue começado a siete años cumplidos.[10]

[And this book was first worked on the eve of Saint John the Baptist,
on the fourth year and twenty-three days of our reign, that began when
the Era of Adam had run the course for five thousand twenty-one years
of the Hebraic calendar, and two hundred eighty days. And in the Era
of the Deluge, four thousand three hundred fifty-three Roman years and
one hundred five more days. And from the Era of Nabucodonosor one
thousand nine hundred ninety-eight Roman years and ninety more days.
And from the Era of Phillip, the great king of Greece, one thousand five
hundred sixty-four Roman years and twenty-two more days. And from
the Era of Caesar one thousand two hundred eighty-nine years, and one
hundred fifty more days. And from the Era of the Incarnation one thousand two hundred and fifty-one Roman years, and one hundred fifty-
two more days. And from the Era of the Arabs six hundred twenty-nine
years, and three hundred one more days. And it was completed in seven
years.]

Although there is mention of the "AEra de la Encarnacion," the era of
the Incarnation is one of the possible chronologies. This passage also includes the difference between *años Romanos* and *años Hebraycos*, a distinction that I gather would presuppose counting the start of the days at
midnight or at dawn. The implications escape me. But note that among the
possible chronologies, the *Siete Partidas* lists the "AEra de los Arauigos."
The Roman count remains the common denominator for the remaining
dating. Is this a gesture that offers equivalence for understanding empire
as comprising all peoples on earth? In a similar light, the Requerimiento
defines the authority over all peoples on earth: "juzgar y governar a todas
las gentes, Christianos, moros, judios, gentiles y de qualquier otra seta o

creencia que fuesen" [to judge and govern all people, Christians, Moors, Jews, and gentiles and from whatever other sect they would belong to].[11] In the Protestant context, we may cite Joseph Juste Scaliger's *De emendatione temporum* (1583), which argues that ancient history should not be confined to that of the Greeks and Romans, but also should include that of the Persians, the Babylonians, the Egyptians, and the Jews. Scaliger goes beyond establishing eras as in the *Siete Partidas* in that he proposed that their different systems of chronology should be compared. In the case of Nahua historians, we find the translation of dates in terms of the correspondence between the two calendars. In some instances, Nahua historians using the alphabet specify the equivalence in terms of anno Domini by stating after the corresponding date, "motlacatillitzino yn totemaquixticatzin Jesu christo" [after our Savior Jesus Christ was born].[12] The rigor with which they document the Mesoamerican calendars allows for the definition of a chronology in terms of the fifty-two-year cycle and the significance dates would have in that system of dating. Let these indications stand as possible ways of complicating the prevalence of anno Domini but also the transparency with which historians and archaeologists date the past—a practice one may identify in the glosses on top of the Mesoamerican calendrical entries on folio 46r. This is an early instance of the use of the Judeo-Christian calendar for dating events in all cultures, whether on the basis of written documentation or archaeological evidence. The "West" may now write the history of all peoples.

In drawing equivalences between the Mesoamerican and the Christian calendars, the glossators of Telleriano-Remensis assumed that the history of people without history—that is, that have been recently incorporated into Christianity—can be written by ascribing events anterior to the beginning of history with historical significance, even if this significance amounts to a homogenization of time. (This historical tenet has gained universal applicability in the last two centuries.) The apostle travels far to bring all peoples into the temporal fold of the Church, imposing upon those he touches with his holy water a flattening of their past into homogeneous time that they must then reconfigure in terms of the time to come, the time that remains after that great break dated by the birth of Jesus Christ—the time of *christos*, of the Messiah, whose forgiveness, whose gift we cannot choose not to accept, "we cannot not periodize." Christology must now rule native time and temporality.

By temporal definition, colonial subjects whose life-forms have been confined to a state of antiquity form part of another history that cannot be understood merely as a variation of Europe or an *alternative modernity*, for that matter. Modernity from the colonial perspective of the Nahuas, of the *tlacuilo* in particular, is not just a form of existence, or even a profound transformation of previous life-forms, or, for that matter, a paradigm shift. It is a regime of truth, of politics, of structures of feeling that the colonial regime imposes on Mesoamerican subjects as the only acceptable form of life. Despite this, the position of exteriority also suggests that this singular modernity has multiple points of entry. The *tlacuilo*, in responding to the request by the missionary, participates in the logic of modernity, inasmuch as she clearly understands the imperative for objectifying her culture, identifying missionary orders, recording Spanish institutions, using the writing technologies of the book, perspective, and the alphabet. But this coevalness that defines the time of the conversation, of the request to produce an objective record of her culture, I must insist again, entails a world that exceeds the statements produced according to a multiplicity of European regimes of truth. This European multiplicity may be conceived, to borrow Lyotard's terms in *The Differend*, as "phrases in dispute." Two such instances would be the divergent, indeed, irreconcilable understandings of Mesoamerica I have traced in the Dominican and the Franciscan ethnographic and evangelical programs. The concept of *elsewhere* calls forth the existence of a world whose regimes of truth cannot be reduced to European equivalents. One may write using the alphabet, paint with perspective, ride horses, use guns, weave wool on standing looms, and so on, from within a Mesoamerican *elsewhere* that the missionaries sought to destroy. While the *tlacuilo* was subjected to social transformations brought about by the colonial order, she remained grounded in Mesoamerica, even when for the missionaries it is a reality that haunts them as a living "antiquity." The project of transformation involves a temporal displacement without which the colonial order cannot conceive itself as such. The colonial order structurally comprises an outside that assumes the form of a perpetual tutelage.

What are the implications of perpetual tutelage for the project of rethinking periodization—the slash that partitions the Middle Ages from the Renaissance? In responding to this question, we must keep in mind that sixteenth-century missionary ethnographers followed in their training the archaeological and linguistic investigations of the pagan, mainly Roman, past. The constitution of dictionaries and grammars of Latin prepared the ground and served as models for the grammars of indigenous languages in the Americas. The tools for reconstructing a dead language now serve to reform, to confine, to reduce to an order: *reducir* was the Spanish technical term applied to the *artes* of living Indian languages.[13]

In analogy to the *reducciones*, the forced settlements that sought to visually subject Indians to a Christian polity, *artes* sought to visually subject language to a grammatical regime. Neither physical nor linguistic *reducciones*, however, would necessarily involve a process of Hispanization. In fact, *reducciones* and *artes* are often conceptualized as spaces for the protection of Indian life under the so-called *repúblicas de indios* and of Indian languages under the assumption that one could identify a "classical" standard. On the other hand, Roman and to a lesser extent Greek pagan culture was the preferred referent in comparative ethnographies. This panorama, however, lacks a central component—the native informant without whom this work could not be produced. In the training of the informant, the missionary undergoes a process of training as well. Even when the imperial mission destines the native population to perpetual tutelage, the colonial structure is much more complex than the binary colonizer/colonized suggests, not because this binary does not exist but because the colonial process cannot be reduced to such simple terms. Along with the informant, we find the native political administration that plays a significant position in the implementation of the colonial order. Native judges, governors, and caciques (without naming the specific titles of local leaders) administer the *república de indios*. The *tlacuilo* that painted the pictorial component of Telleriano-Remensis is but one instance of an adroit informant straddling the semantic fields of Mesoamerican *antiquity* and the Spanish Renaissance/Medieval divide. If Jameson's maxim "We cannot not periodize" retains its pertinence, the colonial divide entails two distinct habitus and backgrounds from which and against which one makes sense of the before and after of the Spanish invasion. Periodization would, in the end, ascertain the efficacy of the narratives that led to ethnosuicide.

DECOLONIZING MEDIEVAL MEXICO

My discussion of Lacan and Lévi-Strauss in Chapter 5 has enabled me to productively complicate the narrative of the "most modern science," that is, the story of how "there was nothing but fantasy regarding knowledge until the advent of the most modern science."[14] Even though Lévi-Strauss sought to erase the criteria for formulating a stagist narrative of human development that would trace a transition from mythical thought to modern science, he could not avoid a qualitative differentiation between the mythical *bricoleur* and the engineer/the physicist. The *tlacuilo* would seem to have partaken of the spirit of modern science in her invention of a pictorial vocabulary for depicting the colonial world and the topology of conquest she draws to reveal the missionaries' fantasies regarding apostasy. We may productively expand the applicability of the concept of *elsewhere* to wrest cultural phenomena that scholars have tended to characterize as "medieval" from the medieval/modern paradigm.

The concept of "medieval Mexico" is a construct that can assume positive, negative, and folkloric values. In recent years, several scholars, including myself earlier in this chapter, have felt the urgency to date the beginnings of modernity with the Spanish colonization of the New World. This call responds to the standard periodization that constitutes modernity in terms of Northern European culture, whether of the so-called classical age of the seventeenth century or the Enlightenment. Tracing the beginnings of modernity back to the sixteenth-century colonial period carries an impetus to claim contributions to modernity, a resistance to a medieval mentality, a need to understand the Spanish process of colonization and empire building as thoroughly modern, and a general tendency to speak in terms of alternative modernities.[15] I mention these questions of periodicity not because I intend to provide new criteria for marking the beginnings of modernity. Rather, my objective here is to study the force of texts that have been classified (pejoratively, I might add) as medieval in and on their own terms, not to claim their status as modern.

I am not interested in tracing medieval phenomena by dwelling within the texts that one may characterize as circumscribed or as participating in a habitus that we may define as medieval. Given the colonial nature of sixteenth-century Mexico, the term *medieval* might include precolonial Mesoamerica as an equivalent to the European transition to capital and modernity, but it might also include the culture Spaniards brought with them to the New World. Whereas the first instance of a habitus leads to the questionable practice of comparing artifacts belonging to two distinct worlds that cannot be subsumed under a third world without exerting violence, the latter understanding of habitus bears the burden of medievalist stereotypes. In order to avoid the semblance of a single world that engulfs all possible horizons of universality, I have developed in this book the notion of *elsewheres* to speak of life-forms that must not be conceived from the standpoint of an anthropological "other" and the mirroring dialectic of Same and Other.[16]

We may further complicate the use of the term *medieval* to encompass all colonial phenomena. As far as the indigenous populations of Mexico are concerned, the criteria for establishing the periodicity of the medieval and the Renaissance (or modern) must include other criteria that would address the transformations the Spanish invasion brought about by creating a colonial divide. In speaking of the colonial divide, the discontinuities and continuities between before and after the conquest cannot be equivalent nor reduced to what Margreta de Grazia has identified as the modern divide.[17] Consequently, the term *medieval* would be equivocal not only with respect to Ancient Mesoamerica but also with respect to the indigenous colonial social and cultural structures. When speaking of medieval Mexico, we must take care to specify that this term refers to lifeforms that have been identified as medieval rather than to stable entities we may unequivocally call medieval. In other words, the term *medieval* itself calls forth the history of its invention as a border period that already carries epistemological violence in the assumption that this period's only significance resides in what comes after—that is, the Renaissance or modernity. My use of the term *medieval* in this essay signals this conventionality. I offer a definition of *nonmodern* that avoids the built-in teleology of the "pre" in *premodern* and the transitional status of the medieval.

Luis Weckmann's two-volume *La herencia medieval de México* provides a thorough, perhaps insuperable, catalogue of "medieval" practices in New Spain, ranging from political institutions to culinary arts. His recuperation of medieval traits of the Mexican nationality, however, is often neutral, sometimes positive, sometimes negative. Some traits pertain to the realm of folklore. Jacob Burckhardt's *Civilization of the Renaissance in Italy* infects Weckmann's project with a teleology manifested in his use of the term *retroceso* (retrogression) to characterize the evolution, or rather devolution, of Spanish institutions taken to the New World. Although this observation serves to characterize cultural differences, the ideology of medievalism circumscribes it. With the exception of isolated responses to a postrevolutionary call to recognize indigenous contributions to the national identity, for Weckmann, the indigenous peoples of Mexico are mere receptors of medieval culture and practices. Their current dress, for example, Weckmann dates back to 1518 when Indians on the Gulf of Mexico accepted wearing Grijalva's "gift" of white shirts and pants made of cloth from Castile "para ocultar su desnudez" [to conceal their nakedness].[18] At least in these locations, Hernán Cortés would have found in 1519 indigenous peoples already wearing European attire. Weckmann, however, chooses to ignore that on the white cloth from Castile, indigenous women would embroider indigenous forms—and eventually wove them into cotton and wool cloth—techniques that have undergone transformations over the centuries but continue to be practiced today. It is a common assertion that contemporary indigenous women wear clothing that merely reproduces what medieval Castilian women wore in the fifteenth century, thereby denying their indigeneity, but the story is a bit more complicated. This reductive understanding of medieval culture reminds us that tracing the medieval in the Americas is hardly an innocent affair.

In tracing the medieval in ancient Mexico, one confronts oneself in the terrain of comparisons that ultimately erase rather than clarify the particular nature of Mesoamerican societies and cultures. I must confess such comparisons are tempting. Arguably, the Medieval and the Mesoamerican lived before the disenchantment of modernity. Comparisons are inevitably caught in the entrails of a third term, the *premodern*, that places modernity as a horizon of both societies: that is, Mesoamerica and fifteenth-century Spain share a premodern mentality, premodern prejudices, obscurantism, orality, and perhaps also brilliance.[19] One risks erasing contemporary as well as historical difference and specificity because Mesoamerican peoples are not confined to a distant past but continue to live in our present. What we say about the indigenous peoples of the sixteenth century and their colonial subjection inevitably affects contemporary indigenous societies. Classifying indigenous cultures, languages, and institutions as medieval is not merely an exercise in historical taxonomy but an insertion within a teleology. The epistemic violence of the comparison may be summed up as saying that just as medieval society was bound to become modern (at different rhythms in various European locations), indigenous cultures today must give way to modernity. The disciplinary crossings of anthropology and history carry the danger of engaging in what Johannes Fabian diagnosed as the denial of coevalness in anthropological discourse.[20] In refuting the denial of coevalness, however, we face the need to speak of coexisting heterogeneous temporalities in both the colonial and contemporary societies. The recognition of multiple temporalities need not force us to view the experience of temporal differences in absolutist terms that exclude each other, but rather can invite us to see porous experiences of time in which a subject may dwell in more than one world. By speaking of contemporary societies as medieval, we place them in a temporality that is not our own but also confine them to sociocultural forms that are incompatible with the modern. We therefore remain oblivious of the medievalist tropes that demand the assumption of the modern as norm.

Postcolonial approaches to Latin American colonial societies have called forth criticisms similar to those medievalists face when adopting postcolonial theory. Critics argue that the postcolonial presentist concerns cannot be transposed to the Middle Ages or to the colonial period without distorting historical specificity or engaging in anachronism. In medieval studies, however, Bruce Holsinger has argued quite convincingly that the traffic of concepts between medieval studies and postcolonial theory was first initiated by Indian subalternists, in particular Partha Chatterjee, who drew from medieval social and economic theory to understand twentieth-century India. This observation solves the question of whether postcolonial theory is "applicable" to the Middle Ages, in that postcolonial theory as practiced by Chatterjee is largely grounded in medieval studies.[21]

The importation of medieval parallelisms for understanding India, however, entails a denial of coevalness; the analogy between the Indian present and the medieval past places the researcher outside the temporality of the object of study. The specter of transition to capital narratives inevitably haunts this sort of parallelism. More recently, Chatterjee has precisely questioned the violence implicit in the teleology and historicism of transhistorical models of transition-to-capital narratives. He is particularly concerned with understanding the coexistence of different temporalities, of what Dipesh Chakrabarty refers to as the "times of the gods and the time of history."[22] But even when Chakrabarty is careful to recommend that historians attend to and learn from the experience of subalterns in writing histories, he avoids conceiving fluid subjects that dwell in multiple temporalities without incurring contradiction. This fluidity could be traced in experiences of the world in the so-called medieval period as well as in both the colonial and postcolonial life of indigenous peoples in Mesoamerica. Although the historical location of temporal heterogeneity in terms parallel to the Middle Ages loses applicability in Chatterjee's more recent work, he suggests that one cannot help being modern, even if one does so under the aegis of "alternative": "Much recent ethnographic work has established that these 'other' times are not survivors from a pre-modern past: they are new products of the encounter with modernity itself."[23]

The solution, to my mind, does not reside in conceptualizing alternative modernities but in conceptualizing ways to speak of the nonmodern in terms that avoid the built-in teleology of the "pre-" in the premodern. To what extent does the concept of the "premodern" form part of the tool kit of medievalism?[24] Can one imagine the Middle Ages without a reference to antiquity and modernity? What is to be gained when we study "medieval" cultural artifacts in their own right, on their own terms, that is, merely as nonmodern? As I have pointed out above, the nonmodern would be understood as an *elsewhere* that lacks the determination of the modern embedded in the premodern. The nonmodern and *elsewhere* pertain to a *without history* that conveys an amphibology comprising both *lack* (substantiation by historical discursive appropriation) and *outside* (determination by historical terms of action). Under this form the "non-" would be a pure negation of the modern rather than an adjective denoting an earlier period. I must underscore that the modern must be understood as a periodizing construct or a rupture with a past that is constituted as medieval—but may also include the savage, the primitive, or the tribal—as transitional life-forms that must give way to more evolved social formations. If the modern is only meaningful within the paradigm that opposes the medieval and the modern, it demands the internalization of what it defines as incompatible. Invoking the modern is never a natural inconsequential affair, but a violent regulatory speech act. But then again, the virtue of the *elsewhere* may also reside in opening to unexpected readings the social and cultural forms known as modernity. This implies that cultural objects defined as modern can also be wrested out of the paradigm that binds the modern to the medieval. In this regard, the term *elsewhere* enables the redefinition of the terms.

This is particularly crucial when addressing life-forms in present-day indigenous societies in which the nonmodern coexists with (as well as eludes, observes, critiques) the modern without incurring contradiction or a sense of temporal anteriority, as manifesting the *remains* of a temporality bound to disappear. This coexistence, that is, contemporaneity of more than one distinct world and temporality, does not necessarily imply that all forms of life exist today under the time of globalization. If the language of periodization saturates the categories we scholars are bound to use in thinking about the past (for example, colonization, domination, empire, etc.), we ought to refrain from saturating the concepts of the *nonmodern* and *elsewhere* with new, perhaps more powerful forms of periodization (for instance, a singular modernity, the age of the Global, the postmodern condition, etc.). In this regard, *elsewhere* and *nonmodern* convey a theoretical virtue that lends itself to repetition, to an eternal return of possible dwellings *without history*.

The constructed nature of the Middle Ages is a truism for medieval scholars, yet Kathleen Davis has furthered our understanding of the Middle Ages as an idea in a study of the role that news about Amerindian cultures played in creating the concept of "feudalism" and in displacing slavery as a practice belonging to Europe's pasts and areas outside "modern" Europe.[25] In the context of the Americas, Mesoamerican societies before (and after) the Spanish invasion are conceptualized, paradoxically, as *living antiquities* that had to be destroyed to give place to a Christian era. And yet "feudalism" is now applied, as if it were a transparent *descriptor*, to the socioeconomic condition of contemporary indigenous societies (or, for that matter, to the colonial period). The use of the term implies that their subaltern condition is a mere effect of the Spanish Conquest and not the result of five hundred years of oppression defined by the evolving modes global capital has assumed. Whether one attributes the backwardness of Mexico and of Latin America in general to the feudal or the mercantile nature of the colonial regime, one operates on a transitional model that postulates causes of a historical lag.[26]

Without relying on the modern as a point of reference, the nonmodern suggests a way to think of Mesoamerica and the Middle Ages as *elsewheres* with their specific habitus. When we reflect on colonial Mesoamerica, we face the task of outlining the means by which Western religious and secular practices, institutions, and systems of representation (for the moment, we can bracket out the question of modernity) invaded various Mesoamerican habitus. There was indeed an attempt at a wholesale replacement of a habitus. We may understand the process of colonization as a confrontation of the practices, institutions, and systems of representation that define the given habitus, and perhaps of generations that are brought to develop and participate exclusively in the habitus of a colonial power. In reading folio 46r, we have observed that the imported life-forms were subjected to interpretation and alteration by the receiving habitus to the degree that those charged with the task of implanting the new culture could never fully anticipate the transformations and inventions that characterized the confrontation of cultures. My point in this chapter is not to celebrate indigenous transcultural forms or to expose the abuses in the *contact zone*, to borrow Mary Louise Pratt's term in *Imperial Eyes*, but rather to examine instances in which European nonmodern forms are embedded or mediate colonial Mesoamerican cultural artifacts and thereby define the terms by means of which we may access worlds that remain outside and lack the determination of the time of *christos*, of the Messiah.

Let me recapitulate: I do not intend to redefine a periodization of the colonial nor to undermine Weckmann's study. My objective, rather, is to outline the depth and complexity of three cultural artifacts from sixteenth-century Mexico that are rooted in European nonmodern life-forms. I will be discussing a Nahuatl *Exercicio quotidiano*, the use of European paper and book forms in manuscripts drafted in collaboration between missionaries and Indian intellectuals, and the Augustinian friar Alonso de la Vera Cruz's *De dominio infidelium et justo bello*. The analysis of these texts should contribute to the insights we have drawn from the detailed readings of folio 46r. Whereas the Nahuatl *Exercicio quotidiano* and Vera Cruz's *De dominio* enable me to explore further the complex and diverse evangelical and ethnographic programs of sixteenth-century Franciscan and Dominican missionaries I learned to identify reading folio 46r, the mid-sixteenth-century *Historia Tolteca-Chichimeca* should enable me to address further the intellectual and material conditions in the production of colonial indigenous pictorial codices. My discussion of these texts is not intended to provide a detailed examination of their materiality and substance, but rather to extract characteristics by means of broad strokes for illustrating *elsewheres* as a method for reading nonmodern texts. By reflecting on these texts, I don't want to claim their modernity in terms of technologies of the self, (self)-ethnographic writing, or imperial political theory. I prefer to recognize the European nonmodern matrix from which they originated.

Note that whereas the first two texts (the *Exercicio quotidiano* and the *Historia Tolteca-Chichimeca*) further complicate the stories we tell about the instruments that were designed to promote ethnosuicide (the *Historia* by means of the use of European instruments of writing and painting, the *Exercicio* by programming spiritual introspection), Vera Cruz's *De dominio* complicates prevailing assumptions about those who produced the instruments of evangelization. Beyond the Franciscan and the Dominican differend, the Augustinian Alonso de la Vera Cruz offers postcolonial critics a category we cannot afford to ignore: *ignoratiam invincibilem*.

I. NATIVE CRITICAL THOUGHT

Este exercicio halle entre los yndios, no se quien le hizo ni quien se le dio tenia muchas // faltas E incongruidades mas con verdad se puede dezir que se hizo de nueuo que no se enmendo. Este año de 1574 fray Bernardino de Sahagún.[27]

[I found this exercise among the Indians. I do not know who produced it, nor who gave it to them. It had many errors and incongruities. But in truth it may be said that it was done anew rather than corrected. In this year of 1574. Fray Bernardino de Sahagún]

This note appears at the end of the Nahuatl *Exercicio quotidiano* that was found among the papers of the Indian historian from Chalco, don Domingo de San Antón Muñón Chimalpahin Quauhtlehuanitzin, most commonly known as Chimalpahin. He penned the copy, which reproduces the note by the great Franciscan ethnographer Bernardino de Sahagún, sometime toward the end of the sixteenth century. One gets the impression from Sahagún's note that he suspected the orthodoxy of the *Exercicio*, even after he rewrote it. One also wonders about the extent to which Sahagún's annotation would have lent legitimacy to a copy held by an Indian. It is clearly not a document that would have been drafted by a Franciscan nor by an indigenous intellectual who would have been educated in their missionary schools, otherwise Sahagún would have recognized the style of thought and the penmanship as indicative of Franciscan teaching. The emphasis this *Exercicio* places on the thorough preparation before baptism and the care it gives to developing a habitus through a series of daily meditations during a weeklong preparation that would ready the Indians for communion and the reception of grace that accompanied the sacrament suggest that the writer was educated by Dominican friars. In passing, I must add that it was not a product of Jesuits, even though the title is similar to Ignacio de Loyola's *Ejercicios espirituales,* since the order did not arrive in Mexico until 1572.

As we have seen in earlier chapters, throughout the sixteenth century, Franciscans and Dominicans engaged each other in heated debates on the proper spiritual preparation of Indians for baptism. The Franciscans tended to favor multitudinous baptisms without catechization, while the Dominicans emphasized a thorough catechization and full consciousness of what it meant (spiritually as well as politically) to be baptized. Again, the Dominicans' emphasis was on developing a habitus not only for the reception of grace implanted by the sacrament of baptism but also for the participation in the political life of the colony as converts. For the Franciscans, the true work of evangelization would follow after the incorporation into the Church; although they never advocated forced conversions, at times, as the Dominican Bartolomé de las Casas puts it, baptism was "a veces medio forzado," at times more or less forced.[28]

Whereas the Franciscans consider that the resistance to evangelization had to do with (ill) will, with a hardened heart that kept Indians from accepting revealed truth, the Dominicans underscored the place of the understanding—hence the development of an intellectual habitus—in processes of conversion. In its extremity, the task could take generations before Indians could be baptized and, in theory, they could then opt to remain outside the fold of the Church. As I have shown in Chapter 5, a pagan was always preferred to an apostate. The *Exercicio* works on the assumption that the addressed neophyte has been thoroughly evangelized and will be ready to prepare the soul for receiving communion with a weeklong series of daily exercises.

We will never know what errors and incongruities Sahagún found in this *Exercicio*, but we could speculate that he might have been concerned with the critical consciousness that results from examinations of conscience. Even though (perhaps because) the Council of Trent instituted general confession, the Church became suspicious about individual examinations of conscience such as those practiced in Santa Teresa's *Las Moradas*. The indigenous historian Chimalpahin, who penned the *Exercicio* and kept it among his papers, opens the first entry of *Diario* precisely in the year of 1577 when Santa Teresa wrote *Las Moradas*: "vii. calli xihuitl, 1577. *v* ypan in yn xihuitl oquimihcuilhui yamoxtzin libro in itoca d las moradas yn la madre Teresa de Jesus" [7 House, year 1577. *v* In this year mother Teresa de Jesús wrote her book named *De las moradas*].[29] Although the *Diario* does not offer a day-by-day account of Chimalpahin's spiritual travails, it clearly provides a critical account of the political events or the responses of his Spanish and indigenous contemporaries to natural phenomena such as a solar eclipse or an earthquake. I lack the space here to develop a thorough analysis of the *Diario* and the *Exercicio quotidiano*, so I limit myself to suggesting the *elsewhere*, the nonmodern, from which Chimalpahin examines exclusionary practices, assesses the superiority of European scientific explanations of the world, and exposes governmental corruption.[30] Readers must keep in mind that Chimalpahin's critique practices the art of balancing *perspicuitas* (explicitness) and *obscuritas* (dissimulation). It is my contention that the *Exercicio quotidiano* involves a form of meditation that promotes the forms of critical thought Chimalpahin practices in the *Diario*.

In tracing a genealogy of the *Exercicio* and considering it a nonmodern text, we should think of the personal tone and introspection of Thomas à Kempis's *Imitation of Christ* rather than the uses of the senses of Ignacio de Loyola's *Ejercicios espirituales*. *Imitation of Christ* has been defined as medieval, whereas there seems to be a consensus that argues that Loyola's text offers modern forms of meditation and self-examination. Loyola is often associated with forms of governmentality that can be found in sixteenth-century Mexico, but Loyola can and has been read outside the paradigm of governmentality. But, what does it mean to insist that the *Exercicio quotidiano* is a nonmodern artifact, one situated in an *elsewhere* that cannot be subsumed under the paradigm that opposes the medieval to the modern? One possible answer is that it functions less as an instrument of colonial governmentality (in spite of all the markings of pastoral power) than as a space for meditation and the creation of a critical consciousness, much in line with Las Casas's emphasis on the understanding in evangelization—a dialogical process that would not necessarily end in a docile subject, but rather would lead Indians to reflect on what it means to be a Christian and (in an extreme case when arguments were exhausted) to refuse incorporation into the Church or the empire. This process involves the possible emergence of a critical consciousness that would remain inaccessible to governmentality and pastoral power. But why and how is it that this critical consciousness is not embedded in categories that are most often associated with modernity?

If we were to take Las Casas's call for the understanding as the only way of calling people to Christianity, then the reflection on Christianity and the colonial regime would involve a dialogue in which the participants — Christian and Indian subjects — would straddle European and Mesoamerican worlds. This indigenous subject would come to know, to understand, and to use colonial institutions to his or her advantage and thereby develop a habitus for undoing the common sense colonial governmentality would seek to implant. But there is no reason to assume that this habitus is the result of a modern or even a Christian pedagogy, even if Las Casas is unusually lucid about the place of the understanding. Indeed, it is because of Las Casas's lucidity, which entails the respect of indigenous reasoning (otherwise, one would be imposing a single view of the understanding), that an indigenous habitus is reinforced while the Indian subjects learn their way around the colonial order. Unless we want to perpetuate the image of Indians remaining static in straddling these worlds, we must allow for the nonmodern to undergo transformations autonomous of the evolution of the self-proclaimed superiority of discourses that define themselves as modern. The nonmodern is not a static, pure form but an existence independent of the historical transformations modernity claims as total. In fact, my contention has been that modern objects, practices, and forms of subjectivity assume a life of their own in the habitus that remain *elsewhere*. Christian doctrines — whether in European or Mesoamerican expressions — would be incorporated into the indigenous nonmodern world.

This is not to say that the nonmodern would exclude all forms of governmentality or that the modern collapses with governmentality, but that the *Exercicio* and Las Casas's emphasis on the understanding in evangelical practices reside outside the logic and practices of governmentality. Chatterjee provides a succinct definition of governmentality: "Governance, that new buzzword in policy studies, is . . . the body of knowledge and set of techniques used by, or on behalf of, those who govern."[31] This definition suggests that the category of governmentality cannot be thought outside the paradigm that defines the modern vis-à-vis the medieval, the tribal, the primitive, and so forth. However, the practices of governmentality—body of knowledge and set of techniques—are not exclusive to the period named *modern*, even if there is an incremental ability to deploy and define techniques of governmentality. By the same token, we ought to avoid limiting all those life-forms we may value—for instance, democracy, critical consciousness, science, enlightenment politics, secularism—to those meanings one generates in deploying the paradigm of modernity. It is not a question of recognizing how all cultures in all times have been modern, as Aníbal Quijano and Enrique Dussel would in deploying the concept of transmodernity,[32] but rather of enabling readings and practices in which we may trace nonmodern life-forms, *elsewheres* not bound by the paradigm of the modern.

In fact, the critical consciousness we can detect in Chimalpahin's *Diario* does not derive its force or its lucidity from European knowledge or political practices but remains embedded in indigenous understandings of the world. The paradox is that if apostates must be feared because in learning Spanish ways they turn into able ladinos, the thoroughly catechized Indians of Las Casas would learn not only Christian doctrine but also the arts of logic and political thought, thus becoming astute ladinos who could straddle and cross the borders of colonial exclusionary institutions. In this example, the difference between the nonmodern and the modern would not reside in defining an inversion or absence of certain traits by means of which the modern constitutes itself vis-à-vis the Middle Ages, but rather in the lessons Las Casas and Chimalpahin would hold for modernity's claims to truth. For instance, the doctrine that truth must come from the outside to subaltern groups—a staple of and impasse in Marxism, more specifically in Leninism, which recurs among postcolonial theorists like Chakrabarty—finds a nonmodern counterpart in Las Casas's and Chimalpahin's assumption that if one cannot avoid engaging the hubris of self-proclaimed superior modern institutions, one may engage them from an *elsewhere* that keeps the exclusionary logic of modernity at bay.[33] In this respect, Las Casas and Chimalpahin anticipate the Zapatista undoing of vanguardist claims to authority by grounding their struggle in indigenous conceptualizations of the political that have contributed to a new revolutionary ethos, as manifested in the Maya Tojolabal expression: "ja ma' 'ay ya'tel kujtiki, mandar 'ay kujtik" [the authorities we elect are governed by us]. The Zapatistas adopted this age-old maxim in 1994 with the succinct expression "mandar obedeciendo" [to govern by obeying].

chacui – chini tanquehue xihuiqui notlatzin ximotlali ypan ycpalli –
chitao [Come, my uncle, sit on the chair]
chacui qieaha tanquehe xihualmohuica ximotlali [Come, sit]
chacui tachi – tanquehue – xihuiqui nococoltzin ximotlali [My grandfather, sit]
chontana dios tachi – ma Dios mitzmohuiquili nocoltzin [My grandfather, go with God]
chini yn chay – tihi – maxoconmiti notlatzin tepitzin [My uncle, drink
a little]
chontana chana Dios ma Dios mitzmohuiquili tlatouane [Oh, *Tlatouani*,
go with God]
caona miercoles – mostla miercoles [Tomorrow Wednesday]
tinquila jueves huiptla jueves [Day after tomorrow Thursday]
quipia onpohualli yhuan matlactlamomome yshuatl lipro de conquista
[Book of conquest has fifty-two folios][34]

This call in Nahuatl and Popoloca for the uncle and the grandfather to
sit and drink sets the scene for a verbal performance of a pictographic
and alphabetical account that traces the origins and the foundation of
Quauhtinchan in the present-day state of Puebla. The use of both languages suggests the multilingual nature of Quauhtinchan, even though the
dominant language was Nahuatl. These annotations inviting the elders to
listen record the bringing together of the community for a particular performance of the stories that had been alphabetically recorded in *Historia
Tolteca-Chichimeca* in the 1540s.[35] The handwriting is from the eighteenth
century and must have been written shortly before the manuscript was
taken from Quauhtinchan some time after 1718, when it is mentioned in
a Nahuatl inventory of the documents of Quauhtinchan that were in possession of the *principal* don Miguel Pérez Velázquez: "yhuan ocse amatli/
conquista mexino [*sic*]/quipia onpohuali yhuan/matlactli omome izhuatl"
[y otro papel/Conquista de Mexico/que tiene cincuenta/y dos fojas."[36]
It became part of Lorenzo Boturini's collection of Nahuatl documents
sometime between 1736 and 1743; Boturini's "Catalogo del museo historico indiano" describes the *Historia Tolteca-Chichimeca* in 1746. Today the
manuscript is held by the Bibliothéque Nationale de France (manuscript
Mexicaine #46–50, #51–53, and #54–58). In accordance with the name
this manuscript has received in modern times, I will speak of it as the *Historia*, but the reader should keep in mind the distance we must retain with

respect to the *elsewhere* from which it was produced rather than assuming a transcultural, indeed, a transhistorical understanding of history, as if this discipline and the forms of memory it privileges embodied universal categories applicable to all times and cultures. The eighteenth-century inventory merely speaks of it as *ocse amatli*, another paper.

Dana Leibsohn has recently argued, in a detailed study of the manuscript, that the *Historia* was first commissioned by a powerful man, don Alonso de Castañeda, a noble man from Quauhtinchan. For Leibsohn, the *Historia* was not only commissioned by don Alonso, but owned by him. Hers is a highly individualized account of the pictorial and verbal narratives of Quauhtinchan. At times, Leibsohn lays out the limits of her assumptions: "Nothing survives to reveal, in any direct or precise way, what don Alonso imagined or sought to do when he commissioned the *Historia*, and so I do not wish to argue that the *Historia* was wholly of his design, or that its execution fully satisfied his aims."[37] Though I find the argument of don Alonso's commission of the manuscript credible, I would put less emphasis on ownership and the personal gain to be derived from the stories it tells than on the guardianship of a document that ultimately was a collective product and represented the interests of the community. This doesn't mean that the Castañeda family did not hold a particularly powerful position in Quauhtinchan. We find mention of guardianships of colonial and ancient manuscripts throughout the colonial and republican period. Notable instances are Fernando Alvarado Tezozomoc, who, at the turn of the seventeenth century, assumed the responsibility of keeping the ancient books, "the account that the aforesaid ancients arranged are in my own personal safekeeping," and Emiliano Zapata, who at the start of the 1910 Mexican Revolution, guarded the documents pertaining to Anenecuilco. "Chief of his village and by necessity a student of its sources," writes John Womack, "Zapata knew in detail how and why it had struggled."[38] The *Historia* is not the product of a single scribe and painter, even though the final copy reflects a single scribe and painter, but a collective effort that called forth the participation of members of the community, in particular the elders who knew the stories to be told when reading ancient pictorial texts. After all, the *Historia* closes with mention of the *tlatoques*, of the leaders, of those who had the assignment to speak in Quauhtinchan: "auh oncan oquilnamicque yn tlatoque yn quauhtinchantlaca y don alonso castañeda yn don diego de Rojas yn don pedro de luna yn don felipe de mendoza don baltazar de tores don diego de galicia yn don baltazar de lopez yn quinquechillico yn mexicatl" [And then the *tlatoque quauhtinchantlaca*, don Alonso Castañeda, don Diego de Rojas, don Pedro de Luna, don Felipe de Mendoza, don Baltazar de Torres, don Diego de Galicia, and don Baltazar de López, remembered the borders the Mexicas established].[39]

The *Historia* consists of pictographs, whose elements, at least partially, could be traced back to an ancient (that is, before the Spanish invasion) pictorial text, and an alphabetical transcription of a verbal performance that supplements the paintings. The *Historia* provides an example of pictorial and alphabetical texts that were produced outside the supervision of missionaries and bureaucrats and was intended for the community itself. In this regard, the *Historia* exemplifies the kinds of hybrid texts—indeed, of wild literacy—Nahuas were producing by the 1540s. The project was not to reproduce the ancient writing systems, as in Codex Telleriano-Remensis or Codex Mendoza, but to produce a new kind of textuality that drew from the ancient pictographic tradition but also made full use of the technology Latin script made available for recording voice.

Although the information contained in the alphabetical text is more accurate than the pictographs, which at times contain "errors" (at least inconsistencies), hence suggesting the existence of an earlier pictographic text that served as the basis for the verbal text, the pictorial component can be read independently of the alphabetical text, even when read in tandem.[40] The verbal performance that led to the alphabetical records must be understood as a collective effort that involved several community members who were brought together for the occasion of telling the founding narratives of Quauhtinchan. We should resist the notion of an individual author who sat down to inscribe the traditions. The final product, however, corresponds to a posterior moment in which the pictorial text was produced and the recorded verbal performance copied from a rough draft of what may be defined as the stenographic moment in the recording of the speech event. Its alphabetical format resembles two-ink demarcations of lines and paragraphs in medieval manuscripts and the paintings "seem" more like illustrations than iconic script, if we were to ignore that the pictographic inscriptions provide a story of their own. I say the pictography in the *Historia* seems to be illustrations of the alphabetical texts and speaks of format rather than form because the verbal form remains Mesoamerican even though the text is compiled as a book and uses European paper.[41]

What does it mean to speak of collecting verbal performances by means of the alphabet and illustration-like pictographs in a book format as a "medieval" (that is, nonmodern) practice? In what follows I retain the term *medieval* as a heuristic notion for locating textual practices in that period called the Middle Ages. Again, the point is not to invert the value of medievalism but rather to identify European practices that promoted dialogical exchanges between indigenous intellectuals and missionaries that enabled Indians to produce artifacts that preserved their memory for posterity or enabled them to negotiate political spaces from within the colonial order. These indigenous texts suggest variations of manuscript culture most often identified with medieval practices of constituting authoritative texts. The format of the book and the alphabetical script define the margins for the inscription of pictographs and the stenographic-like recording of a singular verbal performance. One may argue that the alphabetical transcription destroys orality by embalming a particular narrative, but another way of seeing the written record is to conceive of it as, yes, the embalming of a singular voice that future generations can bring back to life in verbal performances. After all, the reading practices of sixteenth-century Mesoamericans (or of our contemporary Indians for that matter) hardly resemble the silent habits you are practicing in reading my text. Neither did those of the readers of sixteenth-century Spain, who often read letters aloud while viewing a painting of the author.

In defining this practice as part of medieval manuscript culture, I want to emphasize the difference with ethnographic projects that not only translated indigenous narratives to Spanish but also wrote them using Western historiographic conventions. The accounts Spanish and mestizo historians collected for writing their histories erase the Mesoamerican historical genre and silence the informants' voices, reducing their speech to factual information to be processed through European narrative forms. Even though histories by Diego Durán, Juan de Tovar, or Bartolomé de Las Casas (some of the most prominent historians of the sixteenth century) were not published until the nineteenth century, they were intended for publication. As such, they must be understood as forming part of the textual revolution of the printing press. Of course, that they were written texts for the printing press does not necessarily mean that these texts did not partake of nonmodern textual practices.[42] The *Exercicio quotidiano* could very well be seen as written for the printing press and for wide circulation, but, as I have argued above, the discipline and the habitus it sought to implant cannot be reduced to pastoral forms of governmentality. We may further press the issue and state that nonmodern spiritual practices, whether European or indigenous, may convey forms of interiority that governmental vigilance cannot access. By this, I do not suggest that governmentality is an exclusive concern of modernity, but that certain forms of the nonmodern (in the mode of Mesoamerican as well as European *else-wheres*) that scholars have defined as *medieval* have coexisted with modernity even when the modern has defined them as incompatible. This incompatibility of the modern and the nonmodern was an exclusive concern of modernity. Indigenous subjects manifest the ability to dwell in multiple worlds without incurring contradiction. With respect to alphabetical writing, we must underscore the existence of forms of wild or savage literacy, that is, of writing using the Latin script outside the supervision of missionaries and bureaucrats. Sahagún's note at the end of the *Exercicio quotidiano* suggests a brilliant instance of autonomous spaces in the production and proliferation of Latin script in sixteenth-century Mexico.

The use of alphabetical writing to record verbal performance of pictographic texts hardly fits the model of the writer who sits in silence to record his or her thoughts. In the case of the *Historia Tolteca-Chichimeca*, we find a collective effort to produce a pictorial and verbal account for the internal consumption of the community. There are other texts in which indigenous scribes and *tlacuiloque* collaborate with missionaries to produce verbal and pictorial texts that often provided indispensable keys for approaching ancient Mesoamerica. Because these efforts were not restricted by "neutral" scientific methods that regulate the modern ethnographic project, we gain perspective on the confrontation—the dialogical effort of jointly producing a manuscript. If the mediation is through the format of the book and alphabetical writing, the product is Mesoamerican inasmuch as it creates a site of memory for present and future indigenous generations. Indeed, it is an indigenous artifact. As to whether that makes Indians medieval, the suggestion smacks of medievalism as a form of confining indigenous societies and practices to the *retroceso* (retrogression) with which Weckmann identified the Mexican colonial world.

3. *Ignoratiam Invincibilem*

Sequitur ex ista conclusione quod qui sic emptas possidet terras alias cultas, nisi propter ignorantiam invincibilem excusetur, est in peccato et tenetur restituere etiam damnum datum. Et oportet ad hoc quod posit licete possidere per emptionem, quod emptio fiat et venditio per consensum liberum totius populi et interveniat iustum pretium sine extorsione et violentia et sine metu.[43]

[It follows from this conclusion that he who thus possesses lands otherwise cultivated—unless he is excused because of invincible ignorance—

is in sin and is bound to make restitution also of the damage done. In order to licitly possess through purchase, it is necessary that the purchase and sale be made through the free consent of the entire people and that the price be just without extortion and violence and without exerting terror.]

Vera Cruz's *De dominio infidelium et justo bello* consists of a series of lectures he delivered in 1554–1555 for the inauguration of the Universidad de México. The treatise, in addressing the sovereignty of infidels and the legality of war, inevitably must respond to the question of the lawfulness of the wars of conquest and the dominion the pope and the Spanish Crown may claim in the New World. These lectures address eleven doubts or questions pertaining to the pope's right to spiritual dominion over infidels, the emperor's authority to claim sovereignty over the entire world, the legality and justness of the wars of conquest and also discuss the payment of tribute, the appropriation of land, and forced conversions. Vera Cruz's lectures were directed to future confessors of Spaniards, who would thus lead the Spanish elite to examine their conscience and evaluate the justness of their property, the fairness of tribute exacted from Indians, and the legitimacy of Spanish territorial claims. If guilty, then, as a precondition for the absolution of their sins, the Spanish elites (which included the emperor and the Council of the Indies as well as the native elite who had benefited from the new power structures) were expected to restore property and sovereignty and repair damages inflicted.

This treatise is complex and intricate. At the risk of being reductive, Vera Cruz's position is essentially that even if the Spaniards conducted an unjust war, the colonial regime that followed was to be preserved yet perfected to promote the common good: "And since this is morally certain [the Spanish dominion is needed to prevent apostasy, *ita quod retrocederent facile*], no person of sound mind would maintain—even were it evident that in the beginning the emperor's title was founded in injustice—that the emperor is bound to renounce his claim and restore the kingdom to Montezuma and his successors."[44] If it is meaningless to question the emperor's dominion a quarter of a century after the invasion of Mesoamerica, the emperor nonetheless was obliged to make the colonial order a just regime. When reading Vera Cruz, I recalled my former philosophy professor in Mexico, Joseph Ferraro, who had written a doctoral dissertation that synthesized Thomas Aquinas and Marx. Needless to say, his was a liberation theology project. Vera Cruz's insistence upon justice partakes of a communalism, if not a communism, that underscored the need to distribute wealth when excessive accumulation obstructed the promotion of the common good.

The passage I cite at the beginning of this section corresponds to Vera Cruz's Doubt III, which asks "whether the *encomendero* who has just dominion over his charges through the royal grant, may occupy their lands at will, if they are untilled but destined for the grazing of his cattle or for planting or harvesting grain."[45] The conclusion states that the possession of cultivated lands had to have met certain standards of verification that included the consent of the "entire people and that the price be just without extortion and violence and without the use of terror."[46] The *encomienda* was a system of tribute in which the grantees were obliged to promote the spirituality of the Indians. They were not land grants but territories that paid tribute in kind and labor. By the 1550s when Vera Cruz was writing, several plagues had decimated the indigenous population of Central Mexico, making the system of tribute a burden to the indigenous survivors. Toward the middle of the sixteenth century, there was a move among Spaniards to seize lands that were either abandoned by communities that dissolved when facing the impossibility of meeting the tribute payments or were lost to opportunistic sales of land that by definition belonged to the community. This corrupt sale of communal land continues today to affect indigenous communities to whom communal holdings were restored after the revolution of 1910. Many suburbs in Mexico City and adjacent towns have been built on illicit purchases from corrupt leaders who never consulted the community and merely benefited individually.

Vera Cruz lays out the legal and ethical issues that confessors must examine in order to lead the confessed into examining their consciences regarding fair and just possession. One may argue that the text was bound to merely assuage the consciences of the Crown and the viceregal authorities with no real effects. Perhaps. It is not my objective here to document cases in which illicit possessions were taken to court. Rather, I dwell briefly on the concept of *ignoratiam invincibilem* that defines the epistemic limits of the confession and the examination of conscience.

Vera Cruz makes an exception for guilty parties when their "sins" were committed as a result of "invincible ignorance." Confessors in such cases were to lead the confessants to moral diligence and push the limits of ignorance. In fact, *De dominio* seeks to examine doubts to dispel ignorance. Its objective to train confessors was bound to enforce the moral diligence of the elite at the cost of incurring mortal sin if they did not examine their consciences in earnest and pursue the limits of involuntary ignorance rigorously. Presumably, in order for ignorance to remain invincible, one would not be able in the process of examining one's conscience to ascertain, just to cite one situation, whether the purchase of land were licit—knowledge of illicit acquisition impinges on retaining the property. Otherwise, how could one evaluate whether the original purchase was done under invincible ignorance, hence without sin, without becoming cynical: "I did not know, hence I am not under obligation now to restitute the land to the community." Vera Cruz does not pursue this situation, which leads me to suppose that the ignorance would be invincible not only with respect to the past but also with respect to what can be ascertained in the present. It is one thing to say that one could not have sinned because of ignorance, another to say that such ignorance would justify the continuation of holding the land that one now knows was gained illicitly.

Vera Cruz's concept of invincible ignorance may prove handy in examining human rights abuses and restoration claims, but it also offers a method for examining the limits of knowledge. Along with the questions of sin and ignorance, there are other questions pertaining to self-evident truths, truths often defined as natural law. Vera Cruz systematically questions the breach of natural law as a possible justification for wars of conquest. The justification of removing a tyrant is often (and unfortunately continues to be) cited as a legitimate cause for declaring war. In this specific instance, it is worth citing Vera Cruz's particular acumen when he discusses whether Mesoamerican rulers like Moteuczoma or Calzontzin were tyrants: "But whether they really ruled tyrannically and not for the good of the commonwealth, I do not know. Perhaps what seems tyrannical to another nation was appropriate and beneficial for this savage nation [*gentis barbarae*]."[47]

In passing, observe that I am using the 1968 English bilingual edition by the Jesuit Ernest Burrus. More recent editions in Spanish tend to emphasize the modernity of Vera Cruz at the expense of the scholastic method of rigorous examination of doubts and the elements of disputes. The introduction to the 1997 Spanish edition from the Consejo Superior de Investigaciones Científicas offers this justification for producing an abridged version: "Detrás de la estructura académica y más allá del método escolástico, puramente formal, subyace su propio informe o testimonio directo. . . . De aquí nuestro empeño por disociar lo que hay de propio testimonio y de montaje escolástico y académico" [Behind the academic structure and beyond the scholastic method, purely formal, resides his own report and direct testimony. . . . Hence our insistence on dissociating what there is of personal testimony from the scholastic and academic assemblage].[48] The exemplary methodological rigor goes by the wayside in favor of truths and personal testimony that the editors of this purported scientific edition can isolate from the slumber of scholasticism. The desire to extract the kernels of truth in Vera Cruz leads these editors to edit out what they felt was superfluous.

The lessons from Vera Cruz reside in systematically pushing the limits of ignorance, in the movement of ideas that end in phrases like "non constant mihi" [I do not know], "nos de jure disputamos" [we are discussing law], or "Ego non video; fortassis in medio sole decutio!" [I cannot see by what law or right; perhaps I am melting in the midst of the sun!]. These expressions mark an honest pursuit of truth in which one cannot readily ascertain Vera Cruz's personal position. Take as an example his concluding remarks as to whether Indians have a right not to convert to Christianity: "It follows, I say, that although it be claimed that the faith was sufficiently set forth to them and that although they have heard the Christians preaching about God and the faith, such unbelievers do not sin by not believing; since, in order to be guilty of sin, the faith would have to be explained to them sufficiently."[49] In the end, Vera Cruz would propose that the only argument for the adoption of the faith, which by definition cannot be taught, resides in the example of the teachers: "For the faith which is witnessed by so many persons of upright character and confirmed by so many miracles and is so propounded, such faith acquires clarity and stability."[50] This follows a discussion of the corrupt nature of the Spanish Conquest. As Vera Cruz would put it, he is only disputing law. Whether evangelization is thorough, respectful of dialogue, and truly understood must always remain a matter of invincible ignorance. Indeed, the meaning of the gospel, of the call, of its truth ultimately resides in the subject who makes sense of the missionaries' words.

In tracing the "sins" of medievalism, are we bound to the notion of *ignoratiam invincibilem*, which may be reformulated in terms of a collective or individual unconscious, not unlike the habitus that Bourdieu derives from Aquinas? Does our task involve intricate reasoning that leads to knowledge that our ancestors could not actualize? In matters of Spanish imperialism, the knowledge of abuse and illicit claims to dominion has been with us since the sixteenth century, but has disregard—if not the mockery of medieval mentalities, flawed according to the standards of modernity— kept generations from "knowing" the violence and destruction of imperialism, despite or even because of its claims to benevolent civilizing intentions? Then again, can we claim today to have resolved and overcome all the limits the notion of *ignoratiam invincibilem* entails? Is the task of postcolonial studies to pursue the limits of ignorance that haunt our most benevolent intentions? To what extent does this most nonmodern notion of *ignoratiam invincibilem* provide the elements of an ethos for dwelling in multiple worlds?

I have examined Vera Cruz's brilliant exposition of a confessional project for a more just society that places the common good as its highest end. This examination of conscience draws on and is grounded in Scholasticism and more particularly in Thomas Aquinas, but one may also trace a connection with the other two texts that I have briefly discussed. The nonmodern practice of manuscript writing enabled the community of Quauhtinchan to design pictorial and alphabetical memories that traced origins, certified foundations, and delimited the boundaries of communal lands. As for the *Exercicio quotidiano*, we may trace an individual practice of examining conscience that resulted in an autochthonous form of critical thought that enabled Indians to dialogue, confront, and question the colonial authorities.

These examples have enabled me to take the question of the colonial divide a step further. The periodization of the modern, when applied to the indigenous communities living under colonial rule, erases the lived experience and limits the political possibilities of these communities by confining them to instances of a global modernity. The concept of the *nonmodern* has enabled me to undo the descriptive value of the term *medieval*. The confinement of texts to expressions of the modern or the medieval, often depending on readings that privilege traits attributed to characteristic mentalities, gains depth and complexity when read in and on their own terms. It has not been a question of writing against periodization — as if our linguistic habitus could be transformed by a scratch of the pen — nor has it been a question of finding more powerful forms of periodizing, but rather one of sidestepping the comparative frame embedded in periodization. These gestures have allowed me to examine the entrails of periodization. Folio 46r of Telleriano-Remensis has taught me how to avoid generalizing the modern divide, but the glosses it was subjected to point to the comparativism that has haunted all writing about and from the New World (already a loaded comparative category) since the European invasion.

Chapter 8

(IN)COMPARABLE WORLDS

The bracketing of *(in)comparable* at once signals that colonial studies always entail a space of comparison and that an inflection of the voice, *in*comparable, would point to the limits of comparative studies. Beyond a single world, the title calls for reflection on geopolitical categories that remain outside the planetary imaginary of Euro-America. Continuing the discussion of the *elsewheres* (historical, cultural, chronological, spatial, semantic, semiotic, and so on) I have been identifying in reading folio 46r of Codex Telleriano-Remensis (see Figure 1), this chapter addresses the following question: What does it mean to compare, better, to dwell in a space determined by comparison, and yet to remain vigilant of the violence we inflict in comparing worlds? I argue that comparisons are only possible when done from within a common background or habitus. The move to incomparable worlds not only underscores the existence of an indigenous background, of an *elsewhere* from which the *tlacuilo* of folio 46r and other indigenous subjects question the universality of Western categories and interpretative models, but also opens a semantic space in which we can trace the incorporation of Western life-forms into Mesoamerica.

Throughout this book I have built on F. R. Ankersmit's definition of *background* as the absolute presuppositions against which and from which we recognize and understand culture and history: "They [culture and history] belong to the domain of the *absolute presuppositions*, to use Collingwood's terminology. This is also the reason why politics should not interfere with culture."[1] One wonders what Ankersmit would say about "culture wars" in the colonial context of the sixteenth century or, for that matter, in the twenty-first-century debates over multiculturalism. Are these wars and debates about *absolute presuppositions*, which, by extension, we may define as the colonization and/or imposition of a habitus? The phenomenon of "culture wars," however, is not far from Ankersmit's observation that "culture, of which historical writing is part, is rather the background *from which* or *against which* we can form our opinion concerning the usefulness of, for example, certain kinds of scientific research or certain political objectives."[2] Culture as background (and, I would add, as habitus) is hardly a permanent state, but rather a site of struggle. In addressing *elsewheres* and the lessons I have derived from folio 46r, I have argued the need to account for multiple backgrounds and their specific absolute presuppositions. I have furthermore underscored the possibility of multiple backgrounds coexisting in a given culture and individual. Colonialism and liberation contend for the imposition, destruction, and creation of backgrounds. This struggle, however, also calls for the neutralization of horizons of modernity in which there is no room for the nonmodern, as if one could not dwell in multiple worlds without incurring contradiction.

These propositions seek to problematize the existence of an all-encompassing background that would subsume all cultures and life-forms under its explanatory categories, concepts, genres of discourse and what Lyotard has defined as phrase regimes (reasoning, knowing, describing, recounting, questioning, showing, ordering, etc.): "Phrases obeying different regimens are untranslatable into one another. A translation presupposes therefore that a regimen and a genre in one language have their analogue in the other, or at least that the difference between two regimens and/or two genres in one language has its analogue in the other."[3] However useful Lyotard's observation is for conceptualizing multiple universes defined by phrase regimens and genres (*elsewheres* to each other), the limits of comparativism and translation that I am exploring in this chapter are not limited to the varieties—and possible analogues—of phrase regimens in different languages but to *elsewheres* that should not be configured in terms of regimens or genres that we can readily identify and extrapolate.

I have advocated an attitude built on the intuition that recognizes that objects have a life of their own—that objects reveal selves and exceed the apparently unavoidable, all-too-human will to appropriation. Dominion calls for a narrative of ethnosuicide that entails the internalization of phrase regimens and genres that would substitute indigenous life-forms and habitus. From the *tlacuilo* of folio 46 we learn that subjects inducted into the objectification of their culture for the purpose of its destruction actually understood this call from a background and habitus that observed the observers from afar. The ability to dwell in at least two worlds ensures the ability to forestall the narrative of ethnosuicide that seeks to enforce the death of a worldview. Clearly, this conception of multiple backgrounds differs from multicultural projects that assume the immediate accessibility of different cultures in curricula that offer courses and readings on "all" the cultures of the world. Here the recognition of multiple backgrounds has nothing to do with the recognition of a right to exist or be taught, but with the recognition of interpretive limits when facing indigenous life-forms, hence the call to conceptualize the existence of the background as a problem in comparative studies.

I have recognized in the *tlacuilo*'s painting of folio 46r her ability to participate in a plurality of worlds without incurring contradiction. I have read joy in her ability to move between worlds rather than the chagrin of being forced to respond to the missionaries' demands. I have also underscored that I make these observations from within a Euro-American background. By Euro-American, I mean the discursive traditions that build on Western forms regardless of their location in Europe, in the Americas, or, for that matter, in Asia and Africa, and definitely not exclusively the products of Europeans born in the Americas. The "American" component reflects the transformation European culture underwent after the incorporation of the Americas into the European worldview in the aftermath of Columbus's voyage.[4] Unavoidably, one dwells in a Euro-American world when one writes in European languages or when one uses Western categories and frames of reference while writing in non-European languages, but also by the mere fact that you are reading and following the argument in this text. This does not necessarily mean that you may not also dwell in other worlds, but there again we face questions of translation and comparison.

Throughout this chapter, which consists of a series of approximations that address aspects pertaining to the problem of the background in comparative studies, I return to the question of the circumscription by a Euro-American background. If the legacy of colonization (that is, the appropriation of the indigenous life-forms, the demand that the *tlacuilo* of Telleriano-Remensis objectify her world, and the unexpected return of the gaze at the observer) places me in a space of comparativism, in folio 46r I have learned of ways to create montages that suspend full-fledged comparison. The depictions of a Dominican, a Franciscan, an apostate, a viceroy, a wandering Nahua, and a dead conquistador appear as isolated elements in an apparent mere listing of events on a given year in an annalist mode. And yet these discrete events have enabled me to elicit stories that have linked these discrete events from within an ever-so-tenuous narrative without closure. In what follows, I engage key theoretical texts that provide spaces for testing and interrogating the seemingly inevitable appropriation of the world in Western philosophy. As such, this chapter consists of a series of theoretic-narrative loops that explore aspects pertaining to the problem of the background in comparative studies.

THE PROBLEM OF THE BACKGROUND
IN COMPARATIVE STUDIES

This heading draws its inspiration from an essay by Hans-Georg Gadamer, "The Problem of Historical Consciousness." As in the case of Gadamer, my concern is with identifying a "problem." In Gadamer's essay, the problem was the inevitability of thinking from a particular historical moment. As such, historical consciousness defines the limits of objectivity in historiography. In *Truth and Method*, Gadamer connects the question of historical consciousness with the comparative method in his critique of Wilhelm Dilthey: "Comparison essentially presupposes that the knowing subject has the freedom to have both members of the comparison at its disposal. It openly makes both things contemporary. Hence we must doubt whether the method of comparison really satisfies the idea of historical knowledge."[5] Gadamer goes on to indicate that Dilthey "did not regard the fact that finite, historical man is tied to a particular time and place as any fundamental impairment of the possibility of knowledge in the human sciences."[6] Gadamer criticizes Dilthey for taking the comparative method from a subordinate tool to a central position in defining historical knowledge. This promotion leads, according to Gadamer, to arbitrary reflection. I would add that given the terms of Gadamer's critique, one of the problems of the comparative method is that it flattens out cultural and historical differences. Comparisons by definition exclude the singular. The desire to objectify and appropriate by means of the classification and interpretation of indigenous artifacts (again, note that these practices privilege Western categories and conceptual apparatuses) systematically ignores the singular, without even posing the singular as a question or a desirable end. I am particularly concerned with full-fledged comparisons that underscore and spell out commonality between cultural artifacts. If comparisons are unavoidable, my preference is for juxtapositions that lead the reader to conceptualize and imagine life-forms that are not immediately recognizable in the discrete elements of a montage. I will make a case for this latter practice insofar as we can trace the limits in the transformation of the backgrounds that enable montage in the first place.

Comparison operates under a logic that privileges the One, the commonality of the diverse, at the expense of the Multiple.[7] One cannot compare objects that do not share a common background without inflicting epistemic violence. Indeed, an all-encompassing background (as it were, the sum of phrase regimens) subsumes, if not subordinates, objects under comparison. The question of the background in comparative studies in religious, literary, historical, or ethnic studies calls for the interrogation of the third terms that enable comparisons. Third terms in comparative work, in turn, carry an explicit teleology. Teleology is particularly problematic when it grounds and is grounded in a single history and world even when considering that history and the world partake of multiple logics or inexhaustible possibilities in the mode of a *finite infinite*, to paraphrase Nancy.[8] Comparisons manifest an impulse to control, to domesticate, indeed, to appropriate (to make one's own and proper) the anomalous, whatever threatens the integrity of the whole. And yet in their possibility, comparisons convey the impossible dream of closure that Nancy identifies with Derrida's *différance*, where the *a* in its French misspelling of *différence* signals two possible voicings: to differ (differentiate) and to defer (postpone). Writing is *différance* inasmuch as it involves the deferral of sense and differentiation. We must insist, however, that the discovery of *différance* pertains to *our* history: "But who, 'we'? This *we* which has, or have, discerned writing is both the modest authorial 'we' and the royal 'we' of the philosopher. But it is also *ours*: the *we* of a community in its history. 'We' voices the historiality of the discerning of writing."[9] There is so much at stake in the limits of this "we" that conveys a community of thinking that remains bound to the discovery of the endless deferral of sense and differentiation in writing. I find myself circumscribed by this "we" and yet know that the discovery of this community remains bound to what Nancy calls its historiality. At the limits of empire, which includes the "we" comprising "the community of thinking" that now practices writing as *différance*, the will to dominion faces the inability to arrive at univocal meaning. Imperial writers face a constant semantic slippage of categories in the objectification of native culture. The call for ethnosuicide irremediably turns into ethnogenesis. We must abstain from reducing or, for that matter, comparing this semantic slippage to the terms of *our* historiality.

If in folio 46r we can observe and assume an indigenous background that incorporates and develops pictorial vocabularies to depict institutions, objects, and subjects pertaining to the colonial world, the fact remains that the *tlacuilo* responded to an impulse to objectify Nahua culture for a comparative project conceived and articulated from the perspective of Western languages and epistemological regimes. By classifying similarities, establishing differences, and drawing genealogies, missionaries and lay officials at once appropriated non-European cultures and validated their own. Along with the collection of information that subsumed all singularities in (always already translatable) categories crafted in the Greco-Abrahamic traditions, we must interrogate the style of thought in comparative studies.[10] Moreover, I would argue that in our use of Western languages there is no outside to the history and culture of comparative studies of the last five hundred–plus years of European exploration and conquests of the globe. This limitation, however, does not imply the existence of a single world and history.

The problem of historical consciousness and comparative studies exposes a desire to be objective, to erase the subject. If Gadamer's phrasing of the problem of historical consciousness in terms of the impossibility of objectivity was particularly critical for hermeneutics in the first half of the twentieth century, it has become by now a commonplace in historical inquiry. Rare are the comparatists who would pretend today to practice the "discipline" from an objective perspective. More likely, comparatists feel obliged to make manifest her or his identity and the position from which she or he writes. Thus, the subjectivity of the historian and the comparatist is no longer a problem but now a desired epistemological and ethical point of view. This epistemic privilege entails a recentering of the subject in terms of gender, sexuality, ethnicity, race, and class. We are annoyed by, and hence expose, transparent intellectuals who fail to acknowledge their mediation in historical or literary representations. The recentering of the subjects often assumes a positioning with respect to other centerings that are perceived as oppressive—Eurocentrism, logocentrism, phallocentrism, phonocentrism, and so on. One then tends to define alternative locations to these places of power. In other words, we believe that by naming Eurocentrism, phallocentrism, and logocentrism, one escapes their structures of power. The "we" of my discourse is located within a system haunted by centrisms. My take is that we (as individuals and collectivities) think from within a system, and not that a system inhabits us and that the solution would simply be to expel the system from within us or to just step out.

IN COMPLICITY WITH KANT, THE H(A)UNTING OF "MAN IN THE RAW"

In exposing centrisms, we fail to acknowledge that their naming corresponds to a representation by a subject not unlike the Kantian transcendental subject. In Section II of the second edition of the *Critique of Pure Reason*, Kant differentiates the "I think" that underlies all thought, and is inaccessible as such, from the consideration of one's thoughts as "mine" or the experience of "me" in empirical psychology. The naming of the centrisms suggests two possibilities: one would locate the centrisms as outside one's thought (neither I nor my thoughts are Eurocentric); the other would trace the centrisms in one's innermost thoughts (including the "I think" that identifies and names). The first option retains intact the Kantian structure of the "I think" by placing the object, that is, Eurocentrism, outside of consciousness, and by identifying it with a list of undesirable traits that one *ought* to avoid. In this gesture, cognition and obligations entail each other. I must readily recognize the evils of Eurocentrism and ethically respond accordingly. Thus, we stop short of examining the implied universality of the forms that make possible the mapping, cognition, and understanding of Eurocentrism as an object of study and accepting a moral obligation to denounce it. The centrisms would just be one more series of objects in the world to be apprehended. This approach would conceive of itself as non-Kantian, given that Kant tends to be identified as one of the pillars of Eurocentrism. But by an ironic turn, one continues, in the self-certainty of our identification of centrisms, to think "like" Kant and to reproduce the epistemological structure of the *Critique of Pure Reason* as well as the binding of moral obligation on cognition in the *Critique of Practical Reason*. This is not the place to fully expose the logic of the categorical imperative and the "enjambment" of the I/you in the prescription "Act in such a way" that marks the passage from "I am able" to "you ought," thereby creating a universal "we." [11] The second option would reinscribe the critique by questioning the categories and schemas that Kant construed as universal and apodictic. It would outline a critical project in which, as Gayatri Chakravorty Spivak has suggested, we are in complicity with Kant and the centrisms we feel obligated to denounce. In speaking of the need to read Kant, Hegel, and Marx, Spivak writes: "Ostentatiously to turn one's back on, say, this trio, when so much of one's critique is clearly if sometimes unwittingly copied from them, is to disavow agency, declare kingdom come by a denial of history." [12]

Much has been written about Kant's racialized geography. Most of the work has focused on Kant's minor works, *Observations on the Feeling of the Beautiful and the Sublime* and *Anthropology from a Pragmatic Point of View*. Henry Louis Gates, for example, on the basis of the *Observations* asserts that "Kant, moreover, is one of the earliest major European philosophers to conflate color with intelligence, a determining relation he posits with dictatorial surety," and goes on to cite Kant: "This fellow was quite black from head to foot, a clear proof that what he said was stupid." [13] In his conclusions to an essay on Kant's *Anthropology*, Emmanuel Chukwudi Eze writes: "It is clear that what Kant settled upon as the 'essence' of humanity, that which one ought to become in order to deserve human dignity, sounds very much like Kant himself: 'white,' European, and male. . . . The so-called primitives surely ought to be wary of such Kantian 'universalist-humanoid abstraction' [Eze quotes Wole Soyinka], which colonizes humanity by grounding the particularity of the European self as center even as it denies the humanity of others."[14] A Kantian or neo-Kantian philosopher, in the style of Kojin Karatani in *Transcritique*, could dismiss these assessments by arguing that they are incidental statements that do not alter the import of Kant's more rigorous contributions to philosophy in the three critiques, and that ultimately one can trace a relativism in Kant that would enable the supersession of these statements as instances of a common sense that *ought* to be left behind (i.e., face the obligation to accept a new universal taste): "This indeterminate norm of a common sense is, as a matter of fact, presupposed by us; as is shown by our presuming to lay down judgments of taste. But does such a common sense in fact exist as a constitutive principle of the possibility of experience, or is it formed for us as a regulative principle by a still higher principle of reason, that for higher ends first seeks to beget in us a common sense?"[15] In posing this question, Kant opens the road for understanding common sense as historical, in terms of *oughts* that are redefined by (and redefine) universality.

For her part, Spivak, however, focuses on a passage from the *Critique of Judgment* where Kant addresses the humanization of the human through culture: "It is a fact that what we call sublime by us, having been prepared through culture, comes across as merely repellent to a person who is uncultured and lacking in the development of moral ideas."[16] Spivak points out that the correct translation for *dem rohen Menschen*, which Werner S. Pluhar here translates as "uncultured," would be "man in the raw." As such, the emphasis apparently resides in the uncultured, rather than on a racial determination. But Spivak reminds us that for Kant, the uncultured or the uneducated corresponded to children and the poor, whereas women stood for the "naturally uneducable."[17] On the other hand, "man in the raw" belongs to the category of the savage and the primitive. Spivak calls our attention to a later passage in the *Critique of Judgment* where Kant evaluates the purpose of humans in the scheme of nature: "We cannot arrive at a categorical purpose in this way [how cattle need grass, and how man needs cattle] because, after all, we cannot see why people should have to exist (a question it might not be so easy to answer if we have in mind, say, the New Hollanders or the Fuegians)."[18] The Fuegians and the New Hollanders (that is, savages or primitives in general) turn into a limit case of the human and thus provide us with a name for "man in the raw."

Within the purposive scheme of nature, within the teleology and the criteria it sets for comparing humans, the savage (New Hollander or Fuegian) would amount to a degree zero of culture, that is, of "an aptitude for purposes generally."[19] We can only envision the Fuegians (savages in general) as falling short of being representative of the schema in which "man is indeed the only being on earth that has understanding and hence the ability to set himself purposes of his own choice, and in this respect he holds the title of lord of nature; and if we regard nature as a teleological system, then it is man's vocation to be the ultimate purpose of nature, but always subject to a condition: he must have the understanding and the will to give both nature and himself reference to a purpose that can be independent of nature, self-sufficient, and a final purpose."[20] As such, man's appropriation of the world, which is in the scheme of nature, calls forth the definition of purposes that lead to the creation of disciplines for tempering desire and the formation of civil societies that counter the impairing of happiness and restrain the oppression of the lower classes by those with the leisure to develop the arts and sciences: "These others keep the majority in a state of oppression, hard labor, and little enjoyment, even though some of the culture of the higher classes does gradually spread to the lower classes."[21] This trickling-down economy of moral and aesthetic taste would, in principle, also entail the appreciation by the elite of formerly dismissed "savage" arts. Consider the fashion of donning tattoos among suburban (and urban) white middle classes today. Within this system of thought, there would be the possibility of an *ought* that recognizes the beauty of the diverse in a multicultural world.

The question, then, would be whether "man in the raw," or at least some instances of him, could be cultured, and thereby learn to reflect according to the categories and concepts of the three critiques. In his concern with educable races, Kant replays the sixteenth-century debates at Valladolid in which Bartolomé de Las Casas confronted Juan Ginés de Sepúlveda's argument that Native Americans would have to be first subjected politically, if not militarily, and then educated and converted to Christianity. Las Casas, for his part, would uncouple cultural development from the ideals of Christianity, hence his deployment of the noble savage as a rhetorical utopian figure, not an empirical fact.[22] But I would argue that in the context of the Spanish sixteenth-century colonization of the Americas, we do not find a concept of "man in the raw" as not human, not even in Sepúlveda, who used the term *homunculi* (little men, underdeveloped). There may be a trace of "man in the raw" in Joseph de Acosta's most infelicitous statement about nomadic peoples, "que es necesario enseñallos primero a ser hombres, y después a ser cristianos" [who must first be taught how to be men, and then to be Christians].[23] But even here there is no suggestion whatsoever of the denial of humanity that Spivak, Eze, and Gates identify in Kant's racialized geography. And here I have entered a comparative space in which Kant, Northern Europe (which also saturates the South and its intellectuals after the ideals of the Enlightenment), and the eighteenth century would turn out to be the villains of history. The comparison, which would privilege the Spanish ideologues of conquest and empire, would build on a privileged notion that all humans are educable—that is, the potential subjects of empire (and this was Sepúlveda's point, not the denial of humanity). Kant's wondering whether the answer to the purpose of humans would be so readily answered when taking the Fuegians (that is, savages and primitives) in mind leaves open the terrain for extermination with apparently no justification needed, "they have no purpose for existing." As Spivak insists, Kant does not say this explicitly, but merely implies it; however, the actions of nineteenth- and twentieth-century extermination campaigns in the American West (also in the Mexican North, the Argentine Pampas, and Amazonia, to mention just a few examples from the Americas) provide the missing script. Some "men in the raw" were subjected to civilizing processes, others to extermination. It all depended on their willingness to recognize the European moral ideas and be cultured thereby. Today we read that the leaders of ALBA (Alianza Bolivariana para los Pueblos de Nuestra América), in particular Evo Morales and Álvaro García Linera, attribute the limits of intercultural dialogue to a subordination of indigenous groups to the state as the ultimate arbiter of the nation's interests.[24] Are those who now refuse to subordinate themselves to the Bolivian state a new form of indigenous peoples constituting *men in the raw* to be destroyed when they do not "understand" the reasons of the state? In sixteenth-century Spanish anthropology, the dominant trope is not the uncultured "man in the raw" but the recognition (as in cognition, not acceptance) that the main impediment to the conversion of Native Americans resided in their being thoroughly cultured, hence the trope of extirpation of their beliefs.

Paradoxically, Kant can only claim universality to the extent that his thought is only meaningful for a European-like humanity. We can give Kant the benefit of the doubt and lay out a critical program from within Kant himself. In fact, the singular, the particular, and the historical delimit the three critiques internally. Exposing this would take more space than I have here, so let me just indicate that the fear of "man in the raw" in facing the sublime, which separates savages from European humanity, delimits the universal import in the *Critique of Judgment*. But also note that in this critique, the history of taste (manifest in the trickling down of aesthetic sensibility to "lower" social classes but also in the recognition of new aesthetic objects formerly dismissed) undermines the universal claims that Kant seeks to establish with respect to the beautiful and its corresponding feeling of pleasure: "Since the inquiry into our power of taste, which is the aesthetic power of judgment, has a transcendental aim, rather than the aim to [help] form and cultivate taste (since this will continue to proceed as it has in the past, even if no such investigations are made), I would like to think that it will be judged leniently as regards its deficiency for the latter purpose."[25] Kant would further entertain the contingency and historicity of pleasure in the experience of art and nature by conceiving the underlying common sense. The *ought* of the universal in taste cannot remain stable. Clearly, Kant would not have empathized with the pleasure (the beauty) I derive from Codex Telleriano-Remensis, just to mention the main example from Mesoamerican culture that I have proposed as a limit text for comparative projects. Again, little do we gain toward settling our score with Kant by denouncing his "racism" if we continue to think "like" Kant.

We can trace a limit in the three critiques by exposing how they build the universality of their claims and categories on particular forms of humanity (male, white, bourgeois). But we *ought* to observe as well a naturalization of the will to appropriate the world as lord of nature in Kant's definition of man's purposive nature. He points to reversing the oppression of the lower classes but hardly points a way out of the comparativism that evaluates purposes and assumes mastery of the world as an end of the teleology of nature. But note that my writing here, and your reading there, participates in the humanity Kant understood as the audience of his critiques. And I am not thinking of the specialized reader of philosophy for whom Kant writes, but of the specific background that makes possible becoming a reader of Kant.

In the event that we forget that for Kant the transcendental subject eludes representation by definition, we inevitably reproduce forms that until now have escaped our mapping of the undesirable centrisms— namely, the manifest structures of consciousness and the transcendental subject that grounds the processes by means of which we appropriate the world. Let us pause with a reminder by Ankersmit:

> We have become so Kantian that we find it hard, if not impossible, to think of a discipline that does not aim at appropriation. Obviously, if

we can discern an example of an actually existing disciplinary practice (hence, no mere rhetorical model) that contradicts or does not fit within the all-encompassing Kantian tradition, such an example may function as an entryway into a new intellectual world that is so difficult to imagine because of our being conditioned by the Kantian paradigm of knowledge and meaning.[26]

However desirable "an entryway to a new intellectual world" may be, we should not underestimate the difficulties Ankersmit signals here and consider the ways the Kantian paradigm may very well be an integral part of our background and habitus. In Kant's "Critique of Pure Reason," Theodor W. Adorno has succinctly underscored the appropriative nature of Kantian philosophy: "Synthesis in Kant means merely that a manifold, an assemblage of diverse things, is brought together in a unity. It is actually the decisive factor by means of which Kant may be said to have signed up to the tradition of a *philosophy concerned to dominate nature*."[27] The challenge for a philosophy of the future resides in developing forms of thought that undo the pervasive appropriative impulse in Kantian thought, which is not unlike the comparative method that builds unity out of the diverse.

Consistent with Kant, the "I think" of the transcendental subject is universal to the extent that it refers to European man or a Europeanized man; as such, it is a particular form of consciousness that claims truths from within a specific horizon of universality. This again should warn us about the commonplace that attributes appropriation to what we refer to as subalterns (for lack of a better term). If appropriation rules the relationship of the subaltern to dominant thought, what differentiates the transcendental subject underlying the dominant from the subjectivity of the subaltern? Kant or a Kantian philosopher would assume that the transcendental subject is universal and would leave it at that, shrugging off our concerns with oppressive centrisms as if to appropriate the world was in the nature of things. Out of charity for both Kant and subalterns, a twenty-first-century neo-Kantian (say, as Spivak would put it, a philosopher ready to call this "reading of Kant 'mistaken'")[28] would assure us that all of humanity participates in reason as defined by Kant, and that the latter's assertions regarding the differences between European man and "man in the raw" should be read as rhetorical (perhaps excessive) expressions. Now, the project of recentering, as I understand it, would aspire to break away from the determinations of those appropriative forms of the transcendental subject that have been identified under Eurocentrism and the rest of the centrisms. The problem of the background under this formulation would no longer reside in the impossibility of objectivity, as posed by Gadamer, but rather in the transcendental subject that underlies our appropriation and organization of the world, even if under a mode of resistance to the dominant. We may not claim objectivity, but we continue to objectify the world and the self. In the best scenario, philosophers such as Martin Heidegger, Jacques Derrida, and Jean-Luc Nancy have systematically interrogated the limits of Kant's critical project. But note that in naming these philosophers and their project to end the history of mastery and appropriation of the world, I am invoking a teleological process in terms of a single life world. It is as if philosophy had as its destiny the articulation of an exit from the all-encompassing history of Being. From this perspective, there is no possibility of recognizing *elsewheres* from which worlds are made and unmade.

LANGUAGE GAMES, FAMILY RESEMBLANCE, *Mondialisation*

If comparison seems to be engrained in the thought of the Americas, my juxtaposition of Euro-American and indigenous abilities to dwell in a plurality of worlds would seek to identify the existence of different backgrounds and corresponding life forms. Clearly, the point is not to compare these two distinct backgrounds, but rather to explore ways of understanding similarity and difference that do not depend on objectification and reduction. This would imply assessing the extent to which Euro-American philosophies travel beyond their backgrounds and frameworks.

Let's consider, for instance, whether Wittgenstein's concept of "family resemblance" is transcultural.[29] As I look out the window of my office, I perceive shades of red, green, and lilac that in a most elemental language game would presuppose color names as a comparative frame. I can, of course, go on to differentiate flower shapes from leaf shapes, to observe the shades of color, to identify species of plants, to establish that these plants are camellias and lilacs, et cetera. Is the notion of family resemblance universal? What does it mean to ask this question? Are we interrogating the simile of family resemblance or are we questioning the universality of such distinctions as shades of red, green, and lilac? Are the prelinguistic and preconceptual impressions of color on our nervous systems universal? Does it make sense to dream of such a radical empiricism? But even if the perception of color differences is transcultural, does that mean that the sensorial spectrum would be organized with the same categories? Or, perhaps more poignantly, would speech about plants in cultures with different backgrounds be recognized as sharing commonalities defined by family resemblance?

From there, the path to ethnobotany would have a history that in the context of the Americas would begin with Columbus's most basic attempts to describe unknown plants. Arguably, the history of ethnobotany would begin with Columbus's linguistic gaps ("para hazer relacion a los reyes dlas cosas que vian no bastaran mill lenguas a referillo, ni su mano para lo escrivir, que le parecia qu'estava encantado" [in order to report to the sovereigns the things they were seeing, a thousand tongues would not suffice to tell it or his hand to write it; for it seemed that it was enchanted][30]) and would conclude with the transformation of indigenous knowledge into data to be patented by transnational pharmaceutical firms (for example, the consortium of Quest International and the University of Minnesota obtained a patent in the United States [#5919695] for the use of a bacteria they isolated from *pozol*, the Maya beverage based on maize, with nutritional and medicinal properties known for millennia). We could then elaborate a comparison in terms of the appropriation of indigenous knowledge (Columbus's "mill lenguas" stands for informants), and perhaps draw differences from within the disputed ethics of empire.

The standpoint for such an ethics could, perhaps, include the benefits indigenous peoples should derive from the expropriation and patenting of their knowledge. The frame for comparison would entail a teleology in which the West (in consultation with native peoples) would constitute the criteria for a fair and just use of indigenous knowledge. What indigenous peoples think about the intrusion in their territories, the extraction of their knowledge, and the strategies they develop to make sense of this Euro-American process of appropriation tends to be systematically excluded from the discussion. In the best scenarios, such as the plurinational Bolivian state and the call for interculturality, the state appoints itself as absolute arbiter. As I have suggested above, indigenous groups that must be made to "understand" the reasons of the state may be subjected to regulatory violence in the name of the nation's interests.[31] We may benefit here from the following questions (apropos of Yuruba healers) raised by Hallen and Sodipo in *Knowledge, Belief, and Witchcraft*:

> And, finally is it representative to refer to these wise men as our "colleagues"? We might choose to regard them as such, but would they care to look upon us as *their* colleagues? They play a vital, active, and therefore different role in their societies, while the university and its academic "doctors" represent a foreign, closed and ludicrously luxurious educational system whose avowed ideology, to some degree, is to be isolated

from the society at large and to make few direct practical contributions to it.[32]

Beyond the appropriative impulses of transnational or State corporations, Hallen and Sodipo signal the limitations all Western-trained researchers will face in working with healing specialists in the field. Our limitations are partly due to our inability to (re)cognize the background and the framework *from which* and *against which* Indians make sense of Euro-American appropriations. The assumption that an all-encompassing single background ultimately makes sense of indigenous perspectives systematically negates Indian conceptualizations even under the Bolivian claims of *interculturalidad*. For all its claims of *interculturalidad*, the plurinational state makes sense in terms of the single world and history that enables the state to claim the privilege to make sense, that is, interrupt the discussion in the name of the nation. Let us return to the philosophical issues underlying the question of comparativism.

In his essays in *Culture and Value*, Wittgenstein is acutely aware of different life worlds, but he did not contribute much to our understanding of what it means to speak of heterogeneous backgrounds and life worlds beyond recognizing their existence. Wittgenstein would perhaps explore what he called the language games of hypothetical primitive cultures, but I am afraid that these worlds would amount to products of an imagination bound by a background defined by the notions of family resemblance and language games. To his credit, Wittgenstein would agree that these terms, "family resemblance" and "language games," could have different uses and meanings from those current in European languages that share a philosophical tradition.

Can we think without comparing, if metaphor is at the root of all thought, including scientific thought? I prefer to think in terms of juxtaposition and montage rather than of fully articulated comparisons. But in likening the avoidance of comparison to montage, one is in fact elaborating a metaphor and opening a space for comparison. This space would be defined by the differences between outright comparisons (which would be defined by third terms, family resemblance, and teleology) and montage (which would juxtapose life-forms without necessarily objectifying them according to a third term). In creating montages, the project would avoid the reduction of life-forms to elementary aspects that convey a particular language game; instead, it would foreground the fluidity of life-forms with infinite possible variations. The project would thus identify the machinery of terms that Euro-American thought has built to explain cultural difference and similarities. We could, then, speak of third terms that enable comparative projects: that is, the sacred, religion, ritual, literature, and (without listing more specific terms) all those concepts and classificatory practices (that is, Linnaeus's Latinate for naming the whole of nature) that would fall under the notion of *globalatinization*, or *mondialatinisation* in French, as put forth by Derrida in his essay "Faith and Knowledge": "*Globalatinization* (essentially Christian, to be sure), this word names a unique event to which a meta-language seems incapable of acceding, although such a language remains, all the same, of the greatest necessity here. For at the same time that we no longer perceive its limits, we know that such a globalization is finite and only projected. What is involved here is a latinization and, rather than globality, a globalization that is running out of breath [*essouffée*], however irresistible and imperial it still may be."[33]

Is globalatinization an instance of what Ankersmit defines as the *absolute presuppositions* that define the *against which* and the *from which* one draws comparisons in culture and history? If so, the fear of naming or defining universal culture in terms of the background that Derrida calls globalatinization would certainly disturb the apparent complacency of the background. More so when the *from which* and the *against which* of practices that contribute to the "running out of breath" of globalatinization presuppose spaces of contention. But, then, how could the background of contention also be understood as an *absolute presupposition*? Ankersmit's project offers little for thinking outside the West. But Derrida's concept of globalatinization fails to go outside the concept of a single background, outside the *absolute presuppositions* that now have a name. But what is the background *from which* and *against which* Derrida defines globalatinization? His indication that "a meta-language seems incapable of acceding, although such a language remains, all the same, of the greatest necessity here," betrays circularity: a meta-language would imply an exteriority and objectivation that would inevitably infuse new blood into globalatinization rather than contribute to "its running out of breath." Observe the possible transition from comparative projects that would assume the concepts of the sacred, religion, ritual, rite, and so on as givens to a critical reflection in which one notes their "Latin" history, hence their lack of transparency. Globalatinization enables us to be more precise when speaking about Eurocentrism (which often turns into shorthand for the bad thinking of Euro-Americans or, for that matter, of non-Europeans) insofar as the naming of objects in the world, say the planet, has been done using "Latin." But the issue is not just a matter of exposing Latin concepts, even if from within the Indo-European families we may profitably circumscribe the meaning of terms derived from Latin, with the aid of Émile Benveniste's *Le vocabulaire des institutions indo-européennes*. However useful these clarifications may be, they are limited in that their etymologies reduce our observations to the discourses that we tend to view as carrying universal implications. These etymologies might help us understand the globalatinization we bring into play when approaching non-Western languages and cultures, but in thus realizing their particularity, we may begin exploring other linguistic families and the institutions they obtain.

Jean-Luc Nancy has further developed the French concept of *mondialisation* (world-forming), which he differentiates from *globalization* (global expansion of the market, that is, the suppression of all world-forming in "unprecedented geopolitical, economic, and ecological catastrophe"), with an etymological reminder that in Christian creationism, the world is something that grows out of nothing: "I say 'growing' for it is the sense of *cresco*—to be born, to grow—from which comes *creo*: to make something merge and cultivate a growth."[34] For Nancy, a "detheologized" creationism enables him to make the following assertion about materialism: "The *ex nihilo* is the genuine formulation of a radical materialism, that is to say, precisely, without roots."[35] The anticipation, perhaps, as a teleological destiny in Western thought, calls forth the end of the age of representation: "Now, in order to distance such thinking of the world from representation, there is no better way than this one: to grasp the 'world' once more according to one of its constant motifs in the Western tradition—to the extent that it is also the tradition of monotheism—namely, the motif of creation."[36] By appealing to creationism, Nancy points to a way out of subject/object binaries that underlie the impulse to objectification and the reification of the subject of knowledge. Nancy proposes a rigorous thought for learning to grasp the world outside of representation. This poses a problem in that we come to this proposal from the inside of representation and objectification. The motif of creation must first be grasped outside its theological context, but Nancy reminds us that at the end of monotheism there is a world without God, not in an atheistic but rather in an *absent-theistic* mode.

In the curing of globalization, *mondialisation* would call forth the development of an *ethos* or *habitus* (Nancy traces the origin of these words to analogous meanings in "self-standing" and *habere*, "to have"), of an inhabiting of the world that ultimately amounts to "a struggle of the West against itself, of capital against itself. It is a struggle between two infinites, or between extortion and exposition. It is the struggle of thought, very precisely concrete and demanding, in which we are engaged by the disappearance of our representations of the abolishing and overcoming of capital."[37] The representations of capital we have inherited turn out to be part of the problem to overcome—which is far from meaning that Marx's thought is obsolete (Nancy is too careful a thinker to dismiss Marx out of hand)—by conceiving the meaning of the reversal of the relation of production (as I have pointed out above, Kant already anticipated a reversal). Beyond Marx's call for the created value to the creator (as in overcoming alienation), the task now calls for "a labor whose principle is not determined by a goal of mastery (domination, usefulness, appropriation), but exceeds all submission to an end—that is, also exposes itself to remaining without end."[38] Now, Nancy has felt pressed to speak in terms of a single world, one dominated by global capitalism, even when his diagnosis still enables us to perceive its end in a project without end. Although the pull to assert the existence of a single world, hence of a single history (open and yet remaining bound to Christian creationism as the origin of its destiny), is understandable because of the rigor that demands the refusal to find a model or solutions in extant worlds that we may find *elsewhere*:

> To that degree, then, it cannot suffice to search *elsewhere* for other forms or values that one may attempt to graft onto this henceforth global body. There is no *elsewhere* left, or indeed, and in any case, there can no longer be an *elsewhere* in the old Western sense of the term (like the *elsewhere* of an Orient refracted through the prism of orientalism or the *elsewhere* of worlds represented as living in the "primary" immanence of myths and rites).[39]

I cannot rest content with Nancy's insistence on the exhaustion of all *elsewheres*. I would underscore that it remains a fact that globalization, capital, the West and its institutions, and the colonial order are observed, depicted, and made sense of from multiple habitus and ethos that entail forms of inhabiting and creating worlds, that Western modes of dwelling and thinking—however "evolved" and open—cannot encompass or exhaust.

WITCHERY

Let's now address the (im)possibility of reading indigenous pictorial and alphabetical texts. The issue no longer resides in the undoing of the *latinization* of indigenous cultures, namely, in finding ways of contributing to the "running out of breath [*essoufflée*]" of globalization, to borrow Derrida's terms, "however irresistible and imperial it may be."[40] And here we may benefit from Lesley Marmon Silko's 1977 novel *Ceremony*.[41] Silko's narrative tells the story of a Pueblo Indian who seeks healing after his return from World War II. The novel exposes the systematic destruction of ceremonies and rituals since the Spanish invasion in the 1530s. The events following World War II, however, have augmented the plight of and threats to the Pueblo Indians (for example, the community is now contaminated by uranium, alcoholism and violence destroy its tissue, and posttraumatic stress burdens the lives of young and not-so-young men). Her end, however, is not to produce a historical novel but to memorialize the past through poetic ellipsis and the reinvention of narrative as a form of ceremony itself. It is a ceremony haunted by the dangers of reductive historical thinking.

Silko speaks of objectivity as witchery, as an Indian invention of Europe, but warns us that the trickery of witchery resides in witches promoting the belief that all evil resides in white people. As Betonie, the old healer, puts it: "But white people are only tools that the witchery manipulates; and I tell you, we can deal with white people, with their machines and their beliefs. We can because we invented white people; it was Indian witchery that made white people in the first place."[42] Betonie goes on to tell a story of a time when witches met for a contest in dark things; it was a time in which the world was already complete, including witchery. Witches try to outdo each other in forms of evil: one speaks of fooling around in caves wearing the skin of foxes, badgers, bobcats, and wolves; another lifted the lids of big cooking pots to discover dead babies simmering; still another exposed "whorls of skin cut from fingertips/sliced from penis end and clitoris tip," but the last one, the most terrifying of the witches, just told a story. The telling of the story brings about the events it tells of white skin people "like the belly of a fish covered with hair," grow away from the earth, the sun, plants and animals:

> They see no life
> When they look
> they see only objects.
> The world is a dead thing for them
> the trees and rivers are not alive
> the mountains and stones are not alive.
> The deer and bear are objects
> They see no life.[43]

The story goes on to tell the history of colonization, extermination, disease, thievery, and destruction of Indian life, indeed, of life itself. The telling itself sets in motion the destruction and killing of life, the setting in motion for:

> Objects to work for us
> objects to act for us
> Performing witchery
> for suffering
> for torment
> for the still-born
> for the deformed
> the sterile
> the dead.
> Whirling
> whirling
> whirling
> whirling
> set into motion now
> set into motion.[44]

After the witch, "who hadn't shown off charms or powers," finished telling his story as the ultimate act of witchery, the other witches ask him to "Call that story back," and after shaking his head, he concludes:

> It's already turned loose.
> It's already coming.
> It can't be called back.[45]

It's all in the stories we tell, Silko would add, reminding us that *Ceremony* is just that, a story to heal people of the evils of colonialism and expropriation, of nuclear garbage sifting through the ground bringing about havoc and disease. And yet the witchery ultimately resides in blaming white people. Does Betonie's story of witchery resonate with Michael Taussig's concept in "History as Sorcery" that "the history of conquest can itself acquire the character of the sorcerer"?[46] For Taussig, the stories history tells may constitute forms of bewitching the living. The objectification of the past in stories—as in the witch's story of the European invasion—empowers "imagery capable of causing as well as relieving misfortune."[47] In telling the story of objectification, of the sapping of life from the world as the Indian invention of Europe, Silko suggests that the grand act of witchery would consist in the naturalization of the state of the world that comes as a result of seeing and objectifying Europe as the done fact we have to contend with, as if there were no *elsewheres* to globalization, no possibility of healing. But as does Taussig, Silko finds the power to heal in the objectification of the historical events in the ceremony.

Not unlike the *tlacuilo* of folio 46r, the old healer Betonie sees the possibility of dwelling in both Indian and European worlds, of dealing with white people, "with their machines and their beliefs." It is the trickery of modernity to insist on its incompatibility with nonmodern life-forms, to instill the internalization of the denigration of one's own. It is a form of denigration that dismisses Indian life-forms when they "lose" their purity, as if Indian, or, for that matter, European, culture could remain static after conquest. For Betonie also finds witchery in the insistence that *ceremonies* must never change, in the need to create new ceremonies after the white people came: "That's what witchery is counting on: that we will cling to the ceremonies the way they were, and then their power will triumph, and the people will be no more."[48]

Witchery is filled with unexpected turns that we have traced in the transparent identification and objectification of Eurocentrism, which, under analysis, turns into a self-defeating reiteration of the same epistemology one sets out to counter in the first place. It is as if the certification that the "world is a dead thing" would confirm its effects on the totality of possible worlds. For Silko, the grand witch performed the illusion of an all-powerful oppressive destruction of life that she characterizes as the Indian invention of Europe. The *tlacuilo*'s invention of a vocabulary for depicting European colonial objects, subjects, and institutions creates a montage of pictorial forms that we must avoid understanding as forms of representation. The identification and coding of the Dominican and the Franciscan missionaries differentiate their styles of evangelization and yet suspend a full-fledged comparison. Their differences can certainly lead to comparisons, but the implicit objectification in comparing them as stable entities would call forth a third term that would define their "value" from within a teleology—as if there could be an ideal missionary ethos to measure their programs and attitudes.

TELEOLOGY

Teleology in comparative studies constitutes the present as the background that defines the criteria for evaluating historical and cultural phenomena. The present from which we write, the hindsight of how history evolved, cannot but be privileged in comparative studies. *Phenomena* is not a good word, but I cannot think of another, perhaps *artifacts*, but there is an objectifying impulse that saps the life of objects when speaking in terms of artifacts and constructs. Moreover, we tend to ignore the ways our subjectivities and our methods are also artifacts and constructs. This is Michael Taussig's point of departure in *Mimesis and Alterity*, where he insists on the dreadfully static sense of nature that comes with "constructionism."

Is there a mimetic component in comparison? Are comparisons caught in "the soulful power that derives from replication," in which "the image affecting what it is an image of, wherein the representation shares in or takes the power from the represented"?[49] Clearly, there is mimesis in metaphor, in saying "this is that," where beyond identity the "that," as it is altered by its contact with the "this," generates a new object. But also consider the age-old method of analogy in Ancient and Medieval philosophy. In the analogy a-b = c-d, a-b stands for the theme and c-d for the phora, in which one does not affirm symmetrical equality but rather an assimilation where the theme is clarified by what one knows about the phora, such as in "man is to woman" what "culture is to nature" in Sherry Ortner's article "Is Female to Male as Nature Is to Culture?" that (quite literally) applies Lévi-Strauss's binary to clarify the relationship between men and women. (Note that Ortner has repudiated this early essay.) I have said that comparisons invoke a third term, but analogy or even metaphor work with four or two elements. The third term I am thinking of is the background in which nature, culture, women, and men make sense. This background would consist of the acceptance in Ortner's example of binary oppositions as transcultural and transhistorical systems. The structuralist paradigm would constitute the background that would make the analogy meaningful. The teleological component surfaces in the assumption that women have men as their horizon of meaning in the same way that nature is subordinated to culture. Thus, nature functions as an implacable, stable entity that by the mere fact of being named, described, mapped out, becomes culture. So an extension of the analogy would be: man shapes women as culture shapes nature. For analogy to work, it is fundamental that the theme and phora are not homogeneous.

Returning to Taussig's *Mimesis and Alterity*, we learn there of a comparativist project in which the awakening of life in petrified objects in Benjamin's writings on Baroque allegory is likened to the infusion of life into the doll in the shaman's plotting of the woman giving birth in the well-known Cuna example. The background as explicitly stated by Taussig is the Enlightenment: "My concern is to reinstate in and against the myth of the Enlightenment, with its universal, context-free reason, not merely the resistance of the concrete particular to abstraction, but what I deem crucial to thought that moves and moves us—namely its sensuousness, its mimeticity."[50] Implicit to the project and the question of finding oneself in the field of study (the Cuna figures are of Europeans) is the interrogation, even the evisceration, of the anthropological enterprise.

And this return of the gaze is precisely what we learn from the Indian pictorial depictions of colonial types and institutions in Codex Telleriano-Remensis. It is, however, a return of the gaze, a situation in which the observer is observed, that does not necessarily reproduce an objectifying epistemology but rather expresses wonder at the demand to "tell the story of how I was conquered." The development of a pictorial vocabulary that identifies aspects of the colonial order from within a Mesoamerican background entails a language game in which, minimally, a distinction between Indian and not-Indian forms is presupposed; however, the meaning these forms have from within the Indian background remains inaccessible to the background *from which* and *against which* we approximate the vocabularies that have been created for inscribing the colonial order.

We may recognize the uses and practices of turning systems of signification (perspective, grids in townscapes, landscape painting, shading, and so on) into signifiers for signifying worlds that missionaries and administrators could not begin to imagine were possible. In this respect, the signifiers manifest a metaphoricity that displaces the proper site of the signifieds one associates with the effects of pictorial perspective, realistic landscape paintings, Latin script, and so on. I recognize something different in the metaphorical use of signifiers in Indian pictorial texts, but I would need to dwell in the background that makes sense of these practices in order to objectify the habitus, something impossible to do at least from the language I am practicing right now. And then I would have to translate for you, thereby setting in motion the process of mastery. Such an effort would, in fact, be haunted by the background that in turning the indigenous habitus into an object of observation finds itself replicated without possible exteriority: one would have to ask what is the habitus that observes the habitus that makes sense and objectifies the indigenous habitus, a process that would lead to an infinite progression? If this endless process is in itself desirable insofar as it is without end, the impulse, which manifests a desire for mastery and appropriation, remains suspect. Having said this, one may imagine the *tlacuilo* moving back and forth between the two habitus she is asked to inhabit in the process of responding to (understanding and recognizing) the modernist call for her objectification of native culture and writing while doing so from a habitus that remains inaccessible to the missionaries. In so doing, she suspends the teleology that would privilege the missionaries' assumption that they possess the categories that would enable them to master and appropriate indigenous life-forms. From the intentionality we have traced in folio 46r, we learn that the question of objectification and appropriation amounts to episte-mological hubris. In the frontal depiction of the Franciscan, I find a self-referential gesture that points to the eyes of the *tlacuilo* looking back at the missionaries but also at us twenty-first-century viewers of the folio. In her looking back at the spectator, she draws the limits of the missionaries' ethnographic project but also of the knowledge we twenty-first-century scholars produce.

FAMILIARIZATION, DOMESTICATION, APPROPRIATION

As a process of interpretation, comparisons manifest at least two differ-ent processes, namely, one in which the objective is appropriation and its implied familiarization and domestication of alterity, and another in which defamiliarization unsettles fixed ideas about nature and humans. Whereas familiarization constitutes a dominant form and is an expression of the will to power, defamiliarization redefines the terms of the domi-nant. Does defamiliarization open a semantic space in which we can for-mulate thought that is not appropriative? Does montage enable defamil-iarization? Is montage by the mere structure of including two items (I am using this vague term to avoid confining what follows to simple or com-plex clusters of cultural and linguistic examples) a particular trope? Mon-tage clearly avoids the "this is that" of metaphor by prompting a reflection that avoids identity and remains open to further elaboration. The objec-tive of montage is to trigger thought. As critics, we are tempted to draw meanings that seem obvious to us, and in some cases, montages beg for reductive signification, but we should pose the imperative of refraining from interpretation in the modality of appropriation and domestication. Defamiliarization must be pushed to the extreme where it manifests the familiarization of one of the terms. In other words, defamiliarization only makes sense from within the horizon of the familiar.

The concept of the subaltern is in itself a relational concept that en-tails defamiliarization from a comparativist perspective. The notion of the utterly subaltern, as in Spivak's radically heterogeneous subjects, is a theo-retical construct with no stable referent. There is, in fact, a contagion be-tween such concepts as Kant's "man in the raw" and the absolutely other that defines the impossibility of speech of the subaltern. And we should resist universalizing Kant's fiction beyond the specific cultural matrix of the European eighteenth-century Enlightenment. The subaltern as conceived by Spivak lacks the possibility of representation. But then again, would this limitation make sense when representation is an option to be avoided? The dilemma of representation leads to those cultural forms that subalterns produce and circulate among themselves and that end up in the bin of superstition and folklore. We write novels, poetry, songs; make films; and produce plays that are intended to express subaltern perspectives and communicate the sources of subalternity; however, as long as we retain the imperative to represent, the subaltern as a receiver, perhaps as a participant in the cultural expressions, has different degrees of understanding of the processes of subalternization. The comparative frame in subaltern studies foregrounds teleology by measuring self-representation and participation in the dominant system.

More recently, in *Death of a Discipline*, Spivak has called for a comparativist project grounded in what she calls teleopoeisis, a concept she derives from Derrida's *Politics of Friendship*: "The teleopoeisis we are speaking of is a messianic structure. . . . We are not yet among these philosophers of the future, . . . but we are in advance their friends. . . . This is perhaps the 'community of those without community.'"[51] Spivak's version of teleopoeisis addresses how we metropolitan intellectuals may conceive the project of learning from indigenous knowledge: "This is now my own real training ground: learning to learn from below to devise a practical philosophy to train members of the largest sector of the future electorate and to train its current teachers in the habits of democratic reflexes (before one necessarily engages the understanding of specific content) and on a one-on-one basis."[52] "*Learning to learn from below*" is clearly understood as enabling the teaching of aborigines so that they gain access to the public sphere: "to train members of the largest sector of the future electorate and to train its current teachers in the habits of democratic reflexes."[53] This formulation of "learning from below" to better teach calls forth the following passage from her earlier essay, "Can the Subaltern Speak?": "In seeking to learn to speak to (rather than listen to or speak for) the historically muted subject of the subaltern woman, the postcolonial intellectual *systematically* 'unlearns privilege.'"[54] This sequence of passage suggests an aporia structured by the values of learning, teaching, and unlearning privilege that, perhaps, can only be resolved within a strategy that in the end would seek to better implant "our" knowledge. Spivak offers the following analogy:

> Primary health care groups . . . if they are to remain uncoercive, must learn or be at home in the cultural idiom of the place. Otherwise the change does not stick. At this point I am clearly displacing the analogy

further, wishing to add to the role of the interpreter the role of the member of the primary health care group, at home in the idiom of the culture, patiently engaging in uncoercive change in the habit of normality.[55]

One cannot but commend Spivak for her insistence on learning "the cultural idioms of the place" in doing comparative work outside the Euro-American cultural spaces. But what can we say about the strategies to make our knowledge *stick*? Is this a form of (secular?) missionary work despite her claims that it is not? Is it comparable to Las Casas's or Vera Cruz's projects to enable Indians to participate in colonial institutions? The teleopoeisis of the future ideal comparativist—one sensitive to and knowledgeable of the "idioms of the place"—anticipates subaltern subjects becoming savvy in the use of the public sphere.

Spivak does provide an example of her (re)cognition of indigenous knowledge when she writes: "Subaltern aboriginal groups read 'nature' with uncanny precision. Their weather predictions, altogether confined in geographical scope, are always astonishing to someone less used to living in the eco-biome."[56] If this is a clear instance of Spivak's epistemological willingness to learn from indigenous groups, the credited knowledge of the subaltern aborigines remains measured by a precision that astonishes our knowledge of the physical world. The background that evaluates "the predictions" remains Euro-American in its categories and in the teleopoeisis that envisions *cultured* aborigines. This representation of the learning and teaching of aborigines might not entail Kant's "man in the raw," but it certainly conveys a conception of indigenous cultures as ignorant and uneducated except in the displays of a common rationality that the comparative critic will now recognize as almost scientific, "with uncanny precision." In the end, this principle of charity does not deny reason to indigenous peoples but subsumes, if not subordinates, indigenous life-forms to those we metropolitan academics will recognize as true and valid. Indigenous peoples must be educated. And education for Spivak stands for universal (read: Western) knowledge, wherein uneducated means not schooled in the most conventional understandings of the term. I am not saying that this form of education is undesirable—indeed, it is unavoidable—but that for indigenous peoples it may coexist or, even better, it may be understood, perceived, deployed, and imagined *from* and *against* an indigenous background. The subaltern subject of learning perceives the tutor from an *elsewhere* that eludes the comparativist's field of observation. In the end, Spivak's and Derrida's teleopoeisis ends up with a single world and history.

Things somewhat change when we examine "comparison" in the context of Codex Telleriano-Remensis. In this case, the *tlacuilo* depicts two missionaries bearing the traits that identify them as belonging to the Franciscan and the Dominican orders. The work of comparison is left to the reader of the codex. She merely juxtaposes the two figures. Her identification captures the theological differences between the two orders as manifest in their approaches to the sacraments, in particular to baptism. One wonders what the purpose was of objectifying the two orders in the images, if the primary audience was the missionaries that solicited the painting. The image clearly outlived the immediate production for the missionaries. As we look at this page we cannot but think that the *tlacuilo* anticipated that her text would survive the epistemic violence that forced her to paint the conquest and colonization, to respond to the mandate "Tell me the story of how I conquered you." It is as if she anticipated Taussig's understanding of colonial history as sorcery by creating images that lead to healing by sapping the force of the missionaries. Is her return of the gaze an instance of epistemic violence? As in the case of all languages, metaphor played an important role in Nahua culture, and the need to domesticate the alien was probably a common practice, but the impulse for comparison and mastery that we have dated to the Spanish effort to appropriate Nahua life-forms does not seem to have been central to Mesoamerican cultures. Spivak would remind me that this exception suggests an instance of Eurocentrism in that I am privileging Europe: "There is something Eurocentric about assuming that imperialism began with Europe."[57] Silko's diagnosis of witchery in the Indian invention of Europe and my discussion of the objectivist impulse to identify Eurocentrism would confirm Spivak's diagnostic. In passing, we must underscore that we should hesitate before universalizing the term *imperialism* as if it were a transparent concept ready-made for cross-cultural applications that describe state formations in the Americas, as when we unreflectively speak of the Aztec or the Inca Empires. To avoid the term *imperialism* would be consistent with Spivak's call to learn the "idioms of the place."

What is the basis for claiming appropriation as a particular Western form of knowledge? There seems to have been no interest among the ancient Nahua in knowing other Mesoamerican cultures in their specificity. The northern nomads, the Chichimecas, are defined as lacking civilization, but also are traced as an origin. Hence, the Nahua would phrase their identity in terms of "We are all Chichimecas." Does this differentiation matter for my argument on the appropriative impulse in comparative studies?

Let us recall that for Gadamer, failure to produce historical knowledge in comparative studies resided in the adoption of objectivity and the erasure of temporality in contemporaneity. For us, it has less to do with contemporaneity—the conquest does not pertain to the past but to an ongoing process in a now—than with the will to objectify and thus appropriate the world. Are there other terms than one's own in appropriation? In supposing that the *tlacuilo* understands the colonial order from an Indian perspective, I have presumed that she does not partake of a will to objectify. But is this correct? Is the will to objectify something imported from Europe, something datable? Was the *tlacuilo* aware of the witchery of objectification so lucidly exposed in Silko's poem-story? The *tlacuilo*'s inscription of European artifacts and people makes sense in terms of the Indian semantic horizon and social world. In short, the Indian world now comprises Dominicans and Franciscans, including their disagreements and debates. This inscription has less to do with retaining a distance from the "other," from the not-us, than with defining a new one's "own" that appropriates, seizes, and dominates. It is, in the end, a question of telling the story of one's conquest, of observing the observer in the act of appropriation, in participating in the creation of an album of one's forms of life. It is a process in which ethnosuicide leads to ethnogenesis, in which objectification in images bears the twin possibility of "imagery capable of causing as well as relieving misfortune."[58]

ON ENDS AND ENDINGS

If this sounds terribly Heideggerian to you, it is because his *Contributions to Philosophy (From Enowning)* provides a theoretical frame for reflecting on the differences between appropriation and enowning, as the English translators chose to render the German *erignis*: "It is no longer a case of talking 'about' something and representing something objective, but rather of being owned over into enowning. This amounts to an essential transformation of the human from 'rational animal' (*animal rationale*) to Da-sein."[59] This is not the place to elaborate a dissertation on the meaning of Da-sein; the purpose for citing Heidegger is to identify a historical project that would open history beyond ontology and metaphysics.

If we assume that Europe, in the figure of Columbus, begins a process in which the subject is separated from the object because of the epistemological transformation brought about by the need to document unheard-of phenomena, should we also posit such a separation within Amerindian cultures, given that they also faced the need to represent the unknown?[60] Heidegger would seem to allude to this process of appropriation in universal terms that we should perhaps delimit as Western: "Man is so fully blinded by what is objective and machinational that beings already withdraw from him; how much more still does be-ing and its truth withdraw, wherein all beings must originarily first arise and appear strange."[61] Heidegger's "Man" clearly subscribes to a single historical telos, even if as an open question. Juxtapose these thoughts to Silko's story of the objectification of the world and its machinations in Western culture as witchery. Suspend the comparison. Just note how speaking of objectification as witchery from within an English expression of the colonial appropriation of native lands illustrates a form of undoing the pull of appropriation from within globalatinization and Eurocentrism. After all, even if the term *witch* is not a Latinate term, the concepts of objectification and machinery, and the anthropological discourses on ceremonies, rituals, rites, and so on, are.

I have alluded to globalatinization and Eurocentrism in one breath. This gesture runs against the tendency to identify and represent Eurocentrism by means of a given set of traits. My concern, however, is not with elaborating a list of Eurocentric items but with the type of thinking implied in the creation of a list and its objectification of the world. As a reductive gesture, listing would negate the complexity of the thought of such figures as Descartes and Kant, and one wonders if in the end they are not waiting for us with a smile. Confirming the objectification of Eurocentrism is an act of witchery that suspends the possibility of healing. In elaborating a critique of Eurocentrism, we have much to gain from readings of Kant and Descartes that explore their thought, and even the possibility of learning from them. One commonplace in dismissals of European thinkers deemed Eurocentric is their purported dualism as the origin of an endless series of binaries: Europe/rest of the world, man/woman, adult/child, master/slave, reason/emotion, and so on. We can actually trace the logic of these binary oppositions to Aristotle's *Politics*, but this would complicate the narrative that dates the rise of Europe and the formation of Eurocentrism to 1492.

I have no quarrel with this zero point for telling a *story* of Eurocentrism, but I find naive arguments that *naturalize* beginnings in the stories we tell about the past. We should tell stories, though not necessarily using a plot structure that defines beginnings, middles, and ends. This is especially pertinent to the art of telling stories that undo generic plot structures. If all stories must end, we must recall Ts'eh's warning to Tayo in *Ceremony*: "They want to end here, the way all their stories end, encircling slowly to choke the life away."[62] The struggle is within language, with endings perhaps even more urgently than with beginnings. Would the dangers of establishing the beginnings of Eurocentrism consist of assuming that the dating brings about the end, and thereby one would remain oblivious of the Eurocentric spaces from which one makes such pronouncements?

The objectification of Eurocentrism presupposes a space exterior to the cultural, social, political, economic, and aesthetic clusters of forms that we identify as such. There is thus a resistance to understanding the ways in which globalatinization has defined and continues to define the terms we use to conceptualize the world. As it were, we desire the languages embedded in globalatinization to be universal; there is, indeed, a need to separate Europe from Eurocentrism under the illusion that the representation of Eurocentric traits has exhausted the problem. By the magical stroke of naming Eurocentrism, we believe ourselves exempted from its logic. So we go on with our acquired habits and remain caught within Eurocentric systems of thought and styles of reflection.

The task of reading, translating, and teaching indigenous languages and cultures demands that we remain open to the specific worlds they articulate and not rush into incorporating them into our alternative proposals. In fact, our proposals must be articulated from within globalatinization; hence we should refrain from elaborating lists of the sort mentioned above, and if we do characterize globalatinization as logocentrism, fallocentrism, Eurocentrism, anthropocentrism, and all the other centrisms we can imagine, it is with the understanding that our most venerable intentions will necessarily be interpreted in terms of a background in which this centrism makes sense of what we say. Even the difference we seek to articulate will make sense in terms of globalatinization. Beyond globalatinization as background, we encounter the incalculable, the indeterminate, the incomparable, and the undecidable. The telos beyond globalatinization would remain open under these terms—messianic without a messianism, Derrida would argue.[63] But we need to keep in mind that this project (and Heidegger's, but also Spivak's) for a future thinking is articulated from within a specific background that does not exhaust or encompass all possible backgrounds, in particular, indigenous life-forms. If Derrida speaks of the necessity to translate, we should remember that translation is a two-way street and that we are limited to the language and background in which we call for and produce translations. By assuming with Derrida and Heidegger that all cultures and languages share an ultimate background, we will fail to recognize life-forms that do things that we cannot replicate from outside their languages and backgrounds. Derrida's and Heidegger's call for changes in the nature of "Man," in the history of be-*ing*, do not subsume indigenous culture.

I began this chapter by pointing out that to think the Americas has always been a comparative project. Given that all comparisons come into play within a background, I have suggested a semantic shift in the pronunciation of the title of this chapter, from "in comparable Americas," to "*in*comparable Americas." Only then will we (as in I/you that is linked in terms of the "I am able, you *ought*" of the categorical imperative) be able to locate the particularity of the background from which we make sense of the world and begin to recognize the existence of backgrounds that cannot be subsumed under a background that pretends to be the source of universal signification even if under erasure, as in the case of Heidegger, Derrida, and Nancy. The theoretic-narrative loops I have elaborated have begun to explore questions pertaining to what should be seen as an ongoing opening of the problem of the background that sets the limits of nonappropriative comparative work. In our desire to trace the efficacy of power, we may very well participate in the inevitability narratives that ethnosuicide prescribes.

In previous chapters, I have examined how the *tlacuilo*—in responding to the missionaries' request to produce an album that collected forms of iconic script describing the feasts, the ancient calendar, and pre-Columbian Mexican history—faced the task of devising a pictorial vocabulary for depicting the colonial order and her subjection to it. I have also entertained the notion that the friars supervising the production of this book were surprised when they realized that they had requested that the *tlacuilo* objectify the colonial world—indeed that she returned the gaze—a particularly brilliant instance of the observer observed. The friars' discomfort with the turning of the field of vision suggests a plausible explanation of why the project was abandoned only a few pages later when the Dominican Pedro de los Ríos took over the production of the book; the aesthetically pleasing and informative use of color and iconic script were supplanted by boxes enclosing the names of the years written in a shoddy calligraphy (see Figure 8). The friars would soon after abandon this effort when they realized that rather than the inclusion of data, the objective had been to register native forms of writing that not only inscribed knowledge about the pre-Columbian and the colonial worlds, but also offered a window into the mind of the *tlacuilo*. Her mind, however, proved (and continues today, I have argued) to be ungraspable.

Writing *elsewheres* has consisted of drawing the limits of Greco-Abrahamic forms of life.[1] I have conceptualized these limits as the limits of empire, in the sense that these are areas in the process of colonization but also areas comprising life-forms that remain inaccessible. It has been my contention that folio 46r of Codex Telleriano-Remensis (see Figure 1) manifests these limits in a particularly dramatic fashion. As such, the *tlacuilo* provides an instance of the failed narrative of ethnosuicide. She offers a metaphor for speculating on the concept of *elsewheres* and the radical empiricism it forced on viewers then and continues to force on us today. Her metaphor continues to exceed the positive knowledge scholars inscribe in the margins of Codex Telleriano-Remensis. The empiricism in which it situates us cannot but pose a threat to our assurance of mastery.

These inaccessible forms of life should not, however, be conceptualized as endangered cultures in need of protection, but rather as political, aesthetic, logical, and loving articulations of independent worlds. These Nahua worlds, furthermore, manifest the ability to articulate and depict European and modern forms of life from the standpoint of indigenous backgrounds. This would add another twist to Dipesh Chakrabarty's notion of "provincializing Europe," Paul Gilroy's "contending (or convivial) cosmopolitanisms," and James Clifford's "discrepant cosmopolitanisms," inasmuch as we are no longer exclusively speaking of alternatives to modernity conceived outside the geographic or the cultural confines of Europe, but of European discourses coexisting with the articulations of worlds in iconic scripts and nonstandard European languages.[2]

From this perspective, the alternative projects of modernity would become for the *tlacuilo* objects of study and reflection that would not entail abdicating her world. Our *tlacuilo*'s capacity to dwell in a plurality of worlds, which would include the adoption of perspective and Latin script, but also the Spanish legal system, horses, or swords, would certainly enable her to partake of Gilroy's, Clifford's, and Chakrabarty's formulations of alternative modernities, which would not exhaust the terms of the worlds she can create. This enables us to theorize the need for a space—an *elsewhere*—in which Greco-Abrahamic forms and linguistic traditions are conceptualized in categories that resist translation to European languages and elude the imperialist impulse of the Greco-Abrahamic conceptual apparatuses that reduces the totality of the world to its own concepts. This effort also entails the appropriation of terms and categories from non-Western traditions. The Greco-Abrahamic tradition forms part of a process of globalatinization that should not just be understood in terms of socioeconomic process and the high theory that incorporate the totality of the world into a common market or a neoliberal ideological program; it also manifests the wholesale (Latin-inflected) Christianization of the world.[3] As such, globalatinization calls for a process of decolonization and deconstruction that ironically must take "colonization" and "construction" of the world as the point of departure. Globalatinization determines the forms of life *from which* and *against which* we scholars (re) cognize the existence of *elsewheres* that elude us while manifesting themselves. The *tlacuilo*'s depiction of the colonial world conveys a self that remains irreducible to appropriation by the forms we project. As we look at the paintings that depict a joyous Dominican who wears baggy pantaloons while imparting baptism to a willing Nahua jumping into the baptismal font, a severe Franciscan who looks at us in a penitential inquisitive mode, and the topology of conquest that separates yet binds the apostle and apostate, we are surprised by the realization that we cannot fully fathom the place from which the *tlacuilo* returns the gaze. There seems to be no outside to the Greco-Abrahamic, even when we intuit the existence of *elsewheres*. The concept of *elsewheres*, thus, explains the element of surprise when the missionaries realize the gaze of the *tlacuilo* is looking back at them. It also offers the possibility of suspending questions that lead us incessantly to pursue explanatory categories that in the end reproduce our own language. The invention of *elsewheres* begins in conceiving spaces and temporalities that reside outside the determinations of paradigms ruled by semantic binaries structured by the mirroring of Same and Other. By depicting the topology of conquest and conversion, the *tlacuilo* revealed to the missionaries the endless repetition of the Same/Other paradigm. It showed how the apostate mirrors the apostle conceptually and discursively. The world of the insurgent Tenamaztle continues to elude us.

And if the most lucid forms of the Greco-Abrahamic tradition (such as Derrida's or Nancy's) expose the limits of its inscription of the world, they also retain the expectation and assumption that the West and its discourses, in which we must include the postcolonial varieties, might permit privileged access to the mapping and recognition of the aesthetic beauty, intellectual acumen, and ethical force of life-forms whose background resides *elsewhere*.[4] The tendency, then, is to assume that in their (re)cognition one does justice to difference. There is a danger that we might end up just celebrating and reinforcing the assumption that Greco-Abrahamic forms of life are capable of establishing universal principles, with implicit teleologies that postulate epistemological, aesthetic, and ethical ideals of inclusion and exclusion based on standards of rationality.[5] We must beware the dangers of remaining within the limits of a one-way street that ignores the existence of a *tlacuilo* who reflects on the criteria that define the standards of rationality. The concept of *elsewheres* enables us to avoid getting caught up in the paradoxes of "otherness."

If the concept of "otherness" always poses the question *to what?*, the space of *elsewheres* remains indeterminate, if not empty of positive characteristics. It's haunting because it sets the limits of empire, whether understood as a domain of reason or as the space of a gaze that by definition remains inaccessible and troubling. The *tlacuilo* threw off the epistemological certainty of the missionaries, who, after asking her to tell them the story of how she and her people had been conquered—that is, to tell them the narrative of ethnosuicide—realized that they were being observed from a place they could never fully inhabit and expropriate. Missionaries and colonialist types cannot afford, within an economy of conquest and conversion, to assume the relativism (that is, the irreconcilable differences) that plagues their pursuits of and conflicts over universal truths. Their relativism would negate the essence of conversion, which seeks to bring the "other" into universal history, but also the economy of conquest in which the insurgent in the figure of the nude Tenamaztle, conceptualized as apostate, reminds missionaries and lay officials that insurgency can never be fully explained or contained. This was a most unpalatable truth to learn from the *tlacuilo*.

From outside, the Greco-Abrahamic tradition as embodied in the Dominican and Franciscan can only be perceived as irremediably fragmented in its claims to universality. There seems to be an inherent resistance to the notion that one is limited to horizons of universality that can never be final. But then again, if I am making this statement from within the Greco-Abrahamic tradition, am I not just one more intervention in a long history of conflict and debate? What difference does it make to speak in terms of *elsewheres*? At the very least it should force us to acknowledge that the traffic between cultures is a two-way street—a recognition that ought to humble, rather than mark the first moment in the pursuit of mastery. Within this generalized state of struggle, we must insist on the *tlacuilo*'s capacity to dwell in both the modern and the nonmodern without incurring contradiction, despite the inherently jealous nature of modernity. I have traced this capacity in her ability to move between worlds in the joy she expresses when capturing caricaturesque images of missionaries or when displaying her ethnographic acumen in drawing the topology that binds apostate to apostle. I also find the ability in the invention of a pictorial vocabulary to depict the colonial order. This obviously does not mean that she would have felt oppressed by the demands of Christianity. This coexistence within one indigenous subject and culture would entail a porosity between the modern and the nonmodern in which life-forms belonging to these worlds would travel from one location to the other, providing elements for self-critique. But because of the colonial past and imperial vocation of modernity, the nonmodern self-critique would not be subjected to a desire for recognition by the moderns, but rather unfold itself in an ongoing process of autonomization from the legacies of colonization.

The concept of plural-world dwelling enables us to bypass traditional accounts of relativism that assume an intimate connection to either skepticism or cynicism, depending on whether the focus is epistemological or ethical.[6] The discussion shifts slightly when, instead of asserting either the impossibility or the necessity of finding universally valid knowledge in ethical or epistemological matters, we bind the universality of truth statements to singular worlds. Radical relativism offers a perspective in which universalities coexist as independent worlds that can no longer be subsumed into a single all-encompassing world. Radical relativism assumes the burden of retaining the tension between the project of radical atheism and the assumption that the categories pertaining to radical atheism would make no sense outside the world in which they have been formulated. As such, atheism demands both the recognition of multiple gods (no god tradition holds a privileged position) and the expression of a most rigorous reflection on the gods of the West (philosophical, theological, aesthetic). Radical relativism would push the limits of the language of those seeking to establish an end of history (à la Hegel or Heidegger), while at the same time asserting the singularity of a plurality of worlds that cannot be subsumed under the end of philosophy.

This amounts to stating that philosophy belongs to a particular tradition of the Greco-Abrahamic. It clearly underlies the discourse that I am presently articulating, as well as the reader that it calls forth. The readers involved in this horizon of universality would, however, retain the possibility of participating in multiple other worlds. This argument requires a specifically Greco-Abrahamic habitus of reasoning and argumentation, even as it seeks to deploy reading and writing practices that make manifest the limits of empire. I have argued that the *tlacuilo*'s depictions of colonial institutions and discourses, which are readily familiar to those trained in the Greco-Abrahamic tradition, teach us how to see these colonial forms from a consciousness under siege. Her gaze vanishes from sight in the same gesture that offers a glimpse into the *elsewhere* from which she paints. Rather than dismissing the philosophies of the end as mere Western provincialism passing for universalism, one would take on the force of their arguments and the sphere of their influence. Paradoxically, in the pursuit of a never-to-be-completed project to overcome the sacred resides the realization that the categories of the "sacred" as crafted in the Greco-Abrahamic tradition cannot be merely transported to life-forms existing *elsewhere*. I place the term "sacred" within quotes to underscore the particularity of this concept and the need to suspect its universal applicability. Radical atheism underscores that the forms with which Western discourses produce the "other" lack the transparency one often assumes when speaking of magic, the sacred, and spirituality, if not superstition and idolatry, as inherent to "enchanted" worlds. Needless to say, "enchantment" is all too often taken as a cultural descriptor of some sort of premodern mentality, when in fact the project of modernity as disenchantment remains a wish haunted by its own self-induced binary that reproduces the paradigm and its phrases ad nauseam.

From its inception with Plato, philosophy has posed the limits of conveying truth, whether by deploring the invention of writing as a detriment to memory or by posing the limits of transmitting knowledge in terms of language, as in the following passage from the *Seventh Letter*: "There does not exist, nor will there ever exist, any treatise of mine dealing with this thing. For it does not at all admit of verbal expression like other disciplines, but, after one has dwelt for a long time close to *the thing itself* and in communion with it, it is suddenly brought to birth in the soul, as light kindled by a leaping spark; and then it nourishes itself."[7] In either case, Plato assumes the existence of a world different from a world conveyable in any sort of unproblematic way through either speech or writing. Indeed, in the *Seventh Letter*, it is not even in the province of philosophy to transmit *the thing itself*. Plato suggests untransmittable realms not unlike the famous secrets of Rigoberta Menchú, or the doomed inquisitorial investigation of native culture during the conquest not unlike the limits of implanting faith through conversion, the mysteries of grace through baptism, and the spirit of rebellion, perhaps nowhere better expressed than in the Zapatista figure of Votán Zapata, "the guardian and the heart of the people." We can, likewise, trace these themes in folio 46r of the Codex Telleriano-Remensis. The *tlacuilo*'s production of knowledge is itself haunted by the impossibility of transmitting the truths sought by the missionaries. These examples suggest both the existence of worlds that cannot be communicated in philosophy and a frontier between worlds belonging to different traditions. Our task ought to be to sustain these questions, remaining vigilant of the colonial power structures, which, although they are often articulated in highly benevolent terms, plot the demise and destruction of difference—indeed, call forth the narrative of ethnosuicide.

The commentaries I have elaborated in reading folio 46r have had implications beyond the specific circumstances of the colonial setting in which Dominican missionaries requested the *tlacuilo* to produce a painting of the colonial world. In requesting a representation of a *xiuhamatl* (book of the years), the missionaries led the *tlacuilo* to produce an account that marked the colonial divide, but did so from within a continuous narrative that flows seamlessly, at least formally, from the ancient to the colonial world. She reproduces the Mexica prototype of a continuous open-ended narrative. Elizabeth Hill Boone has captured well this continuum when she writes: "They [postconquest annals] continue to address the concerns of the *altepetl* by bringing the Spaniards into their ongoing story."[8] The colonial divide itself, as I have argued in Chapter 7, is a periodization the missionaries sought to implant by calling forth the narratives of ethnosuicide. The *tlacuilo* offers a painting that reflects, indeed that enables us to reflect, on the limits of conversion and conquest and the necessity to recognize the existence of *elsewheres* that elude the categories the West has created to inscribe all cultures into a single history. The *tlacuilo* shows us an instance of thought that conceptualizes the colonial world without being circumscribed by the missionaries' horizon of universality.

The history of philosophy can be summed up as series of attempts to solve (while, obviously, constructing) the problems posed by relativism. By the "history of philosophy," I mean the history of the disciplines that first originated in Greece and have been cultivated by a long line of thinkers in, for the most part, either Indo-European or Semitic languages. I would like to briefly underscore that if the goal remains the validation of the rationality developed in the West as universally applicable, as superseding and/or subsuming other horizons of universality not grounded in Western forms of rationality, then little is gained from tracing the origins of Greek thought to Egypt. The trick, again, consists in asserting the capacity to dwell in multiple worlds. Indeed, we must emphasize that the beginning of philosophy, history, and, arguably, literature among the Greeks was a self-conscious effort to differentiate their style from all previous cultures. Nineteenth-century German and British scholars only built on these gestures of separation. Many have philosophized in other languages, of course, by incorporating the concepts and categories, as well as the problems, first formulated in Ancient Greece specifically, and within the Greco-Abrahamic tradition more generally. One can introduce concepts derived from non-European languages and thus alter the character of philosophical reflection. But in so doing, one must keep in mind that the discipline and its branches — ontology, metaphysics, epistemology, aesthetics, and logic — have a history inseparable from the languages in which terms and categories were first formulated, thereby determining and circumscribing the new vocabularies we may derive from other languages. As we relate the new concepts with the old, we find ourselves irremediably in a terrain of linguistic relativism, facing the aporias of translation. Beyond drawing comparisons, the concept of *elsewheres* reveals the limits of the worlds in which terms and statements have a life of their own inaccessible to philosophy and, by implication, to imperial power.

There are no self-evident reasons other than political expediency and fascination—and this last one is, indeed, very important—why a non-Greco-Abrahamic culture would find the need to incorporate (Western) philosophical categories into its languages and practices. We can envision individuals, perhaps whole communities, seeking recognition for their ability to master Greco-Abrahamic discursive forms to gain political status by proving their thorough conversion and acculturation. We can also envision a mastery of European forms, which, like the Hegelian Master/Slave dialectic, would set new models for the dominant culture, but we must also recall Hegel's dismissal in *Phenomenology of Spirit* of the new master as a piece of ingenuity left behind by the emergence of Reason: "Having a 'mind of its own' is simply stubbornness, a type of freedom which does not go beyond the attitude of bondage. . . .[I]t is rather a piece of cleverness which has mastery within a certain range, but not over the universal power nor over the entire objective reality."[9] In other words, within the Hegelian dialectic, the new master-form ends up co-opted by Reason as the new dominant figure. The past was Hegel's all-encompassing time, contrary to the philosophical *topoi* of the present as including the past and the future. Individuals and collectivities are bound by the figures that make up the Absolute at the end, which is also the beginning, of the *Phenomenology of Spirit*. The whole dialectic, however, makes sense only if one believes in the concept of a dominant culture; to my mind, the construct of the dominant is a self-induced trompe-l'oeil. The past haunts us in multiple ways that cannot simply be identified with a particular thought, even if it aspires to embody the Absolute. But even if we were to accept the notion that the Hegelian Absolute circumscribes and exhausts Greco-Abrahamic totality, this would not mean that it encompasses or exhausts life-forms belonging to other linguistic families and horizons of universality. In fact, we can conceive of an elaboration of a Hegelian synthesis that would be consistent with its own criteria of truth, but would not necessarily extend to all possible styles of thought within the West.

The concept of the dominant, like that of the hegemonic, must be thought of in the plural. Our task is to invent forms of thought that avoid the determinations of the past not only by elaborating cartographies of power, but also by constituting ourselves as desiring *elsewheres*. The opening of affect to objects *acting* on us from *elsewheres* entails a desire to dwell outside the totalizing impulses of periodizations that insist on the inescapability of the last era, age, or moment defining *our* history, whether in the name of alternative modernities, the age of the "global," or a singular modernity. It involves desiring a *without history* (as absence and out-side) that enables us (not unlike the impossible-to-define space and time of the apostate Tenamaztle) to avoid circumscription ruled by the iron-fisted logics of history—that is, by inventing ourselves in terms of an *elsewhere* that cannot be written into history by either legal and intellectual recognition or by political representation in state apparatuses.

Fascination opens up precisely the ways Indians take in Greco-Abrahamic forms of life—not seeking recognition of good behavior and the mastery of Western forms, but rather running with the new forms in never fully anticipated directions. We cannot but sense the genuine wonder about the mysteries of Catholicism captured in the *tlacuilo*'s depiction of the Dominican and Franciscan. The lucidity of the *tlacuilo*'s codification of Catholic diversity reveals her status of *tlamatini* (a term most often translated as *sabio*, "wise") and not a mere scribe. But we should retain *tlamatini* as such and not turn the *tlacuilo* into a philosopher. The recognition that Native Americans practiced law, philosophy, history, literature, or art is fraught with contradiction: as one seeks to identify these particular traits *elsewhere*, the same criteria that the Greco-Abrahamic devised to single out its practices end up universalized. Thus, León-Portilla has argued that Mesoamerica at the time of the Spanish invasion was on the brink of an intellectual revolution akin to the emergence of philosophy in 5 BC Greece, and Elizabeth Hill Boone has found the urgency to identify "why" questions as a staple (even if just implied) in Mesoamerican ancient history, just to mention two of the better-known projects.[10]

Are philosophy, history, literature, art, and law not universal discourses? Shouldn't we be suspicious of any attempt to validate indigenous practices by insisting that we would find these disciplines and fields if we looked close enough? What is to be gained by defining philosophy as a universal practice, rather than as a set of disciplines particular to Greco-Abrahamic worlds? Clearly, these disciplines may function as universal frameworks for actual discourses that seek to inscribe themselves within their definitions, problems, and categories. We may speak of Aztec philosophy or, for that matter, of Hindu philosophy by teasing *philosophemes* out of statements not intended to fulfill the definition of philosophy in the first place, but what do these traditions gain by doing so? Why would all cultures want to identify themselves as cultivating history, literature, philosophy, or art? Why should one feel the need to validate one's culture by proving the existence of these disciplines? One can certainly remember, make beautiful objects, tell wonderful stories, or concern oneself with truth without sharing the preoccupations and criteria for establishing beauty and truth, or the narrative structures that have defined history, philosophy, art, and literature in the Greco-Abrahamic traditions.

Let us not forget that the inquisitorial investigations of missionaries and lay authorities in the sixteenth-century Americas used these fields to chart and assess Amerindian cultures; finding the existence of art, literature, philosophy, and history in ancient America, along with the Indians' capacity to learn European forms, proved to be a mixed blessing. Spanish authorities sought to learn the Indians' history, philosophy, literature, art, and writing systems, wherefrom they would proceed not only to evaluate the accomplishments of the peoples they desired to dominate, but to extract knowledge to be derived from translations into European idioms. In this regard, sixteenth-century Spaniards constitute a paradigmatic instance of the philosophical imperialism that Lacan has outlined in debunking the Hegelian Master/Slave dialectic. Lacan argues in *Seminaire XVII: L'envers de la psychanalyse* that the master extracts the knowledge, *savoir*, from the slaves, and that work (rather, spoliation) produces no knowledge, contrary to what the Hegelian dialectic suggests, or so some of its interpreters would have us believe: "Philosophy" writes Lacan, "in its historical function is this extraction, this treason, I would say, of the knowledge of the slave, to obtain a transmutation as knowledge of the master."[11] This statement would make suspect any attempt to elaborate a version of history in which the future of knowledge resides in slaves' work (read: spoliation), in the shadows of the master. While today's pharmaceutical patenting of knowledge derived from indigenous sources, or biopiracy, constitutes a blatant example of this colonization of knowledge, there are other more subtle forms of violence implemented through the ruses of universality in translation.

One can certainly study and translate discourses of universality into other forms of life, but the limits of translation would reside precisely in the impossibility of translating the translation of one's culture to the universality of another—that is, translating what makes the translation meaningful. On the one hand, we would assume that the questions and categories of European philosophy are universal, and can thus be incorporated and elaborated in Nahuatl; on the other hand, we would assume a whole array of Nahuatl categories and questions that would reflect on the enterprise of philosophy using terms not yet formulated, indeed impossible to formulate, in European thought. A Nahuatl reflection on European philosophical concepts would, thus, amount to an explanation and translation to Nahua life-forms. This would not be unlike the cross-cultural discourse practiced by Barry Hallen and J. Olubi Sodipo in *Knowledge, Belief, and*

Witchcraft, where they outline a series of experiments on African philosophy, taking as a point of departure Willard Van Orman Quine's thesis on the indeterminacy of translation.[12] Quine's thoughts on the indeterminacy of translation, for instance, would be subjected to Nahuatl categories rather than merely mimicked in a Nahuatl translation borrowing his categories and methods. As such, the meaning of a Nahuatl reflection on Quine (read: Europe) would remain inaccessible to Europe, thus leading to a translation of the translation, which would inevitably lead to infinite interlingual discourse.

We can now further connect the aporias of translation with the frontiers of empire. European thought translated into Indian languages entails an endless progression in which the translation of the Indian categories used to discuss European thought in turn gives place to the translation of the European categories used to think the Indian categories, used to translate European categories, and so on ad infinitum. The infinite process of translation resides in the impossibility of constituting a universality encompassing the other language's horizons of universality. The limits of translation and universality would indefinitely pose a limit to empire's desire to subsume all languages. The task of radical relativism would consist of mapping the limits of empire while not building bridges that would further subsume other worlds. Translation will obviously continue as a practice, but we would recognize that translations also move from Europe to non-Europe, and that what actually happens in that process cannot be translated back to a European lingo without incurring an infinite progression. Again, this process of translation into non-Europe would not merely consist of translating European texts—for example, the Christian *doctrinas* into Nahuatl—but of reflecting in Nahuatl categories on such terms as *dios* (god), *la trinidad* (the trinity), *la gracia* (grace), or *el diablo* (the devil).

Let me conclude by tracing these thoughts on translation back to the work of the *tlacuilo*. The Dominican and Franciscan figures have introduced not only the mysteries of grace but also the messianic as the history of salvation into Indian life. There is a merging of historical horizons in the translation of Mesoamerican time to the Christian calendar, work done primarily by the Christian glossator in his effort to make sense of the indigenous calendar. Note that the glossator, perhaps by an accidental additive effect, opens the possibility of reading both dating systems according to their own chronologies: "Este año de dies casas y de 1541" [This year of ten houses and of 1541]. The missionaries failed to grasp the meaning of the depicted events in Mesoamerican time, and yet the glossator testifies to the possibility of reading the calendrical notations with both keys.

The Mesoamerican key, however, remains inaccessible to modern scholars even in their hermeneutic willingness to understand the world of the *tlacuilo* in and on her terms. The translation of the events into messianic time would partake of the revelation of a pure language as an overcoming of the Tower of Babel.[13] The *tlacuilo* could very well entertain these thoughts, given the apocalyptic and millenarian expectations of a sector of the missionaries, particularly some of the Franciscans. On the other hand, the *tlacuilo* captures the incomprehensibility to the uninitiated of the world of Tenamaztle's rebellion. We may even wonder whether the *tlacuilo* herself knew this world, or whether she simply located the limits of empire on the river to symbolically and naturally separate Tenamaztle's world from Mendoza's. But beyond the (im)possibility of transmitting the spirit of rebellion, we can assemble the *tlacuilo*'s topologies of conquest. Observe the parallelism between the feather-attired, otherwise naked Tenamaztle confronting Mendoza across the river, and the naked Indian wearing nothing but a cloak, a *tilmatli*, jumping into the baptismal water; the depicted water establishes at once symbolic and natural references.

If the messianic is an inevitable component of indigenous life following the introduction of Christianity, it must be understood as an indigenous messianic whose key translational terms are no longer the Greco-Abrahamic historical horizon, such as the Tower of Babel. We remain barred from the indigenous messianic not because its symbols prove incomprehensible or inaccessible, for anthropological tracts abound, but rather because its existential truth evades us. I am tempted to speak of transculturation, but little would be gained with respect to the life of the indigenous messianic. As for the nativistic world of Tenamaztle, in spite of his baptismal given name Francisco, the *tlacuilo* depicts it in direct opposition to the world being imposed by Mendoza. The *tlacuilo*'s reflection on the messianic and the nativist rebellion bears the imprint of categories and sensibilities that we cannot simply translate back to a Greco-Abrahamic idiom without incurring infinite interlingual progression.

This aporia of translation requires that we conceive of the past in the present through a plurality of forms pertaining to different worlds. The Greco-Abrahamic past haunts the project of a critique of *writing violence* by circumscribing us to the categories and disciplines in which we reflect on the coloniality of knowledge. It constitutes a past in a present with which we inevitably grapple during the process of inventing *elsewheres*, or worlds that would radically alter the same symbolic system for sensemaking from within Western discourses. One way of pursuing this impossibility is to open discourses in European languages to categories derived from subjected cultures. The limitation here is that the transformation of the disciplines (i.e., ontology, epistemology, metaphysics, logic, as well as literature and history) would make sense only to the extent that the new terms and categories were subsumed under the old semantic fields. The radical questioning of the Western philosophical tradition is, indeed, itself a component of that tradition. Our relationship to this tradition, as critics of empire, should not be trivialized as preference for one set of thinkers over another, as in the servile choice of Foucault over Derrida, Nancy, and Lacan, or vice versa. I list these French theoreticians, but the choices could include a different set of Euro-American thinkers. I leave the filling of the blanks to the reader. We should note that the best of these thinkers reside precisely in those places where they fail. Only then will we be able to take Greco-Abrahamic thought to its extremes. But in doing this, in inventing *elsewheres*, we must keep in mind the existence of worlds with different pasts. From the *tlacuilo* in Telleriano-Remensis we learn that we the observers (and this category should include indigenous as well as European subjects) have been observed in terms that have all along eluded our symbolic systems. Rather than imagining a Nahuatl *tlamatini* becoming a philosopher by philosophizing (thinking in the terms and categories of philosophy) in Nahuatl, we should speculate on the possibility that this *tlamatini* will not only reflect on the strangeness of the philosophical project in Nahuatl categories (as a safeguard against infection), but also cross over and practice (the demise of) philosophy in European languages—indeed, participate in the struggle of the West against itself.

NOTES

CHAPTER ONE

1. I follow Quiñones Keber, *Codex Telleriano-Remensis*.

2. For a detailed description of the Codex Telleriano-Remensis and discussion of these transformations in Telleriano-Remensis, see Chapter 2. In *Codex Telleriano-Remensis* (115–132), Quiñones Keber offers exhaustive analyses of the history of the manuscript, its materials, provenance, and dating.

3. See Sommer, *Proceed with Caution*, 10.

4. The literature I am alluding to here comprises the work of philosophers such as Jacques Derrida, Jean-Luc Nancy, Giorgio Agamben, and Jean-Luc Marion, but also the work of proponents of decolonization of the coloniality of power such as Walter Mignolo, Aníbal Quijano, and Enrique Dussel. Note that the gesture here has less to do with undermining their work than with situating my project as inevitably grounded in Western thought. The *elsewhere* we intuit in folio 46r, however, disrupts the assurance that this invasion of the West has imposed a singular world and history. The assumption of singularity, paradoxically, recurs in the proponents of decolonization who choose to ignore the fact that the definition and identification without ambiguity of an undesirable form of thought—namely, Eurocentrism—could very well partake of the same epistemological regime they set out to dismantle. I address this issue in Chapters 8 and 9. For recent collections of essays on the coloniality of power in the context of the Americas, see Moraña, Dussel, and Jáuregui, *Coloniality at Large*, and Branche, *Race, Colonialism, and Social Transformation*.

5. Bourdieu, "Postface," 226. I complement Bourdieu's definition of *habitus* with F. R. Ankersmit's understanding of the concept of *background* as the absolute presupposition against which and from which we make (or do not make) sense of the world. For Ankersmit, the concept of *background* allows for a conscious use of limited concepts and categories and is thereby less determined, even when seeing remains blind to what makes seeing possible in the first place (Ankersmit, *History and Tropology*, 164). In this book I tend to use the terms *habitus* and *background* interchangeably, though they merit a more serious consideration of their differences. There is something static to the concept of background that the notion of habitus would avoid by conveying an intentionality that acts on the world but

would also respond to confrontations with other habitus, such as in colonialist impositions.

6. See Bourdieu, *Outline*, 72–75 and passim.

7. My reading of Codex Telleriano-Remensis and in particular of folio 46r has little to add to the manuscript studies that have done extensive work on the materiality of this codex and other colonial and ancient Mesoamerican codices. However, when required, I have questioned the categories privileged in manuscript studies. One cannot do justice to the immense bibliography on the archaeology of Mesoamerica in the span of a footnote. I limit my observations to texts I have benefited from in this book. Quiñones Keber's edition of Codex Telleriano-Remensis provides indispensable information on the systems of writing, the materiality of the paper and the book format, the different hands that wrote the glosses, and ample references to other codices that treated similar materials and to Codex Rios, also known as Codex Vaticanus A, which forms part of the same family as Telleriano-Remensis. I have also consulted and benefited from E. T. Hamy's edition. In addition to these specific editions of Codex Telleriano-Remensis, we could mention the numerous critical editions in facsimile of Mesoamerican codices that were published throughout the twentieth century and continue to be produced. Notable is the pioneer work of Alfonso Casos's decipherment of Codex Selden, Codex Bodley, and Codex Colombino. These sources in archaeology can also be productively expanded with Elizabeth Hill Boone's in-depth studies of Mesoamerican historiography, *Stories in Red and Black*, and of the divinatory books *Cycles of Time and Meaning in the Mexican Books of Fate*. Gordon Brotherston's *Feather Crown* offers invaluable insights on Mesoamerican calendars and the perception of European calendars by Mesoamerican *tlacuiloque*.

8. For a detailed study of the ambivalences incurred in translating Christianity, see Burkhart, *Slippery Earth*.

9. I find Brotherston's use of the concept of iconic script to speak of Mesoamerican writing systems more neutral, perhaps more descriptive than the category of hieroglyphic writing and the corresponding use of the term *glyph*. See Brotherston, *Book of the Fourth World*. In some places, I also speak of pictography.

10. For a critical edition and translation of Tezozomoc and Chimalpahin, see, for example, Chimalpahin, *Codex Chimalpahin*. On the question of voices and the creation of a Mesoamerican archive, see Rabasa, "Ecografías de la voz" and "In the Mesoamerican Archive," Chapter 11 of *Without History*.

11. Klor de Alva's essay "Contar vidas" offers a most rigorous discussion, inspired by Foucault's *History of Sexuality*, of the transformation of the body and ethos of the Nahuas that the confession, the telling of one's conversion, sought to implement. The paradigm is, of course, St. Augustine's *Confessions*.

12. The literature of the instruments for evangelization is enormous. I limit myself to citing a few examples: Valtón, *Cartilla para enseñar a leer*; Molina, *Confesionario mayor*; and Sahagún, *Psalmodia Christiana*.

13. I owe the concept of ethnogenesis to James Clifford (personal communi-

cation, 2010). The specific turn I give this concept in tandem with ethnosuicide might not have captured the gist of Clifford's observation, however.

14. Bhabha, "Of Mimicry," 89.

15. Nancy, *A Finite Thinking*, 87.

16. This discussion of the limits of "alternative" modernities has benefited from recent work by historians from the Subaltern Studies collective. I find particularly lucid Dipesh Chakrabarty's essay "The Time of History and the Times of the Gods." Also of interest is his discussion of what he calls History 1 and History 2 (that is, the difference between the abstract categories of capital we may deploy and the temporalities the social sciences cannot exhaust) in *Provincializing Europe* and *Habitations of Modernity*. Partha Chatterjee, for his part, argues in the *Politics of the Governed* that nonmodern temporalities are actually the product of modernity rather than the remains of precapitalist worlds.

17. Cf. Nancy, *Being Singular Plural*; also see Cavarero, *For More Than One Voice*.

CHAPTER TWO

1. In 1982, journalist José Luis Castañeda took a Central Mexican codex known as Tonalamatl Aubin from the Bibliothèque Nationale de France. He donated the codex to the Instituto Nacional de Antropología e Historia (INAH). The INAH and the Mexican government refused to return the codex to the Bibliothèque when the French embassy requested its return. To justify its repatriation, the Mexican government argued that it was stolen from Mexico in the nineteenth century. Castañeda emerged as a patriot in this repatriation feat. In 2009, INAH confirmed that INAH and the Bibliothèque were working on defining the status of Tonalamatl Aubin as on "permanent loan" to Mexico.

2. See Berdan and Anawalt, *Codex Mendoza*.

3. For a detailed account of the collection history of Codex Telleriano-Remensis, see Quiñones Keber, *Codex Telleriano-Remensis*, 115-117.

4. See Quiñones Keber, *Codex Telleriano-Remensis*, 117-118, for a detailed discussion.

5. Panofsky, *Perspective*, 27.

6. For a discussion of the implications of requesting Indians to "tell the story of how they were conquered," see Chapter 6.

7. See Robertson, *Mexican Manuscript Painting*, 109-110.

8. Illich, *In the Vineyard*, 21.

9. Ibid., 95.

10. Even a brief review of the literature on orality, literacy, and the printing press goes beyond the objectives of this book. I am here drawing from Illich more for his insights than for his exhaustive treatment of the subject. As Illich puts it, "I have not written this book to make a learned contribution. I wrote it to offer a guide to a vantage point in the past from which I have gained new insights into the

present" (5). In passing, we may mention two commonly cited studies from which the reader can glean alternative stories to Illich's. Whereas Walter Ong, in *Orality and Literacy*, and Elizabeth Eisenstein, in *The Printing Press as an Agent of Change*, attribute these profound transformations to the printing press, Ivan Illich offers a more nuanced explanation in the passage from slow reading in loud voice that emphasized deep reflection in Hugh to the pursuit of efficient knowledge collection among the Scholastics of the thirteenth century.

11. I owe this insight on the phenomenology of reading books to Jesús Rodríguez Velasco.

12. Dürer's definition of perspective is cited from Panofsky, *Perspective*, 27.

13. Ibid., 40–41 and 68 respectively.

14. See, for instance, Tello, *Crónica miscelánea* and *Fragmentos*. I examine these sources in Chapter 10 of *Without History*.

15. We may consider these Nahuatl warriors from Central Mexico as instances of indigenous conquistadors that Florine Asselbergs, in *Conquered Conquistadors*, has identified in her systematic study of the Lienzo de Quauhquechollan. Also see Wood, *Transcending Conquest*, and the essays collected in Matthew and Oudijk, *Indian Conquistadors*.

16. Tello, *Fragmentos de una historia*, 2, 389.

17. I owe this reference to Johannes Neurath, personal communication, 2006.

18. All passages from Las Casas's *Brevísima* are cited by page number in the text.

19. Francisco Tenamaztle, in collaboration with Las Casas, presented a case against the Crown in 1555 demanding the restitution of sovereignty and reparations. For a collection of the documents, see León-Portilla, *La flecha en el blanco*.

20. Zumárraga, *Doctrina cristiana*, 2v.

21. Motolinía, *Memoriales*, 412.

22. Quoted in Parish and Weidman, *Las Casas en México*, 101–102.

23. For an approximation of grassroots literacy and reading autochthonous texts, see Fabian, "Keep Reading."

CHAPTER THREE

1. Hereafter citations of the *Tractatus* are in the text and follow the paragraph numbering in original.

2. White, *Wittgenstein's Tractatus*, 49.

3. For a discussion of the gramophone example in the *Tractatus*, see Sterrett, "Pictures of Sound." Wittgenstein's example remains viable in the transition from analogue to digital formats.

4. Sterrett observes that for Wittgenstein, "This would mean that the peculiarities of an individual performance, unless they are captured in both the musical score and the gramophone lines, are not considered part of the logical structure of the symphony performance" ("Pictures of Sound," 360).

5. If she saps the power of deities in the process of their objectification, the same effect can be attributed to the depiction of the friars' evangelical preferences and liturgy. Obviously, the depiction of deities in ancient times fulfilled the function of invoking their power, perhaps of taming from within the Mesoamerican body of beliefs. Likewise, the images and statues of saints in churches were intended for their cult and for creating a mesmerizing effect on the community of believers. The creation of album images, however, entails an objectification that removes the images and the *tlacuilo* from the Mesoamerican and the Christian fields of symbolic forces. In this regard, the depiction of the missionaries parodies the production of images of the gods. The *tlacuilo* invents traits that define the essence of the orders in ways that reiterate the use of accoutrements associated with the ancient deities.

6. Daston and Galison, *Objectivity*, 392.

7. Ibid., 375.

8. Latour, *Pandora's Hope*, 272.

9. In addition to Latour's offering an alternative story of the desire to become absolutely modern (i.e., objective and nonideological), we may note Michel Foucault's *Les mots et les choses*, translated into English as *The Order of Things*; Martin Heidegger's "The Age of the World Picture"; Jacques Lacan's "La science et la vérité." Foucault, Heidegger, and Lacan, in their distinct ways, trace the chiasmus between the subject and the object to Descartes.

10. Marin, "Questions, Hypothesis, Discourse," 22.

11. On the irreducibility of the subject of knowledge (*savoir*) to the subject of science, Lacan has written the following on magic: "Le savoir s'y caractérise non pas seulement de rester voilé pour le sujet de la science, mais de dissimuler comme tel, tant dans la tradition opératorie que dans son acte. C'est une condition de la magie" ("Science et vérité," 236–237). On perspective, the subject of science, and the analogies between the pronominal shifters *I/you/it* in utterances and the deitic shifters *here/there/over there*, see Damish, *L'Origine de la perspective*; Grootenboer, *The Rhetoric of Perspective*; Escoubas, *L'Espace pictural*.

12. See Bouza Álvarez, *Corre manuscrito*. In *The Mapping of New Spain*, Barbara Mundy has made an analogous observation with respect to the distribution of tasks in responses to the questionnaires of the Relaciones Geográficas. She argues that Spanish officials assigned the drafting of the *pinturas* to Indians because they felt that painting was below their status.

13. Panofsky, *Perspective*, 27; parenthetical English translation in original.

14. Ibid.

15. Ibid., 31.

16. Damisch, *L'Origine*, 23.

17. Edgerton, *Heritage*, 10.

18. See Gombrich, *Art and Illusion*, 359–360. Edgerton writes: "I have found that they [American college students] can listen to the basic directions and then draw a picture in accurate perspective of a simple rectilinear room with door and

windows, furniture and human occupants to scale, all within one hour" (*Heritage*, 6).

19. Marin, "Representation and Simulacrum," 313.

20. Hence the analogies we may draw between linguistic shifters and space locations. For relevant literature, see note 11.

21. On the use of trompe l'oeil in murals in colonial buildings in Mexico, Gruzinski has written: "Trompe l'oeil was commonly used, and even deliberately promoted in Mexico, for it enabled one to obtain the equivalent of decorative sculpture at little cost. But ultimately its usefulness was restrained, or annulled: not only was the Indian not accustomed to 'reading' these projections, but also, because he had no knowledge of Europe, he could hardly conceive of the shapes, motifs, architectonic effects—the caisson ceiling, for example—to which the procedure alluded and sought to suggest. Far from proposing substitutes to the eye, the trompe l'oeil risked being reduced, in the native gaze, to an additional decorative variation" (*Images at War*, 81). Given Gruzinski's conception of linear perspective as a "code" that needed to be learned, it is, perhaps, consequential that for him trompe l'oeil implied an exercise in "reading." The strangeness of objects under trompe l'oeil, however, does not seem to imply the inability to *fall* for its illusionist effect.

22. For samples of types of woodcuts and paintings the *tlacuilo* could have experienced, see Lyell, *Early Book Illustration in Spain*; Toussaint, *Pintura colonial en México*.

23. Edgerton, *Heritage*, 8.

24. Ibid., 5.

25. One may fruitfully complicate the assumption that the missionaries placed an emphasis on perspective and the capturing of the real with Stuart Clark's insistence that "between the fifteenth and seventeenth centuries . . . European culture experienced not so much the rationalization as the de-rationalization of sight" (*Vanities of the Eye*, 329). Clark's detailed intellectual history, if pertinent to the Protestant Reformation and the rise of science in seventeenth-century Northern Europe, remains limited when reflecting on such contexts in which the Catholic Mass offered windows (scenes) into the mysteries of revealed truths or in which the influence of the devil remained all too real. One must also wonder to what extent the call for de-rationalization (and the implied de-mystification) remains a project, a desired end of the modern ethos. Clearly the *tlacuilo*'s relativization of the ethnographic and evangelical programs of the missionaries, which the *tlacuilo* effects in her depiction of perspective as one more appurtenance for characterizing the Franciscan order, should be understood outside the rationalization/de-rationalization debate.

26. This most schematic discussion of Lacan follows the section "Of the Gaze as *Object Petit a*," in Lacan's *Four Fundamental Concepts of Psychoanalysis*, 115. Lacan's discussion of the eye and the gaze builds on the section titled "The Entertwining—The Chiasm" in Merleau-Ponty, *The Visible and the Invisible*. For an

earlier formulation of a reversal of vision in which things see the subject, see his "Eye and Mind."

27. Merleau-Ponty, "Eye and Mind," 186.

28. Taussig, *Mimesis and Alterity*, 13.

CHAPTER FOUR

* Consider that the friars and the secular clergy each has its own form of penance; consider that the Franciscan friars have one manner of doctrine and one way of life and one dress and one way of prayer; and the Augustinians another; and the Dominicans another; and the secular clergy another . . . and it was also like this among those who kept our gods, so that the ones from Mexico had one way of dress and prayer . . . and other towns had another; each town had its own way of sacrificing.

1. *Procesos de indios*, 3. The ideas expressed in this chapter were first discussed in my inaugural lecture at Berkeley in 1998, "Dominicans and Franciscans under the Gaze of a *Tlacuilo*: Plural-World Dwelling in a Mexican Pictorial Codex." This was the first exploration of the performative force of folio 46r. Over the last ten years I have worked on different aspects that were first laid out in the lecture. In the current version, the emphasis is placed on the dispute of the friars.

2. O'Gorman, *Fundamentos*, 34.

3. Chimalpahin, *Las ocho relaciones*, 2:195. I have benefited from Rafael Tena's translation.

4. Ricard, *La conquista espiritual*, 174.

5. The *Requerimiento* was a document that was read to Indians explaining to them that they were obligated to recognize the sovereignty of the Spanish Crown. The obligation was based on the authority the pope supposedly had to distribute the lands of infidels between Spain and Portugal. Indians were given the choice of either accepting the summons or being subjected to war and enslavement. On the identity of Tenamaztle, see León-Portilla, *La flecha en el blanco*, 25.

6. Parish, *Las Casas en México*, 101–102.

7. Motolinía, "Carta al Emperador Carlos V, 1555," in *Memoriales*, 411.

8. Las Casas, *De unico modo*, 378. My translations of *De unico modo* have benefited from Parish's translation in Las Casas, *The Only Way*.

9. See Gruzinski, "Confesión"; Díaz Balsera, *Pyramid*.

10. *Copia y relación*, 97 and passim. Also see Ricard, *La conquista espiritual*, 209.

11. For a copy and translation of Zumárraga's *Manual para bautizar*, see Focher, *Manual del bautismo*.

12. See the detailed review of the literature on Tezcatlipoca and the Mixtón War in Román Gutiérrez and Olivier, "Tezacatlipoca y la guerra del Miztón." The main Nahuatl accounts of the Five Suns are *Leyenda de los soles*, translated into English as *Legend of the Suns*, and *Historia de los mexicanos por sus pinturas*.

Among the numerous studies of the return of Quetzalcoatl, see the recent arguments by Nicholson in The "Return of Quetzalcoatl" and Graulich in Montezuma, ou l'apogée. For an exhaustive study of Tezcatlipoca in indigenous and Spanish sources, see Olivier, Mockeries and Metamorphoses of an Aztec God. For a critique, see Townsend, "Burying the White Gods," in which Townsend offers a review of the literature that also includes the debates over the deification of Captain Cook as Lono during his first visit to Hawaii in 1779 and his later sacrifice when he returned under less auspicious times. Her position leaves no room for doubt that the story is a Spanish fabrication—the cards seem loaded from the start. From a perspective that underscores the elsewheres from which indigenous peoples might have understood conquerors-as-ancestors, one would remain cautious of assuming that the rationalism that came to prevail in the seventeenth century is a universal trait of all humans in all times. I draw the conquerors-as-ancestor motif from Gose's study of colonialism in the Andes, Invaders as Ancestors.

13. Huizinga, Erasmus, 23. For the influence of Erasmus in Spain, Marcel Bataillon's Erasme et l'Espagne remains the authoritative text.

14. Alain de Libera, in his La philosophie médiévale, provides a most poignant observation regarding the humanist tradition and the systematic undermining of Arab philosophy as manifest in Juan Vives's Contra pseudodialecticos and De causis corruptarum artium: "Entre la chute de Granade et la reconquete de l'Aristote grec, il y a un point commun: l'arabe, l'homme et la langue, sont chases du patrimonie. Le mouvement ne s'arrete pas lá. La expulsion des juifs efface Tolède. Il n'y a plus de dette extérieure. Byzance est morte. La Grèce est là, intacte. Sur ces trois disparus, la Renaissance peut bâtir ses identités nouvelles" (487).

15. This bull is included as an appendix in Focher, Manual del bautismo, 123–131, 124.

16. See Appendix C in Parish and Weidman, Las Casas en México, 320.

17. See Focher, Manual del bautismo.

18. Cited in Gante, Doctrina Christiana, 68.

19. Chimalpahin, Codex Chimalpahin, 2:183.

20. Ibid., 133.

21. Cited in Gante, Doctrina Christiana, 69.

22. Las Casas, De unico modo, 106.

23. Ibid., 72.

24. Ibid., 78–80.

25. Ibid., 88–90.

26. Ibid., 94.

27. Ibid., 350.

28. Las Casas, Apologética, 1:339.

29. Las Casas, De unico modo, 178.

30. For a repertoire of the songs that Sahagún and his collegians collected and that served as sources of metaphors and models of speech, see Bierhorst, Can-

tares Mexicanos. More recently, Bierhorst has edited and translated the other great collection of Nahuatl songs, *Ballads of the Lords of the New Spain*, the sixteenth-century codex known as Romances de los Señores de la Nueva España.

31. Here I have benefited from discussion of attrition and contrition as well as of Duns Scotus and Biel in Oberman, *Harvest*. For a historical account of the debates on confession, see Delumeau, *L'aveu*.

32. These passages from Aquinas and Duns Scotus are cited by Richard Cross, *Duns Scotus*, 9.

33. Sahagún, *Psalmodia*, 24–25.

34. Cross, *Duns Scotus*, 9.

35. Sahagún, *Psalmodia*, 32–33.

36. I have particularly benefited from Heiko Augustinus Oberman's *Harvest*.

37. Libera, *La querelle*, 263 and passim.

38. Aquinas, *Summa Theologica*, Q. 50, Art. 3.

39. Duns Scotus, *A Treatise*, 224.

40. Wolter, *Philosophical Theology*, 148.

41. Ibid., 149.

42. Ibid.

43. Ibid., 162.

44. See Adams, *William Ockham*, 1:105 and passim; Libera, *La querelle*, 352–355; Panaccio, "Intuition, abstraction et langage mental."

45. See Whorf, "Relation of Habitual Thought."

46. See Durán, *Historia*, 1:5.

47. Ibid., 4. I follow Horcasitas and Hayden's translation in Durán, *Books of the Gods*, 52. I modified their versions when necessary to convey semantic nuances lost in theirs.

48. *Books of the Gods*, 4–5; *Historia*, 53.

49. *Books of the Gods*, 78; *Historia*, 150.

50. *Books of the Gods*, 78; *Historia*, 150.

51. *Books of the Gods*, 237; *Historia*, 410.

52. *Books of the Gods*, 237; *Historia*, 410.

53. *Books of the Gods*, 41; *Historia*, 103.

54. *Books of the Gods*, 18; *Historia*, 72.

55. *Books of the Gods*, 79; my translation.

56. Molina, *Vocabulario*, n.p.

57. For a discussion of ecclesiastical positivism and nominalism, see Oberman, *Harvest*, 91, 361–365.

58. See Klor de Alva, "Contar vidas"; López Austin, *Cuerpo humano e ideología*.

59. Sahagún, *Primeros memoriales*, Códice Matritense, fol. 254r.

60. Sahagún, *Florentine Codex*, 1:54.

61. Ibid., 98.

62. Cf. Spinosa and Dreyfus, "Two Kinds"; also see Badiou, *Logiques des mondes*.

1. "*Without* History?: Apostasy as a Historical Category" corresponds to Chapter 10 of my *Without History*.

2. Agamben, *The Time That Remains*, 39–40.

3. Evans, *Introductory Dictionary*, 116.

4. On the traversing of fantasy, the *traversé du fantasme*, see Lacan, *Seminar, Book 11*, 273. In the first chapter to *Seminar, Book 11*, Lacan provides the following insight for understanding the truth the *tlacuilo* conveys to the missionaries: "But if the truth of the subject, even when he is in the position of master, does not reside in himself, but, as analysis shows, in an object that is, of its nature, concealed, to bring this object out into the light of day is really and truly the essence of comedy" (5).

5. See Guha, *Elementary Aspects of Peasant Insurgency*.

6. See León-Portilla, *La flecha en el blanco*. Also see relevant documents in Carrillo Cázares, *El debate*.

7. León-Portilla, *La flecha en el blanco*, 143; Carrillo Cázares, *El debate*, 516. I am including page numbers from both León-Portilla's and Carrillo Cázares's editions of Tenamaztle's letters. As Carrillo Cázares points out, Leon-Portilla's edition has many errors.

8. León-Portilla, *La flecha en el blanco*, 140; Carrillo Cázares, *El debate*, 514.

9. León-Portilla, *La flecha en el blanco*, 140; Carrillo Cázares, *El debate*, 514.

10. León-Portilla, *La flecha en el blanco*, 143; Carrillo Cázares, *El debate*, 516.

11. León-Portilla, *La flecha en el blanco*, 146; Carrillo Cázares, *El debate*, 518.

12. León-Portilla, *La flecha en el blanco*, 146; Carrillo Cázares, *El debate*, 518.

13. I draw this passage from the article on *suzerain* in the *Trésor de la langue française* (http://atilf.atilf.fr/). I owe this reference to Jesús Rodríguez Velasco, who was also kind enough to run coordinates for the earliest uses of the words *soberanía* and *soberano*, indicating first adoption in the early fifteenth century to address questions of the power of the Crown (*jurisdicción real*) and the power of the nobility (*jurisdicción nobiliaria*), a question already in the process of being sorted out in the thirteenth century.

14. Morales Padrón, *Teoría y leyes*, 339.

15. Note that in the *Nuevas Leyes* of 1542, which sought to correct the abuses Las Casas denounced in the *Brevísima relación de la destrucción de las Indias*, the *encomienda* had been dismantled. We know the laws were revised and that in the printed version of the *Brevísima*, Las Casas laments that the laws were not followed, but that does not mean that in the Las Casas–Tenamaztle discourse the *encomienda* was considered a valid regime. In fact, the language of the *encomienda* disappears from later legislation even though the *encomiendas* were not dissolved in their entirety. We must also recall that the *encomienda*, as a system of tribute in labor and kind, had become, for all practical purposes, obsolete with the demographic collapse of potential tributaries. First the *repartimiento* (labor drafts partly

remunerated) and then *peonaje* (free laborers) became more suitable systems of labor. For an account of the transformation of the laws in the sixteenth century, see Rabasa, *Writing Violence*, 84–137.

16. Nancy, *Creation of the World*, 98.
17. Las Casas, *De unico vocationis modo*, 379.
18. Vera Cruz, *De dominio*, 399.
19. Ibid., 361.
20. Ibid., 409.
21. Lacan, *On Feminine Sexuality*, 127.
22. Lévi-Strauss, *The Savage Mind*, 15.
23. Ibid., 20; emphasis in original.
24. Ibid.
25. Lacan, *On Feminine Sexuality*, 127.

CHAPTER SIX

1. Sahagún, *Florentine Codex*, Part 1, 101. Sahagún's *Historia general de las cosas de Nueva España*, also known as the Florentine Codex, which was produced in collaboration with trilingual collegians who spoke Nahuatl, Spanish, and Latin and interviewed elders in different locations in the Valley of Mexico, consists of twelve books in which he collected samples of proper Nahuatl speech about social and natural phenomena: the gods, the feasts, the calendar, fauna, flora, the human body, rhetoric, and so on. Sahagún solicited both literal and figurative meanings. These records of speech were intended to serve as models for sermons and to aid priests in confession. *Book XII* collected a sampler of the language of war by asking informants to tell the story of the conquest from the point of view of the Indians of Tlatelolco, who, along with their cousins, the Tenochcas, resisted the Spaniards to the end. The Tlatelolcas and Tenochcas, the two branches of the Mexicas, shared the central island on Lake Texcoco—today the Avenida Reforma in downtown Mexico City separates the two neighborhoods. I purposely avoid the term "Aztecs" because it erases the specificity of the ethnic groups that inhabited the Valley of Mexico at the time of the Spanish invasion; in fact, its use in sixteenth- and seventeenth-century texts is very sporadic and alternates with the variation "Aztlanecas," from Aztlan, the mythical region in the north from which both the Mexica-Tlatelolcas and the Mexica-Tenochcas migrated. I prefer to speak of the Nahuas and Nahuatl language when generalizing and to provide the specific names of the *altepetl* (*altepemeh*, pl., from *atl* = water + *tepetl* = hill, the term commonly used for the political and territorial units in Central Mexico). Tlatelolco was subjected as a tributary of Tenochtitlan in 1475, and the Tlatelolcan version of the fall of Tenochtitlan-Tlatelolco to the forces of Cortés collected by Sahagún reflects this bitter past. One cannot underscore enough that this is a particular version that should not be taken as representative of all the *altepemeh* of Central Mexico.

2. Freud, "Mourning and Melancholia," 14, 258. Freud further refined his

understanding of mourning, melancholia, and mania in *The Ego and the Id* (*Standard Edition*, 19, 3–66) and in *Group Psychology and the Analysis of the Ego* (*Standard Edition*, 18, 65–143). To my mind, Judith Butler's "Psychic Inceptions: Melancholy, Ambivalence, Rage" in *The Psychic Life of Power* provides a most thorough close reading of Freud's thoughts on mourning and melancholia; the comments that follow have benefited from Butler's essay.

3. Bhabha, "Postcolonial Authority," 66.

4. I develop the full implications of the concept of the Greco-Abrahamic tradition in Chapter 9. For now, take the Greco-Abrahamic as a heuristic principle that situates the languages and histories academic discourses inevitably reproduce, and yet may aspire to disrupt.

5. Quine, *Word and Object*, 58.

6. To my mind, the best study of queer tropes in native colonial culture is Michael J. Horswell's *Decolonizing the Sodomite*.

7. Bhabha draws his concept of "minimal rationality" from Charles Taylor and Satya Mohanty. Quine generalizes the provincialism of all cultures, which enables us to conceptualize a form of radical relativism grounded in the necessity to retain a linguistic and cultural *elsewhere* to which all translation must return for the verification of accuracy — a movement between languages that necessarily involves a process of infinite regress. Quine allows for the possibility of more or less precise translations on the basis of our dictionaries and linguistic knowledge; however, his concept of "radical translation" would ultimately constitute the background for translations of languages and cultures outside the semantic fields of Greco-Abrahamic traditions. Because we make them sound Greek, it does not mean that we have captured their own provincial mode of naming and understanding the world. Minimal rationality merely proves that *elsewheres* are much like us; we would still need to ask if it is so.

8. Sahagún, *Florentine Codex*, Part 13, 26. A full analysis of the terms I am here subsuming under melancholy would demand a paper of its own; here I mention that Alonso de Molina does not include an entry for "melancolía" in his authoritative *Vocabulario en lengua castellana y mexicana y mexicana y castellana*. The early-twentieth-century French scholar of Nahuatl Remi Simeon provides *"el que es melancólico"* as an option for translating the verb *tequipachiui*, which is composed of *tequitl* (tribute) and *pachiui* ("destruirse, hundirse en algo, asi como la sepultura").

9. In tracing a Moteuczoma afflicted by acedia, I have privileged the Nahuatl verbal account, but one may also conduct a reading of the visual text. Building on the assumption that the pictorial component should be read as an independent third text (beyond the Spanish and Nahuatl verbal texts), Diana Magaloni-Kerpel has shown the deployment of images of the passion in rendering Moteuczoma's downfall (see Magaloni-Kerpel, "Visualizing the Nahua/Christian Dialogue"). I would argue that *Book XII* cannot be reduced to a single meaning, but that it lends itself to multiple readings.

10. In his *Historia de las Indias de Nueva España e islas de Tierra Firme*, Fray Diego de Durán describes Moteuczoma sobbing when he addresses the rulers of Texcoco and Tlacopan, the other two *altepemeh* that constituted the triple alliance (misnamed as the Aztec Empire), before Cortés's entrance to Tenochtitlan with thousands of Tlaxcalteca allies, but the scene is far from suggesting the pathological melancholy of *Book XII* (Durán, *Historia*, 2, 535).

11. The literature on the speech-vs.-writing binary is vast, so here I limit myself to citing two key texts in the context of Latin American literary and cultural studies, Lienhard, *La voz y su huella*, and Mignolo, *The Darker Side of the Renaissance*. For a critique of the binary that opposes writing and speech as if this opposition always had the same values, see Certeau, *The Practice of Everyday Life*. David Rojinski's *Companion to Empire* dismantles the universality of this binary by reminding us of how writing operates as a fetish that magically erases oral culture, in what can only be an equally fetishistic construction of orality.

12. For a brilliant exposition of this prejudice, see Brotherston's *Book of the Fourth World*.

13. See the volume edited by Jonathan Boyarin, in particular Johannes Fabian's "Keep Listening: Ethnography and Reading," 80–98.

14. For an edition of the *Historia de Tlatelolco* and *Codex of Tlatelolco*, see Berlin, *Anales*.

15. Lockhart, *We People Here*, 259, 313.

16. On resistance as preceding power, see Hardt and Negri's comments on Deleuze and Foucault in *Empire*, 25.

17. Cadava, *Words of Light*, 30.

18. Ibid., 18. For a most elaborated thesis on the invocation of ghosts in native colonial songs, see Bierhorst's introduction to his edition and translation of the *Cantares Mexicanos*. The Dominican Fray Diego de Durán was well aware of native songs that called forth the warriors of old, and in response to these practices he conceived his version of the rise of Tenochtitlan in his *Historia de las Indias* as a resurrection of the ancient grandeur: "Ha sido mi deseo de darle vida y resucitarle de la muerte y olvido en que estaba, a cabo de tanto tiempo" [My desire has been to give it life and resurrect it from the death and oblivion in which it has rested for such a long time] (2, 27–28). However, we should read this passage in terms of a Western historiographical tradition that seeks to produce scriptural tombs to prevent the return of the dead (see Certeau, *The Writing of History*, 2).

19. Berlin, *Anales*, 31.

20. For a detailed reading of Codex of Tlatelolco, see R. H. Barlow's interpretation in Berlin, *Anales*.

21. Cited by Barlow in Berlin, *Anales*, 114.

22. Lockhart, *We People Here*, 273.

23. Lockhart, *We People Here*, 273; Mengin, *Unos annales*, 162; cf. Berlin, *Anales*, 76.

24. Mengin, *Unos annales*, 162; cf. Berlin, *Anales*, 76.

25. See my discussion of the term *exappropriation* in Chapter 7.

26. Cline, *Conquest of New Spain*, 147.

27. The images must have used earlier pictorial accounts as a point of departure. We cannot document such a process in *Book XII* simply because we lack instances of the earlier paintings, but given the indications by Sahagún that informants were asked to paint and then speak about the pictorial texts, there is no reason to assume that he proceeded differently in *Book XII*. The paintings *seem* to be illustrations because of the polished manuscript in which they are painted but not necessarily in terms of the pictorial code. In the end, the disagreement on whether they constitute an independent text or merely illustrate the alphabetical version might boil down to arguments on the purity of the pictorial code, as if European components could not serve semantic and semiotic functions in native paintings that differed from their usage in European texts. The symbolic use of perspective I have identified in folio 46r can also be traced in *Book XII*. See my reading of the pictorial section of *Book XII* in *Inventing America*. Gruzinski reduces the paintings to illustrations in *The Conquest of Mexico*. For a less categorical view, see Lockhart, *The Nahuas*, 10. I agree with Magaloni-Kerpel's argument in "Visualizing the Nahua/Christian Dialogue" that the pictorial component of *Book XII* should be read as an independent text.

28. Cline, *Conquest of New Spain*, 147–148.

29. Ibid., 148.

30. Lockhart, *We People Here*, 96–99.

31. Cline, *Conquest of New Spain*, 176.

32. Ibid., 147.

33. Of course, the *colegiales* and Sahagún determine the responses by the questions they ask, and by constituting an artificial ethnographic setting, one would be hard-pressed to prove that the *Historia general* records authentic precolonial speech forms rather than the specific speech event in the colonial setting.

34. I am, however, aware that this thesis on the neutrality of writing flies in the face of much recent work that has emphasized the power of alphabetical writing, of what Mignolo has defined as the "tyranny of the alphabet" in *The Darker Side of the Renaissance*. For a contrasting opinion, see Cummins and Rappaport, "The Reconfiguration of Civic and Sacred Space."

35. For an initial mapping of voices, see my "Ecografías de la voz" and "In the Mesoamerican Archive: Speech, Script, and Time in Tezozomoc and Chimalpahin," Chapter 11 of *Without History*.

36. Carochi, *Grammar*, 15.

37. See Durston, *Pastoral Quechua*; Hanks, *Converting Words*.

38. See Karttunen and Lockhart, *Nahuatl in the Middle Years*.

39. Cf. Bierhorst, *Ballads of the Lords of New Spain*, 2–5 and passim. I have addressed the *letrado* quality of Chimalpahin Nahuatl writings in "In the Mesoamerican Archive," Chapter 11 of my *Without History*.

40. Elliot, *Imperial Spain*, 233.

41. For an example of a trilingual Nahuatl, Latin, Spanish *cartilla*, see Valtón, *Cartilla para enseñar a leer*. Also see the facsimile reprints of Spanish sixteenth-century *cartillas*, which include a bilingual *cartilla* in Spanish and Arabic, in Infantes, *De las primeras letras*. On Hispanization policies, see Contreras García, *Bibliografía*. In passing, I would remind the reader that the first instruction of Indians in the 1520s was in Latin. Indians learned prayers and articles of the faith in Latin to the effect that the friars abandoned the practice because they seemed oblivious of the content of their recitations. For a study of the instruction of Latin, see Osorio Romero, *La enseñanza del latín*.

42. The vast numbers of notarial documents in Nahuatl would seem to contradict this corollary, but at least in cases involving land and territory there is a constant reference to pictorial texts that have been misplaced or lost. For studies that have underscored the rhetorical force of pictography in courts, see, for instance, Mundy's discussion of the *mapas de mercedes* in *The Mapping of New Spain*. Pace Mundy's contention that the members of the Consejo de Indias who were responsible for the questionnaire and ultimately for the interpretation of the data would not have been able to decipher native paintings, the assignment of the pictorial component to *tlacuiloque* is indicative of the value given to the information recorded by pictographic writing. I have argued that Codex Mendoza provides pictographic evidence that carried more force than any alphabetical texts for documenting how the *encomienda* and colonial forms of slavery were a continuation of forms of tribute paid to the Mexicas in ancient times; Codex Mendoza was produced in the context of the drafting of the New Laws of 1542 that were to dismantle the *encomiendas* and outlaw slavery (see "Pre-Columbian Pasts and Indian Presents in Mexican History," Chapter 1 of *Without History*). Stephanie Wood has examined a wide array of hybrid pictorial-alphabetical "little-known testimonials" that were produced away from the supervision of missionaries and lay officials. For Wood, these texts offer candid views on the Spaniards that otherwise would have been censored. Even if the production of these manuscripts was intended for preserving a local memory of events and territorial claims, not for presenting legal cases, this intent does not exclude the likelihood that the production of these texts could anticipate the eventuality of using them in courts.

43. Berdan and Anawalt, *Essential Codex Mendoza*, 4, 148.

44. For a reading of Codex Mendoza, see my "Pre-Columbian Pasts and Indian Presents in Mexican History," Chapter 1 of *Without History*.

45. See Quiñones Keber, *Codex Telleriano-Remensis*; and Anders and Jansen, *Religión*.

46. From this perspective, we may read Max Weber's definition of modernity and science in "Science as a Vocation" as the possibility of explaining the totality of life as one more instance in Nancy's genealogy of *mondialisation*, as described in *The Creation of the World or Globalization*.

CHAPTER SEVEN

*And now we, ourselves, will destroy the ancient wisdom?

1. The first part of this chapter first appeared with the title "The Colonial Divide" in a special issue of *The Journal of Medieval and Early Modern Studies*. The essays collected in this volume were originally presented as papers at two conferences with the common title "Medieval/Renaissance: Rethinking Periodization" that were held at Stanford University in October 2006 and at the University of Pennsylvania in November 2006. The broad strokes defining the terms of the periodization with a slash purposefully, perhaps a bit cheekily, elide the distinctions scholars have drawn between the concepts of Renaissance, Modern, and Early Modern. To my mind, the goal of the conferences was to "rethink" periodization, that is, to engage critically the transparency of prevailing periodizing categories. Here I am mainly concerned with the differences we must draw when thinking of the colonial and the modern divide, rather than with drawing subtle differentiations between the Modern, the Early Modern, and the Renaissance. The second part was first published in *Medievalisms in the Postcolonial World*, a collection of essays edited by Kathleen Davis and Nadia Altschul on the practice of medieval studies outside Europe. This volume has its origin in a session on "the other medievalisms" at the American Comparative Association Conference held at Princeton in 2006.

2. See Nancy's discussion of "destruction" as originating in the conquest of the Americas in *A Finite Thinking*, 82–83.

3. Agamben, *The Time That Remains*, 39–40.

4. Jameson, *A Singular Modernity*, 29.

5. Sahagún, *Colloquios*, 152.

6. See Sahagún, *Florentine Codex*, Part 1. See Luhmann, *Observations on Modernity*.

7. For a sustained argument for the necessity of this incorporation in the usages of alphabetical writing by native historians, see Rabasa, "Ecografías."

8. Derrida and Stiegler, *Echographies of Television*, 37.

9. For a discussion and generic classification of Mesoamerican pictographic history in terms of annals, res gestae, and cartographic histories, see Elizabeth Hill Boone, *Stories in Red and Black*. These historical forms, according to Boone, emphasize, in different degrees, time, space, and genealogy. Although Boone's typology offers an understanding of the different formats, there is a danger of erasing the specificity of the Mesoamerican genre. In spite of a long-standing tradition in ethnohistory that speaks of annals as if this category offered a transparent description, I will insist on using *xiuhamatl* (book of the years) or *xiuhpohualli* (count of the years). For a critique of Boone's use of European concepts, see Navarrete, "Path from Aztlan to Mexico," 31–48.

10. Alfonso X, *Las siete partidas*, "Prologo," 4v.

11. Morales Padrón, *Teoría y leyes*, 339.

12. Chimalpahin, *Codex Chimalpahin*, 1:66.

13. See Hanks, *Converting Words*. Also note that in the *Diccionario de autoridades* (1737) there are fourteen entries for the word *reducir*, whereas in Sebastián de Covarrubias Orozco's *Tesoro de la lengua castellana o española* (1611), a meager entry sufficed: "*Reducirse* es convencerse. *Reducido*, convencido y vuelto a mejor orden" [*To reduce* is to be convinced. *Reduced*, convinced and turned into a better order]. The *Diccionario de autoridades* includes a special entry for "convertir o convencer al conocimiento de la verdadera religion" [convert or convince to the knowledge of the true religion]. The word *vuelto* in Covarrubias's definition, meaning "turned" or "returned to," approximates the Latin term *reducere*, "to lead back," which could have conceivably played a role in the writing of grammars of indigenous languages that had undergone changes that missionaries sought to control. I can only mention here that missionaries often expressed concern about what they viewed as a loss of the purity of the indigenous languages, hence the invention of "classical" versions. I am here following an observation by David Wallace in personal communication with me (2006) on the Latin term *reducere*.

14. Lacan, *On Feminine Sexuality*, 127.

15. This has been particularly prominent in the work of Aníbal Quijano, Enrique Dussel, and Walter Mignolo. These authors pay particular attention to the place of Atlantic exploration and the consequent discovery of the Americas in the formation of a modern global world system. I have traced the emergence of a modern form of subjectivity in *Inventing America* and the juridical and legal rationalization of the Spanish Empire in *Writing Violence on the Northern Frontier*. J. Michelle Molina has argued that in Ignacio de Loyola's *Ejercicios espirituales*, one may trace forms of governmentality that are most commonly dated to the seventeenth century, most particularly in the work of Michel Foucault. In *Fundamentos de la historia de América*, Edmundo O'Gorman has traced the place of Bartolomé de Las Casas as a transitional figure between Scholastic philosophy and René Descartes. In passing, I would like to underscore that these exercises in periodization respond in part to a need to counter the bias to date and identify modernity in Northern Europe. It is less a celebration of the South, at least in my work, than an attempt to gain an understanding of the emergence of modernity within historical formations that cannot be reduced to variations of northern versions of modernity. As such, the pursuit of postcolonial studies in the context of the Americas has little to do with imposing later forms of colonization and empire building and more with tracing the sixteenth century in the philosophical shifts of the Cartesian revolution or imperial projects of the post-Enlightenment period. See Davis's "Sovereign Subjects," chapter 1 in *Periodization and Sovereignty*, for a study of the role references to Amerindian cultures played in the definition of the Middle Ages. Her essay resonates with O'Gorman's argument in *Fundamentos* that after the "discovery" of America, Europe becomes Euro-America.

16. My conceptualization of multiple autonomous worlds that cannot be com-

pared without assuming a single world that engulfs them has benefited from Alain Badiou's *Logiques des mondes*. Badiou argues that comparisons can only be effected between elements from one same world: "Evidemment, comme nous montrons qu'*il n'y a pas* d'universe, il appartient à la essence du monde qu'il y ait plusieurs mondes, car s'il n'y en avait qu'un il serait l'universe" (*Logiques des mondes*, 112). On the ruses of comparativism, see Chapter 8.

17. See De Grazia, "The Modern Divide." De Grazia's essay on the modern divide appeared in the same issue of *The Journal of Medieval and Early Modern Studies* where my piece on the colonial divide first appeared. See note 1 above.

18. Weckmann, *La herencia*, 2:729.

19. Karl Anton Nowotny, the great German scholar of precolonial writing systems, draws a parallel in his *Tlacuilolli* that uses the concept of feudal society as a transparent third term: "Medieval Europe and pre-Columbian Mexico were each ruled by a feudal class of nobles" (3). Nowotny adds the following comparison: "To understand the art of Mexican pictorial manuscripts, it is useful to consider what European art owes to medieval book illustration" (4). The parallelism often favors Mesoamerica, but as in all comparisons, the third term may lead to an inversion of values. Martín Lienhard, in his otherwise brilliant study of orality in the Americas, *La voz y su huella*, compares precolonial America to Mesopotamia: "En este sentido, el uso de los sistemas de notación por los grupos dirigentes de los grandes Estados hidráulicos y urbanos de la América prehispánica ofrece un paralelismo notable con el que se observa en los Estados relativamente comparables de la Mesopotamia Antigua" (61). Implicit in both assessments is a radical break between precolonial Amerindians and the postconquest cultures that have survived to the present. For both, alphabetical writing destroyed the integrity of pictography. Consider Nowotny's statement: "The Colonial Period pictorial manuscripts of this area are notebooks fashioned by Spanish monks with Indian paintings and mostly agricultural contents. . . . The figures have lost their firm footing on the ground, are executed with uncertainty, and are ugly. Obviously, if an amazed Indian observed one European painting one single time, this was enough to rob him for all time of the sure-handed application of his old artistic style. This change of style in colonial Mexico makes clear a psychological problem of which too little notice has been taken in judging the drawings of European children" (7). So, the third term now is "European children." For a more continuous view of the interconnections between pictography and the Latin alphabet, see Lockhart's *The Nahuas*, especially 326–373. I further develop this critique of comparativism in Chapter 8.

20. See Fabian, *Time and the Other*.

21. Also see Barbara Fuchs's discussion in "Imperium Studies" and my essay "Colonial/Postcolonial Studies."

22. Chakrabarty first conceptualized this dichotomy in "The Time of History." He has further developed it without abandoning the radical incompatibility of these temporalities in *Provincializing Europe* and *Habitations of Modernity*.

23. Chatterjee, *Politics of the Governed*, 7.

24. For a brilliant articulation of the premodern as a way to avoid the transitional character of the medieval, see David Wallace, *Premodern Places*. Yet Wallace finds himself placing the texts he studies in relation to later developments in the literatures of colonization.

25. Davis, "Sovereign Subjects," chapter 1 in *Periodization and Sovereignty*.

26. In addition to the literature reviewed by Bruce Holsinger in "Medieval Studies," see Marcello Carmagnani's *Formación y crisis de un sistema feudal* for a causal explanation of Latin America's "backwardness" in the feudalism first imported in the sixteenth century. One cannot speak of backwardness and feudalism without an inbuilt teleology. The literature on the feudal versus capitalist origins of Latin America is plentiful, and it is not within the scope of this essay to review it. Note that the category of the feudal and the medieval in this literature is transparent, whatever the models scholars use for explaining the transition to capital.

27. Chimalpahin, *Codex Chimalpahin*, 2:182.

28. Parish and Weidman, *Las Casas en México*, 101–102. See chapter 4 for a detailed discussion of the differences between the Dominican and the Franciscan orders.

29. Chimalpahin, *Annals of His Time*, 27.

30. The title of Chimalpahin's *Diario* is under debate. Since the eighteenth century, the title has traditionally been given as *Diario*. James Lockhart, Susan Schroeder, and Doris Namala, in their recent and otherwise superb edition and translation, provide the following rationale for the title *Annals of His Time*: "They are no diary; Chimalpahin's own activities are barely mentioned, his feelings fully and openly expressed only on rare occasions" (Chimalpahin, *Annals of His Time*, 4). I would argue that his criticism of the secular and religious authorities, diagnosis of mass hysteria among the Spanish colonists, and often sarcastic, if not ironic, tone are more prominent than Lockhart, Schroeder, and Namala recognize. Though I appreciate their effort to trace continuity with the ancient Mesoamerican annalist traditions and the care in the edition and translation of Chimalpahin's text, one must attend to the daily records. To my mind, the definition of the text as an annal misses Chimalpahin's care in recording the days, in some instances by the hours, a practice without precedent in the alphabetical or pictographic Mesoamerican annalist traditions. Unless we want to argue that the diary form and the keeping of hours by the church bells were integral components of the Mesoamerican annalist traditions, we must pay special attention to Chimalpahin's careful recordings of what must have been for sixteenth-century Nahuas a radically different experience of time, let alone the confrontation of calendars that one can trace in the *Diario*. I have discussed these issues and entries in some detail in "In the Mesoamerican Archive," Chapter 11 of my book *Without History*. For a Spanish edition and translation of the *Diario*, see Rafael Tena's edition (Chimalpahin, *Diario*).

31. Chatterjee, *Politics of the Governed*, 4.

32. See Quijano, "Coloniality of Power"; Dussel, *1492*.

33. In his response to my chapter in Davis and Altshul's *Medievalisms in the Postcolonial World*, Chakrabarty protests my attribution of Leninism, quite rightly, since I offer no documentation (Chakrabarty, "Historicism and Its Supplements"). Observe that my attribution of Leninism was not intended as a dismissal or a pejorative attribute, rather as a description of an impasse in Marxist thought. For a critique of the place Chakrabarty grants to "good" history in providing subalterns with the tools for engaging the state or international organizations like the International Monetary Fund (IMF), a position I believe Chakrabarty has not disentangled himself from as of today, see "The Comparative Frame in Subaltern Studies," Chapter 7 of my *Without History*. Is there Leninism in the mediating role Chakrabarty grants to the historian? Perhaps not. But perhaps because recent subaltern studies seem to have arrived at the consensus that the state is a desired institution, and that we cannot but live under the age of "globalization" or the global "now" (the quotation marks are Chakrabarty's; 109, 116). The iron-fisted logic of the globalization of Christianity remains in force, even though the time of *christos* is now concealed under the call for "good" history, and the periodizing hesitant.

34. *Historia Tolteca-Chichimeca*, fol. 1r.

35. For a reading of the verbal accounts in tandem with the pictographs, see Rabasa, "Ecografías."

36. See "Prólogo," *Historia Tolteca-Chichimeca*, 5.

37. Leibsohn, *Script and Glyph*, 8.

38. Chimalpahin, *Codex Chimalpahin* 1:65; Womack, *Zapata and the Mexican Revolution*, 400.

39. *Historia Tolteca-Chichimeca*, 233.

40. See "Descripción y análisis," *Historia Tolteca-Chichimeca*, 9. Cf. Leibsohn, *Script and Glyph*, 24, 37.

41. On the circulation of European books and manuscripts that could have served as models for the *Historia*, see Leibsohn, *Script and Glyph*, 9.

42. For a study of reading practices; the circulation of manuscripts; and the regimes of truth of orality, writing, and painting, see Bouza Álvarez, *Comunicación, conocimiento y memoria* and *Corre manuscrito*. In *Observations on Modernity*, Niklas Luhmann has argued that the impact of the printing press is negligible before the mid-seventeenth century, when one can trace a radical transformation in the systems of communication in what he calls second-order observers. This paradigm shift, according to Luhmann—and more recently to Jameson, who has used Luhmann to build his argument in *A Singular Modernity*—would have structural universal implications, hence the *singular* in Jameson's title. I have sought to complicate these arguments in earlier chapters with evidence drawn from folio 46r of Codex Telleriano-Remensis—as well as from the Tlatelolca version of the conquest that Sahagún and his collegians collected and revised—that suggests that the ethnographic investigations of the sixteenth century entailed the creation of indigenous observers of the observer that led to the invention of pictorial vocabular-

ies from within Mesoamerican life-forms to record colonial political, cultural, and semiotic institutions. These indigenous observers cannot be assimilated into the structural modernity of Luhmann and Jameson without erasing the Mesoamerican habitus and background from which and against which they make sense of the colonial order.

43. Vera Cruz, *De dominio infidelium et justo bello*, 142. For a detailed reading of Vera Cruz's *De dominio*, see "*Without* History? Apostasy as a Historical Category," Chapter 10 of my book *Without History*.

44. Vera Cruz, *De dominio*, 447.

45. Ibid., 137.

46. Ibid., 143.

47. Ibid., 415.

48. Vera Cruz, *De Justo Bello contra Indios*, 62.

49. Vera Cruz, *De dominio*, 399.

50. Ibid., 407.

CHAPTER EIGHT

1. Ankersmit, *History and Tropology*, 165. We may further expand the concept of background with John Searle's definition in *The Construction of Social Reality*: "I have thus defined the concept of the 'Background' as the set of nonintentional or preintentional capacities that enable intentional states to function" (129). Searle's definition addresses the same sort of phenomena included in Pierre Bordieu's concept of habitus. As Searle points out, there is a long tradition in modern philosophy that goes from Hume to Nietzsche: "In the history of philosophy, I believe Hume was the first philosopher to recognize the centrality of the Background in explaining human cognition, and Nietzsche was the philosopher most impressed by its radical contingency. Nietzsche saw, with anxiety, that the Background does not have to be the way it is" (132).

2. Ankersmit, *History and Tropology*, 164.

3. Lyotard, *The Differend*, 48–49.

4. Clearly, the term "Euro-America" is not restricted to the United States. Following Edmundo O'Gorman's arguments in *Fundamentos de la historia de América*, one may argue that starting with the "discovery" of America, a new consciousness emerges that can only be Euro-American. In this book, O'Gorman analyzes two key moments in Western philosophy: Las Casas's thought as an intermediary between Scholasticism and Descartes and the conceptualization of universal history in Hegel. With a stroke of the pen, O'Gorman alters Eurocentric criteria that limit themselves to seeing European thought in terms of a pure cultural space. This incorporation is not limited, of course, to thought but also leads to the consolidation of a capitalist economy and to the circulation of such consumer goods as tobacco, chocolate, tomatoes, and so on that have become integral components of European culture. If these products alter the definition of what is European,

one must observe that Europe does not stop being Europe in its new modality of Euro-America. Needless to say, Euro-American thought assumes its own particular forms in American lands. By the same token, as I have been arguing in this book, we must also consider the other direction in the traffic of ideas, concepts, technologies, and material goods that implies that Mesoamerica may incorporate European culture without stopping being Mesoamerica. For an argument that builds on O'Gorman for examining sixteenth- and seventeenth-century Nahua historians, see Rabasa, "Ecografías."

5. Gadamer, *Truth and Method*, 234.

6. Ibid.

7. For a discussion of the One and the Multiple, see Badiou's critique of Deleuze's predilection for the One in *Deleuze*. Also observe that the Multiple, in Badiou's *Logiques des mondes*, is limited to a specific discursive world regardless of how multiple the propositions and perspectives may turn out to be with respect to a given being or problem. From this perspective, the existence of *elsewheres* from which one may read Badiou can only be conceived as a possibility, or perhaps as a logical necessity to be extrapolated from his system.

8. See Nancy, *A Finite Thinking*, in particular his reading of Derrida in chapter 5, "Elliptical Sense," 91–111. Consider the following statement: "Here *we* are at this limit: the waning [*occidents*] of sense, the distension of its foci, frees up the task of thinking (though in what sense is it still "thinking") the sense of our finite existence" (108).

9. Nancy, *A Finite Thinking*, 107.

10. On the concept of the Greco-Abrahamic, see note 4 in Chapter 6. I return to this concept in Chapter 9.

11. For a discussion of the linkages of cognition and obligation in Kant, see the section on obligation in Lyotard, *The Differend*, 107–127. I find particularly useful his discussion of the categorical imperative of the passage from "I am able" to "you ought."

12. Spivak, *Critique of Postcolonial Reason*, 9.

13. Gates, "Editor's Introduction," 10–11.

14. Eze, "The Color of Reason," 130–131.

15. Kant, *Critique of Judgment*, 85. See Karatani, *Transcritique*.

16. Cited in Spivak, *Critique of Postcolonial Reason*, 124.

17. Ibid., 13.

18. Ibid., 258.

19. Kant, *Critique of Judgment*, 319.

20. Ibid., 318.

21. Ibid., 320.

22. See Rabasa, "Utopian Ethnology." On utopia as a figure and form of discourse, see Marin, *Utopics*.

23. Acosta, *Historia*, 320.

24. See "Estados del ALBA: No pediremos permiso a los indígenas para gober-

nar." http://www.bolpress.com/art.php?Cod=2010062701. Accessed on June 28, 2010.

25. Kant, *Critique of Judgment*, 7.

26. Ankersmit, *History and Tropology*, 19.

27. Adorno, *Kant's*, 196; emphasis in the original.

28. Spivak, *Critique of Postcolonial Reason*, 9.

29. See Wittgenstein, *Philosophical Investigations*.

30. Columbus, *Diario*, Tuesday, November 27, 1492.

31. See "Estados del ALBA: No pediremos permiso a los indígenas para gobernar." http://www.bolpress.com/art.php?Cod=2010062701. Accessed on June 28, 2010.

32. Hallen and Sodipo, *Knowledge*, 9.

33. Derrida, "Faith and Knowledge," 67. As far as I know, Derrida first conceptualized the concept of the Greco-Abrahamic in "Faith and Knowledge." In this essay, Derrida maps out the insuperable tension between faith and reason and proposes the concept of *globalatinization* to characterize how Western discourses have colonized the whole sphere of life with Latin, or Latinized, concepts. Jean-Luc Nancy has defined the project of *destroying* the legacy of globalization or *mondialisation* of Christianity as the end of philosophy—as philosophy's task and overdue in coming. See Nancy, *Creation of the World*, and the essays collected in *Dis-Enclosure*, most particularly "A Deconstruction of Monotheism," "The Deconstruction of Christianity," and "Dis-Enclosure." Also see Anidjar's discussion of globalatinization and critique of Christianity in "Secularism."

34. Nancy, *Creation of the World*, 51.

35. Ibid.

36. Ibid., 50.

37. Ibid., 53.

38. Ibid., 54.

39. Nancy, *Dis-Enclosure*, 30; my emphasis.

40. Derrida, "Faith and Knowledge," 67.

41. I first presented these thoughts on Silko's *Ceremony* in "The Problem of the Background in Comparative Studies," a paper read at the conference "In Comparable Americas: Colonial Studies after the Hemispheric Turn," April 30–May 1, 2004, Newberry Library, at the University of Chicago and the Newberry Library. Unbeknownst to me, Mario Blaser was working on a paper titled "Border Dialogue" that shares many aspects of my reading of Silko's *Ceremony*. His concept of border dialogue resonates with the concept of *elsewhere* I have developed in this book, in particular the sharp differentiation he draws between Walter D. Mignolo's concept of "border thinking" in *Local Histories* and his own "border dialogue": "Border dialogue and border thinking differ on the locus of enunciation. For Mignolo, border thinking implies the capacity 'to think from [two] traditions and, at the same time, from neither of them.' In this sense, border thinking emerges from a locus of enunciation that is already *in the border*. In contrast, border dia-

logue signals the movement from one 'tradition' towards the border as a result of dialogue" (Blaser, "Border Dialogue," 158). Blaser's insistence on retaining the two "traditions" as discrete enables him to tell the story of his conversion from an academic who privileged Enlightenment discourses to an anthropologist who was willing to be "contaminated" by the knowledge of the cultures under study. Note that it is the anthropologist who displays agility in the border dialogue, not the "informant." To my mind, the lesson to be derived from Silko, the "ceremony" that one must conduct over and over, is the exposure of the grandest witch of all as he or she who tells the story of Europe's (i.e., the white man's) insuperable power.

42. Silko, *Ceremony*, 132.

43. Ibid., 135.

44. Ibid., 137–138.

45. Ibid., 138.

46. Taussig, *Shamanism*, 373.

47. Ibid., 367.

48. Silko, *Ceremony*, 126.

49. Taussig, *Mimesis and Alterity*, 2.

50. Ibid.

51. Quoted by Spivak in *Death of a Discipline*, 31.

52. Spivak, *Death of a Discipline*, 35–36.

53. Ibid.

54. Spivak, "Can the Subaltern Speak?" 295; emphasis in original.

55. Spivak, *Death of a Discipline*, 39.

56. Ibid., 68.

57. Spivak, *Critique of Postcolonial Reason*, 37.

58. Taussig, *Shamanism*, 367.

59. Heidegger, *Contributions*, 3.

60. See Rabasa, *Inventing America*.

61. Heidegger, *Contributions*, 78.

62. Silko, *Ceremony*, 231–232.

63. See Derrida, *Specters of Marx*, 168–169.

CHAPTER NINE

1. On the concept of the Greco-Abrahamic tradition, see note 4 in Chapter 6.

2. I can only suggest here a difference between the *tlacuilo*'s articulations of a plurality of worlds and these postcolonial theorists. Chakrabarty's, Gilroy's and Clifford's formulations act on, *a fortiori*, the languages and disciplines (even if under the banner of Subaltern Studies or Cultural Studies) of the Greco-Abrahamic world. There is, moreover, a danger that alternative modernities elide nonmodern worlds either by assuming that they stand for other linguistic communities or by reinforcing the notion that there are no worlds outside of the modern. See Dipesh

Chakrabarty, *Provincializing Europe*; Clifford, "Travelling Cultures," in *Routes*; and Gilroy, *Postcolonial Melancholia*.

3. For articulations of *globalatinization* or *mondialisation* in French, see Nancy, *Creation of the World*; Derrida, "Faith and Knowledge"; and Anidjar, "Secularism."

4. See Ankersmit, *History and Tropology*, 164.

5. Among the most forceful expositions of an ethics of recognition and the ideals of a transmodern rationality is Enrique Dussel's *Underside of Modernity*. This book collects and translates representative pieces of Dussel's work over the past two decades. As the subtitle implies, his is an effort to elaborate a critique of some of the most influential Euro-American philosophers in the second half of the twentieth century. Dussel aims to introduce questions pertaining to inequality and poverty, topics that he finds for the most part ignored by U.S. and European philosophers of multiculturalism, but that are inevitably central when one reflects from Latin America. Dussel, however, does not question the universality of reason, the one he practices in his philosophical discussions and assumes as transcultural and transmodern. In this he is a true disciple of Las Casas, who argued in his sixteenth-century tract *De unico vocationis modo* that there was one single method for the conversion of all peoples in all times: through the understanding. However, to my mind, as I have argued in Chapter 4, Las Casas offers a much more nuanced alternative by suggesting that to conduct a truly dialogical exchange one must presuppose that Amerindians would engage the missionaries in their own languages and categories, and that consequently the missionaries would transform their own use of the understanding in the process of making sense of indigenous discourses. The process, as in translation, is haunted by infinite interlingual progression.

6. The position on radical relativism that I advance in this essay has benefited from Spinosa and Dreyfus's work on antiessentialism in "Two Kinds of Antiessentialism and Their Consequences." Cf. Mohanty's call in "Us and Them" for a common ground between cultures in order for social and political criticism to be effective.

7. Quoted by Agamben in "The Thing Itself," 28–29.

8. Boone, *Stories in Red and Black*, 229.

9. Hegel, *Phenomenology of Spirit*, 240.

10. Miguel León-Portilla and Elizabeth Hill Boone have very different motivations in their attributions of philosophy and history. León-Portilla's objective in *La filosofía náhuatl* is to characterize Mesoamerican society as on the brink of a scientific revolution similar to the Greeks of 5 BC, thereby naturalizing a teleology that posits the West as a paradigm of universal culture. In *Stories in Red and Black*, Elizabeth Boone seeks to correct the denial of history to Mesoamerican cultures by colonial secular and religious administrators.

11. Lacan, *Seminaire XVII*, 22.

12. Hallen and Sodipo, *Knowledge, Belief, and Witchcraft*; Quine, "Translation and Meaning" in *Word and Object*, 26–79.

13. From within a European tradition, we could say with Walter Benjamin, as has been read recently by Giorgio Agamben, that in a messianic conception of history and language, what is revealed in translation is the Idea of pure language itself. But this notion of a messianic horizon of language and translation as the revelation of the Idea of language would need to be translated, say, to Nahuatl, that is, elaborated from within a linguistic community in which the messianic, revelation, and the Idea of pure language would be extraneous, perhaps incomprehensible concerns. See Benjamin, "The Task of the Translator," in *Illuminations*; and Agamben, "The Idea of Language," in *Potentialities*.

BIBLIOGRAPHY

Acazitli, Francisco de Sandoval. *Relación de la jornada que hizo Don Francisco de Sandoval Acazitli*. In *Colección de documentos para la historia de México*, ed. Joaquín García Icazbalceta, 2:307–332. Facsimile edition. Mexico City: Editorial Porrúa, 1971 [1858–1866].

Acosta, Joseph. *Historia natural y moral de las Indias*. Ed. Edmundo O'Gorman. Mexico City: Fondo de Cultura Económica, 1979 [1590].

Adams, Marilyn McCord. *William Ockham*. 2 vols. Notre Dame, IN: University of Notre Dame Press, 1987.

Adorno, Theodor W. *Kant's "Critique of Pure Reason."* Trans. Rodney Livingstone. Stanford: Stanford University Press, 2001.

Agamben, Giorgio. *Homo Sacer: Sovereign Power and Bare Life*. Trans. Daniel Heller-Roazen. Stanford: Stanford University Press, 1998.

———. "The Idea of Language." In *Potentialities: Collected Essays in Philosophy*, trans. Daniel Heller-Roazen, 39–47. Stanford: Stanford University Press, 1999.

———. *Remnants of Auschwitz: The Witness and the Archive*. Trans. Daniel Heller-Roazen. New York: Zone Books, 2005.

———. "The Thing Itself." In *Potentialities: Collected Essays in Philosophy*, trans. Daniel Heller-Roazen, 27–38. Stanford: Stanford University Press, 1999.

———. *The Time That Remains: A Commentary on the Letter to the Romans*. Trans. Patricia Dailey. Stanford: Stanford University Press, 2005.

Albornoz Bueno, Alicia. *La memoria del olvido: El lenguaje del Tlacuilo: Glifos y murales de la iglesia de San Miguel Arcángel, Ixmiquilpan, Hidalgo, teopan dedicado a Tezcatlipoca*. Pachuca, Mexico: Universidad Autónoma del Estado de Hidalgo, 1994.

Alfonso X, Rey de Castilla y León. *Las siete partidas del sabio Rey don Alonso el Nono, nueuamente glosadas por el Licenciado Gregorio Lopez, del Consejo Real de Indias de su Magestad*. 3 vols. Madrid: Imprenta Nacional del Boletín Oficial del Estado, 1974 [1555].

Anders, Ferdinand, and Maarten Jansen. *Religión, costumbres e historia de los antiguos mexicanos. Libro explicativo del llamado Códice Vaticano A. Codex Vatic. Lat. 3738 de la Biblioteca Apostólica Vaticana*. Mexico City: Fondo de Cultura Económica, 1996.

Anidjar, Gil. "Secularism." *Critical Inquiry* 33 (2006): 33–77.

Ankersmit, F. R. *History and Tropology: The Rise and Fall of Metaphor*. Berkeley: University of California Press, 1994.

Aquinas, Thomas. *Summa Theologica*. 2nd rev. ed. Trans. Fathers of the English Dominican Province. London: Burns Oates and Washbourne, 1928.

Asselbergs, Florine. *Conquered Conquistadors: The Lienzo de Quauhquechollan: A Nahua Vision of the Conquest of Guatemala*. Boulder: University Press of Colorado, 2004.

Badiou, Alain. *Deleuze: The Clamor of Being*. Minneapolis: University of Minnesota Press, 2000.

———. *Logiques des mondes: L'Être et l'événement*. Vol. 2. Paris: Editions du Seuil, 2006.

———. *Manifest for Philosophy*. Albany: SUNY, 1990.

Barlow, R. H., and George T. Smisor, eds. and trans. *Nombre de Dios, Durango: Two Documents in Náhuatl Concerning Its Foundation*. Sacramento, CA: The House of Tlaloc, 1943.

Bataillon, Marcel. *Erasme et l'Espagne*. Geneve: Droz, 1991.

Bautista, Juan. *Sermonario en lengua mexicana*. Mexico City: Diego Dávalos, 1606.

Benjamin, Walter. *The Origin of German Tragic Drama*. Trans. John Osborne. London and New York: Verso, 1998.

———. "The Task of the Translator." In *Illuminations*, trans. Harry Zohn, 69–82. New York: Schocken Books, 1969.

Benveniste, Émile. *Le vocabulaire des institutions indo-européennes*. 2 vols. Paris: Les Editions Minuit, 1969.

Berdan, Frances F., and Patricia Rieff Anawalt, eds. *The Codex Mendoza*. 4 vols. Berkeley: University of California Press, 1992.

Berlin, Heinrich, ed. *Anales de Tlatelolco y Códice de Tlatelolco*. Versión preparada y anotada por Heinrich Berlin, con un resumen de los anales y una interpretación del códice por Robert H. Barlow. Mexico City: Antigua Librería Robredo, 1948.

Bhabha, Homi. "Of Mimicry and Man: The Ambivalence of Colonial Discourse." In *The Location of Culture*, 85–92. New York: Routledge, 1994.

———. "Postcolonial Authority and Postmodern Guilt." In *Cultural Studies*, ed. Lawrence Grossberg, Cary Nelson, and Paula A. Treichler, 56–68. New York: Routledge, 1992.

Bierhorst, John. *Ballads of the Lords of New Spain: The Codex Romances de los Señores de la Nueva España*. Transcribed and translated from the Nahuatl by John Bierhorst. Austin: University of Texas Press, 2009.

———. *Cantares Mexicanos: Songs of the Aztecs*. Translated from the Nahuatl, with an introduction and commentary, by John Bierhorst. Stanford: Stanford University Press, 1985.

Blaser, Mario. "Border Dialogue: An Essay on Enlightened Critique, Witchcraft and the Politics of Difference." *Dialectical Anthropology* 29:2 (2005): 139–158.

Boone, Elizabeth Hill. *Cycles of Time and Meaning in the Mexican Books of Fate.* Austin: University of Texas Press, 2007.

———. *Stories in Red and Black: Pictorial Histories of the Aztecs and Mixtecs.* Austin: University of Texas Press, 2000.

Boturini Benaduci, Lorenzo. "Catalogo del museo historico indiano del Cavallero Lorenzo Boturini Benaduci." In *Idea de una nueva historia general de la América Septentrional.* Mexico City: Instituto Nacional de Antropología e Historia, Consejo Nacional para la Cultura y las Artes, 1999.

Bourdieu, Pierre. *Outline of a Theory of Practice.* Trans. Richard Nice. Cambridge: Cambridge University Press, 1977.

———. "Postface to Erwin Panofsky, *Gothic Architecture and Scholasticism.*" Trans. Laurence Petit. In Holsinger, *The Premodern Condition*, 221–242.

Bouza Álvarez, Fernando J. *Comunicación, conocimiento y memoria en la España de los siglos XVI y XVII.* Salamanca, Spain: Seminario de Estudios Medievales y Renacentistas, 1999.

———. *Corre manuscrito: Una historia cultural del Siglo de Oro.* Madrid: Marcial Pons, 2001.

Branche, Jerome, ed. *Race, Colonialism, and Social Transformation in Latin America and the Caribbean.* Gainesville: University of Florida Press, 2008.

Brotherston, Gordon. *Book of the Fourth World: Reading the Native Americas through Their Literature.* Cambridge: Cambridge University Press, 1992.

———. *Feather Crown: The Eighteen Feasts of the Mexica Year.* London: British Museum, 2005.

Burckhardt, Jacob. *The Civilization of the Renaissance in Italy.* London and New York: Penguin, 1990 [1860].

Burkhart, Louise M. *Slippery Earth: Nahua-Christian Dialogue in Sixteenth-Century Mexico.* Tucson: University of Arizona Press, 1989.

Butler, Judith. *The Psychic Life of Power: Theories in Subjection.* Stanford: Stanford University Press, 1997.

Cadava, Eduardo. *Words of Light: Theses on the Photography of History.* Princeton: Princeton University Press, 1997.

Carmagnani, Marcello. *Formación y crisis de un sistema feudal: América Latina del siglo XVI a nuestros días.* Trans. Félix Blanco. Mexico City: Siglo XXI, 1980.

Carochi, Horacio. *Grammar of the Mexican Language: With an Explanation of Its Adverbs/Arte de la lengua mexicana con la declaracion de los adverbios della (1645).* Bilingual ed. and trans. James Lockhart. Stanford: Stanford University Press, 2001.

Carrillo Cázares, Alberto. *El debate sobre la guerra chichimeca, 1531-1585: Derecho y política en la Nueva España.* 2 vols. Zamora, Michoacán, and San Luis Potosí, San Luis Potosí: El Colegio de Michoacán and El Colegio de San Luis, 2000.

Cavarero, Adriana. *For More Than One Voice: Toward a Philosophy of Verbal Expression.* Trans. Paul A. Kottman. Stanford: Stanford University Press, 2005.

Certeau, Michel de. *The Practice of Everyday Life*. Trans. Stephen F. Rendall. Berkeley: University of California Press, 1984.
———. *The Writing of History*. Trans. Tom Conley. New York: Columbia University Press, 1988.
Chakrabarty, Dipesh. *Habitations of Modernity: Essays in the Wake of Subaltern Studies*. Chicago: University of Chicago Press, 2002.
———. "Historicism and Its Supplements: A Note on a Predicament Shared by Medieval and Postcolonial Studies." In Davis and Altschul, *Medievalisms*, 109–119.
———. *Provincializing Europe: Postcolonial Thought and Historical Difference*. Princeton: Princeton University Press, 2000.
———. "The Time of History and the Times of the Gods." In Lisa Lowe and David Lloyd, eds., *The Politics of Culture in the Shadow of Capital*, 35–60. Durham: Duke University Press, 1997.
Chatterjee, Partha. *The Politics of the Governed: Reflections on Popular Politics in Most of the World*. New York: Columbia University Press, 2004.
Chimalpahin Quauhtlehuanitzin, Domingo Francisco de San Antón Muñón. *Annals of His Time*. Ed. and trans. James Lockhart, Susan Schroeder, and Doris Namala. Stanford: Stanford University Press, 2006.
———. *Codex Chimalpahin: Society and Politics in Mexico Tenochtitlan, Tlatelolco, Texcoco, Culhuacan, and Other Nahua Altepetl in Central Mexico*. 2 vols. Ed. Susan Schroeder. Norman: University of Oklahoma Press, 1997.
———. *Diario*. Ed. and trans. Rafael Tena. Mexico City: Consejo Nacional para la Cultura y las Artes, 2001.
———. *Las ocho relaciones y el memorial de Colhuacan*. Vol. 2. Ed. and trans. Rafael Tena. Mexico City: Consejo Nacional para la Cultura y las Artes, 1998.
Clark, Stuart. *Vanities of the Eye: Vision in Early Modern Culture*. Oxford: Oxford University Press, 2007.
Clastres, Pierre. *La société contre l'état*. Paris: Minuit, 1974.
Clifford, James. *Routes: Travel and Translation in the Late Twentieth Century*. Cambridge: Harvard University Press, 1997.
Cline, S. L., ed. *The Conquest of New Spain: 1585 Revision by Bernardino de Sahagún*. Trans. Howard F. Cline. Salt Lake City: University of Utah Press, 1989.
Columbus, Christopher. *The Diario of Christopher Columbus's First Voyage to America, 1492–1493*. Ed. Oliver Dunn and James E. Kelly. Norman: University of Oklahoma Press, 1989.
Copia y relación del orden que los frailes desta Nueva España tienen en administrar á los indios todos los sanctos sacramentos de la iglesia. In *Nueva colección de documentos para la historia de México*. Vol. 2, *Códice franciscano*, ed. Joaquín García Icazbalceta. Nendeln/Liechtenstein: Kraus Reprint, 1971 [1889].
Cornejo Polar, Antonio. "Una heterogeneidad no dialéctica: Sujeto y discurso migrante en el Perú moderno." Special issue, *Crítica cultural y teoría literaria*

latinoamericanas, ed. Mabel Moraña. *Revista Iberoamericana* 176–177 (1996): 837–844.

Cross, Richard. *Duns Scotus*. Oxford: Oxford University Press, 1999.

Cummins, Tom, and Joanne Rappaport. "The Reconfiguration of Civic and Sacred Space: Architecture, Image, and Writing in the Colonial Northern Andes." *Latin American Literary Review* 26:52 (1998): 174–200.

Damisch, Hubert. *L'Origine de la perspective*. Paris: Flammarion, 1987.

Daston, Lorraine, and Peter Galison. *Objectivity*. New York: Zone Books, 2007.

Davis, Kathleen. *Periodization and Sovereignty: How Ideas of Feudalism and Secularization Govern the Politics of Time*. Philadelphia: University of Pennsylvania Press, 2008.

Davis, Kathleen, and Nadia Altschul, eds. *Medievalisms in the Postcolonial World: The Idea "of the Middle Ages" Outside Europe*. Baltimore: Johns Hopkins University Press, 2009.

De Grazia, Margreta. "The Modern Divide: From Either Side." Special issue on Medieval/Renaissance: After Periodization, ed. Jennifer Summit and David Wallace. *The Journal of Medieval and Early Modern Studies* 37:3 (2007): 453–467.

Delumeau, Jean. *L'aveu et le pardon: Les difficultés de la confession XIIIe–XVIIIe siècle*. Paris: Fayard, 1990.

Derrida, Jacques. "Cogito and the History of Madness." In *Writing and Difference*, trans. Alan Bass, 31–63. Chicago: University of Chicago Press, 1978.

———. "Faith and Knowledge." In *Acts of Religion*, ed. Gil Anidjar, 42–101. New York: Routledge, 2002.

———. *The Politics of Friendship*. Trans. George Collins. London and New York: Verso, 1997.

———. *Specters of Marx: The State of the Debt, the Work of Mourning, and the New International*. Trans. Peggy Kamuf. New York: Routledge, 1994.

Derrida, Jacques, and Bernard Stiegler. *Echographies of Television*. Trans. Jennifer Bajorek. Cambridge: Polity Press, 2002.

Díaz Balsera, Viviana. *The Pyramid and the Cross: Franciscan Discourses of Evangelization and the Nahua Christian Subject in Sixteenth-Century Mexico*. Tucson: University of Arizona Press, 2005.

Duns Scotus, John. *Duns Scotus on the Will and Morality*. Ed. and trans. Allan B. Wolter. Washington, D.C.: The Catholic University of America Press, 1986.

———. *Philosophical Writings*. Trans. Allan B. Wolter. Indianapolis: Hackett Publishing Company, 1987.

———. *A Treatise on Memory and Intuition: From Codex A of the Ordination IV, Distinctio 45, Question 3*. Ed. with an introduction by Allan B. Wolter and Marilyn McCord Adams. *Franciscan Studies* 53 (1993): 175–230.

Durán, Diego. *Books of the Gods and Rites and the Ancient Calendar*. Trans. Fernando Horcasitas and Doris Heyden. Norman: University of Oklahoma Press, 1971.

————. *Historia de las Indias de Nueva España e islas de Tierra Firme.* 2 vols. Ed. Ángel María Garibay K. Mexico City: Editorial Porrúa, 1984 [ca. 1570].

Durston, Alan. *Pastoral Quechua: The History of Christian Translation in Colonial Peru, 1550–1650.* Notre Dame, IN: University of Notre Dame Press, 2007.

Dussel, Enrique. *1492: El encubrimiento del otro. (Hacia el origen del "mito de la modernidad").* Santa Fe de Bogotá: Ediciones Antropos, 1992.

————. *The Underside of Modernity: Apel, Ricouer, Rorty, Taylor, and the Philosophy of Liberation.* Trans. Eduardo Mendieta. Atlantic Highlands, NJ: Humanities Press, 1996.

Edgerton, Jr., Samuel Y. *The Heritage of Giotto's Geometry: Art and Science on the Eve of the Scientific Revolution.* Ithaca: Cornell University Press, 1991.

Eisenstein, Elizabeth L. *The Printing Press as an Agent of Change: Communications and Cultural Transformations in Early-Modern Europe.* 2 vols. Cambridge: Cambridge University Press, 1979.

Elliot, John Huxtable. *Imperial Spain, 1469–1716.* New York: St. Martin's Press, 1964.

Escoubas, Éliane. *L'Espace pictural.* Paris: La Versanne, 1995.

"Estados del ALBA: No pediremos permiso a los indígenas para gobernar." http://www.bolpress.com/art.php?Cod=2010062701. Accessed on June 28, 2010.

Evans, Dylan. *An Introductory Dictionary of Lacanian Psychoanalysis.* London: Routledge, 1996.

Eze, Emmanuel Chukwudi. "The Color of Reason." In *Postcolonial African Philosophy,* ed. Emmanuel Chukwudi Eze. Cambridge, MA: Blackwell, 1997.

Fabian, Johannes. "Keep Listening: Ethnography and Reading." In *Ethnography of Reading,* ed. Jonathan Boyarin, 80–98. Berkeley: University of California Press, 1993.

————. *Time and the Other: How Anthropology Makes Its Other.* New York: Columbia University Press, 1983.

Focher, Juan. *Itinerario católico de los misioneros que marchan a convertir infieles.* Bilingual edition. Ed. Antonio Eguiluz, O.F.M. Madrid: Librería General Victoriano Suárez, 1960.

————. *Manual del bautismo de adultos y del matrimonio de los bautizados (Enchiridion baptismi adultorum et matrimonii baptizadorum).* Trans. José Pascual Guzmán de Alba. Mexico City: Frente de Afirmación Hispanista, 1997.

Foucault, Michel. *The History of Sexuality.* Volume 1: *An Introduction.* Trans. Robert Hurley. New York: Pantheon Books, 1978.

————. *Madness and Civilization.* Trans. Richard Howard. New York: Vintage, 1973.

————. *Les mots et les choses.* Paris: Gallimard, 1966. Translated into English as *The Order of Things.* New York: Vintage, 1973.

Freud, Sigmund. "Mourning and Melancholia." In *The Standard Edition of the Complete Psychological Works of Sigmund Freud,* 14:239–258. Trans. James Strachey. London: Hogarth Press, 1957–1974.

————. *The Standard Edition of the Complete Psychological Works of Sigmund Freud*. 24 vols. Ed. James Strachey. London: Hogarth Press, 1957–1974.

Fuchs, Barbara. "Imperium Studies: Theorizing Early Modern Expansion." In Ingham and Warren, *Postcolonial Moves*, 71–90.

Gadamer, Hans-Georg. "The Problem of Historical Consciousness." In *Interpretive Social Science: A Reader*, ed. Paul Rabinow and William M. Sullivan, 103–160. Berkeley: University of California Press, 1979.

————. *Truth and Method*. 2nd rev. ed. Translation revised by Joel Weinsheimer and Donald G. Marshal. New York: Continuum, 1994.

Gante, Pedro de. *Doctrina Christiana en Lengua Mexicana*. Facsimile edition. Ed. with a critical study by Ernesto de la Torre Villar. Centro de Estudios Fray Bernardino de Sahagún. Mexico City: Editorial Jus, 1982.

Gates, Jr., Henry Louis. "Editor's Introduction: Writing 'Race' and the Difference It Makes." In *"Race," Writing, and Difference*, ed. Henry Louis Gates, Jr., 1–20. Chicago: University of Chicago Press, 1986.

Gilroy, Paul. *Postcolonial Melancholia*. New York: Columbia University Press, 2004.

Gombrich, E. H. *Art and Illusion: A Study in the Psychology of Pictorial Representation*. Princeton: Princeton University Press, 1972.

Goodman, Nelson. *Ways of Worldmaking*. Indianapolis: Hackett, 1978.

Goody, Jack. *The Domestication of the Savage Mind*. Cambridge: Cambridge University Press, 1977.

Gose, Peter. *Invaders as Ancestors: On the Intercultural Making and Unmaking of Spanish Colonialism in the Andes*. Toronto: University of Toronto Press, 2008.

Grafton, Anthony. *New Worlds, Ancient Texts: The Power of Tradition and the Shock of Discovery*. Cambridge, MA: Belknap Press, 1992.

Graulich, Michel. *Montezuma, ou l'apogée et la chute de l'empire aztèque*. Paris: Fayard, 1994.

Grootenboer, Hanneke. *The Rhetoric of Perspective: Realism and Illusionism in Seventeenth-Century Dutch Still-Life Painting*. Chicago: University of Chicago Press, 2005.

Gruzinski, Serge. "Confesión, alianza y sexualidad entre los indios de Nueva España (introducción al estudio de los confesionarios en lenguas indígenas)." In *El placer de pecar y el afán de normar*, ed. Seminario de Historia de las Mentalidades y Religión en México Colonial, 171–215. Mexico City: Instituto Nacional de Antropología e Historia/Joaquín Mortiz, 1987.

————. *The Conquest of Mexico: The Incorporation of Indian Societies into the Western World, 16th–18th Centuries*. Trans. Eileen Corrigan. Cambridge: Polity Press, 1993.

————. *De l'idolâtrie: Une archéologie des sciences religieuses*. Paris: Seuil, 1988.

————. *Images at War: Mexico from Columbus to Blade Runner (1492–2019)*. Trans. Heather MacLean. Durham: Duke University Press, 2001.

————. *The Mestizo Mind: The Intellectual Dynamics of Colonization and Globalization.* Trans. Deke Dusinberre. New York: Routledge, 2002.

Guha, Ranajit. *Elementary Aspects of Peasant Insurgency in Colonial India.* Durham: Duke University Press, 1999 [1983].

Gumperz, John J., and Stephen C. Levinson, eds. *Rethinking Linguistic Relativity.* Cambridge: Cambridge University Press, 1996.

Hallen, Barry, and J. Olubi Sodipo. *Knowledge, Belief, and Witchcraft: Analytic Experiments in African Philosophy.* Stanford: Stanford University Press, 1997.

Hanks, William F. *Converting Words: Maya in the Age of the Cross.* Berkeley: University of California Press, 2009.

————. "Language Form and Communicative Practices." In Gumperz and Levinson, 232–270.

Hegel, G. W. F. *Phenomenology of Spirit.* Trans. J. B. Baillie. New York: Harper Torchbooks, 1967.

Heidegger, Martin. "The Age of the World Picture." In *The Question Concerning Technology and Other Essays,* trans. William Lovitt. New York: Harper Torchbooks, 1977.

————. *Contributions to Philosophy (From Enowning).* Trans. Parvis Emad and Kenneth Maly. Bloomington and Indianapolis: Indiana University Press, 1999.

Historia de los mexicanos por sus pinturas. In *Nueva colección de documentos para la historia de México,* ed. Joaquín García Icazbalceta, 3:209–240. Mexico City: Salvador Chávez Hayhoe, 1941.

Historia Tolteca-Chichimeca. Ed. Paul Kirchhoff, Lina Odena Güemes, and Luis Reyes García. Mexico City: INAH-SEP, 1976.

Holsinger, Bruce. "Indigeneity: Panofsky, Bourdieu, and the Archaeology of the *Habitus.*" In Holsinger, *The Premodern Condition,* 94–113.

————. "Medieval Studies, Postcolonial Studies, and the Genealogies of Critique." *Speculum* 77 (2002): 1195–1227.

————. *The Premodern Condition: Medievalism and the Making of Theory.* Chicago: University of Chicago Press, 2005.

Horswell, Michael J. *Decolonizing the Sodomite: Queer Tropes of Sexuality in Colonial Andean Culture.* Austin: University of Texas Press, 2005.

Huizinga, Johan. *Erasmus and the Age of Reformation.* Trans. F. Hopman. New York: Harper and Row, 1957.

Illich, Ivan. *In the Vineyard of the Text: A Commentary to Hugh's Didascalicon.* Chicago: University of Chicago Press, 1993.

Infantes, Victor. *De las primeras letras: Cartillas españolas para enseñar a leer de los siglos XV y XVI: Preliminar y edición facsímil de 34 obras.* Salamanca: Ediciones Universidad de Salamanca, 1998.

Ingham, Patricia Clare, and Michelle R. Warren, eds. *Postcolonial Moves: Medieval through Modern.* New York: Palgrave, 2003.

Jameson, Frederic. *A Singular Modernity: Essay on the Ontology of the Present.* London: Verso, 2002.

Kant, Immanuel. *Anthropology from a Pragmatic Point of View*. Trans. Victor Lyle Dowdell. Carbondale: Southern Illinois University Press, 1978.

———. *Critique of Judgment*. Trans. Werner S. Pluhar. Indianapolis and Cambridge: Hackett, 1987.

———. *Critique of Practical Reason*. In *Practical Philosophy*, trans. Mary J. Gregor, 133–271. Cambridge: Cambridge University Press, 1999.

———. *Critique of Pure Reason*. Trans. Werner S. Pluhar. Indianapolis and Cambridge: Hackett, 1996.

———. *Observations on the Feeling of the Beautiful and the Sublime*. Trans. John T. Goldthwait. Berkeley and Los Angeles: University of California Press, 1961.

———. *Practical Philosophy*. Trans. Mary J. Gregor. Cambridge: Cambridge University Press, 1999.

Karatani, Kojin. *Transcritique on Kant and Marx*. Trans. Sabu Kohso. Cambridge: MIT Press, 2003.

Karttunen, Frances, and James Lockhart. *Nahuatl in the Middle Years: Language Contact Phenomena in Texts of the Colonial Period*. Berkeley: University of California Press, 1976.

Kempis, Thomas á. *Of the Imitation of Christ*. Trans. Abbot Justin McCann. New York: Mentor Edition, 1957.

Klor de Alva, J. Jorge. "Contar vidas: La autobiografía y la reconstrucción del ser nahua." *Arbor* 515–516 (1988): 49–78.

Lacan, Jacques. "Of the Gaze as Objet Petit a." In *The Four Fundamental Concepts of Psychoanalysis: The Seminar of Jacques Lacan, Book XI*, trans. Alan Sheridan, 67–119. New York: W. W. Norton, 1998.

———. *On Feminine Sexuality, the Limits of Love and Knowledge, 1972–1973: The Seminar of Jacques Lacan, Book XX, Encore*. Ed. by Jacques-Alain Miller and trans. by Bruce Fink. New York: W. W. Norton, 1998.

———. "La science et la vérité." In *Écrits* II, 219–244. Paris: Éditions Seuil, 1971.

———. *Seminaire XVII: L'envers de la psychanalyse*. Ed. Jacques-Alain Miller. Paris: Seuil, 1991.

———. *The Seminar of Jacques Lacan, Book 11: The Four Fundamental Concepts of Psychoanalyis*. Ed. Jacques-Alain Miller and trans. Alan Sheridan. New York: W. W. Norton, 1998.

———. "The Topic of the Imaginary." In *The Seminar of Jacques Lacan, Book 1: Freud's Papers on Technique, 1953–1954*, ed. Jacques-Alain Miller and trans. John Forrester, 73–88. New York: W. W. Norton, 1991.

Las Casas, Bartolomé de. *Apologética historia sumaria*. 2 vols. Ed. Edmundo O'Gorman. Mexico City: Universidad Nacional Autónoma de México, 1967 [ca. 1555].

———. *Brevísima relación de la destrucción de las Indias*. Ed. André Saint-Lu. Madrid: Cátedra, 2001 [1552].

———. *De unico vocationis modo omnium gentium ad veram religionem*. Ed. and trans. Paulino Castañeda Delgado and Antonio García del Moral. In *Obras completas*, vol. 2. Madrid: Alianza, 1988.

———. *The Only Way*. Ed. Helen Rand Parish and Francis Patrick Sullivan. Mahwah, NJ: Paulist Press, 1992.

Latour, Bruno. *Pandora's Hope: Essays on the Reality of Science Studies*. Cambridge: Harvard University Press, 1999.

Legend of the Suns. In *History and Mythology of the Aztecs: The Codex Chimalpopoca*, trans. John Bierhorst, 142–162. Tucson: University of Arizona Press, 1998.

Leibsohn, Dana. *Script and Glyph: Pre-Hispanic History, Colonial Bookmaking, and the Historia Tolteca-Chichimeca*. Washington, D.C.: Dumbarton Oaks, 2009.

León-Portilla, Miguel. *La filosofía náhuatl estudiada en sus fuentes, con un nuevo apéndice*. Mexico City: Universidad Nacional Autónoma de México, 1997.

———. *La flecha en el blanco: Francisco Tenamaztle y Bartolomé de Las Casas en lucha por los derechos de los indígenas 1541-1556*. Mexico City: Editorial Diana, 1995.

———. *Francisco Tenamaztle, primer guerrillero de América, defensor de los derechos humanos*. 2nd rev. ed. of *La flecha en el blanco*. Mexico City: Editorial Diana, 2005.

Lévi-Strauss, Claude. *The Savage Mind*. Chicago: University of Chicago Press, 1966.

Leyenda de los soles. In *Codex Chimalpopoca: Anales de Cuauhtitlán y la leyenda de los soles*, trans. Primo Feliciano Velázquez, 119–128. Mexico City: Universidad Nacional Autónoma de México, 1992.

Libera, Alain de. *La querelle des universaux: De Platon à la fin du Moyen Age*. Paris: Éditions du Seuil, 1996.

Lienhard, Martín. *La voz y su huella: Escritura y conflicto étnico-social en América Latina, 1492-1988*. Hanover, NH: Ediciones del Norte, 1991.

Lockhart, James. *The Nahuas after the Conquest: A Social and Cultural History of the Indians of Central Mexico, Sixteenth through Eighteenth Centuries*. Stanford: Stanford University Press, 1992.

———, ed. and trans. *We People Here: Nahuatl Accounts of the Conquest of Mexico*. Berkeley: University of California Press, 1993.

Lockhart, James, Susan Schroeder, and Doris Namala, eds. and trans. *Annals of His Time: Don Domingo de San Antón Muñón Chimalpahin Quautlehuanitzin*. Stanford: Stanford University Press, 2006.

López Austin, Alfredo. *Cuerpo humano e ideología: Las concepciones de los antiguos nahuas*. 2 vols. Mexico City: Universidad Nacional Autónoma de México, 1980.

Lucy, John. "The Scope of Linguistic Relativity: An Analysis and Review of Empirical Resarch." In Gumperz and Levinson, 37–69.

Luhmann, Niklas. *Observations on Modernity*. Trans. William Whobrey. Stanford: Stanford University Press, 1998.

Lyell, James P. R. *Early Book Illustration in Spain*. New York: Hacker Art Books, 1976.

Lyotard, Jean-François. *The Differend: Phrases in Dispute.* Trans. Georges Van Den Abbeele. Minneapolis: University of Minnesota Press, 1988.

Magaloni-Kerpel, Diana. "Visualizing the Nahua/Christian Dialogue: Images of the Conquest in Sahagún's *Florentine Codex* and Their Sources." In *Sahagún at 500: Essays on the Quincentenary of the Birth of Fr. Bernardino de Sahagún*, ed. John Frederick Schwaller, 193–221. Berkeley: Academy of American Franciscan History, 2003.

Mannheim, Bruce, and Krista Van Vleet. "The Dialogics of Southern Quechua Narrative." *American Anthropologists* 100:2 (1998): 326–346.

Marin, Louis. "Questions, Hypothesis, Discourse." In *To Destroy Painting*, trans. Mette Hjort, 15–29. Chicago: University of Chicago Press, 1995.

———. "Representation and Simulacrum." In *On Representation*, trans. Catherine Porter, 309–339. Stanford: Stanford University Press, 2001.

———. *Utopics: The Semiological Play of Textual Spaces.* Trans. Robert A. Vollrath. Atlantic Highlands, NJ: Humanities Press International, 1990.

Marion, Jean-Luc. *In Excess: Studies of Saturated Phenomena.* Trans. Robyn Horner and Vincent Berraud. New York: Fordham University Press, 2002.

Matthew, Laura E., and Michel R. Oudijk, eds. *Indian Conquistadors: Indigenous Allies in the Conquest of Mesoamerica.* Norman: University of Oklahoma Press, 2007.

McCormack, Sabine. *Religion in the Andes: Vision and Imagination in Early Colonial Peru.* Princeton: Princeton University Press, 1991.

Mengin, Ernst, ed. *Unos annales históricos de la nación mexicana: Die Manuscrits mexicains nr. 22 und 22 bis der Bibliothèque Nationale de Paris.* Berlin: D. Reimer, 1939–1940.

Merleau-Ponty, Maurice. "The Entertwining—The Chiasm." In *The Visible and the Invisible*, trans. Alphonso Linguis, 130–155. Evanston, IL: Northwestern University Press, 1968.

———. "Eye and Mind." In *The Primacy of Perception*, trans. Carleton Dallery, 159–90. Evanston, IL: Northwestern University Press, 1964.

Mignolo, Walter. *The Darker Side of the Renaissance: Literacy, Territoriality, and Colonization.* Ann Arbor: University of Michigan Press, 1995.

———. *Local Histories/Global Designs: Coloniality, Subaltern Knowledges, and Border Thinking.* Princeton: Princeton University Press, 2000.

Mohanty, S. P. "Us and Them: On the Philosophical Bases of Political Criticism." *Yale Review of Criticism* 2:2 (1989): 1–31.

Molina, Alonso de. *Confesionario mayor en la lengua mexicana y castellana.* Facsimile edition with an introduction by Roberto Moreno. Mexico City: Instituto de Investigaciones Bibliográficas, Universidad Nacional Autónoma de México, 1975 [1569].

———. *Vocabulario en lengua castellana y mexicana y mexicana y castellana.* Facsimile edition with an introduction by Miguel León-Portilla. Mexico City: Editorial Porrúa, 1992 [1571].

Molina, J. Michelle. "Spirituality and Colonial Governmentality: The Jesuit *Spiritual Exercises* in Europe and Abroad." In Ingham and Warren, *Postcolonial Moves*, 132–152.

Moore, Robert I. *The Formation of a Persecuting Society.* Oxford: Blackwell, 1990.

Morales Padrón, Francisco. *Teoría y leyes de la conquista.* Madrid: Ediciones Cultura Hispánica and Centro Iberoamericano de Cooperación, 1979.

Moraña, Mabel, Enrique Dussel, and Carlos A. Jáuregui, eds. *Coloniality at Large: Latin America and the Postcolonial Debate.* Durham: Duke University Press, 2008.

Motolinía, Toribio de Benavente. *Memoriales o libro de las cosas de la Nueva España.* Ed. Edmundo O'Gorman. Mexico City: Universidad Nacional Autónoma de México, 1971.

Mundy, Barbara. *The Mapping of New Spain: Indigenous Cartography and the Maps of the Relaciones Geográficas.* Chicago: University of Chicago Press, 1996.

Nancy, Jean-Luc. *Being Singular Plural.* Trans. Robert D. Richardson and Anne E. O'Byrne. Stanford: Stanford University Press, 2000.

———. *The Creation of the World or Globalization.* Trans. François Raffoul and David Pettigrew. Albany: State University of New York Press, 2007.

———. *Dis-Enclosure: The Deconstruction of Christianity.* Trans. Bettina Bergo, Gabriel Malefant, and Michelle B. Smith. New York: Fordham University Press, 2008.

———. *The Experience of Freedom.* Trans. Bridget McDonald. Stanford: Stanford University Press, 1993.

———. *A Finite Thinking.* Ed. Simon Sparks. Stanford: Stanford University Press, 2003.

Navarrete, Federico. "The Path from Aztlan to Mexico: On Visual Narration in Mesoamerican Codices." *Res* 37 (2000): 31–48.

Nicholson, Henry B. *The "Return of Quetzalcoatl": Did It Play a Role in the Conquest of Mexico?* Lancaster, CA: Labyrinthos, 2001.

Nowotny, Karl Anton. *Tlacuilolli: Style and Contents of the Mexican Pictorial Manuscripts with a Catalog of the Borgia Group.* Ed. and trans. George A. Everett and Edward B. Sisson. Norman: University of Oklahoma Press, 2005.

Oberman, Heiko Augustinus. *The Harvest of Medieval Theology: Gabriel Biel and Late Medieval Nominalism.* Cambridge: Harvard University Press, 1963.

O'Gorman, Edmundo. *Fundamentos de la historia de América.* Mexico City: Imprenta Universitaria, 1942.

———. *La invención de América: Investigación acerca de la estructura histórica del Nuevo Mundo y del sentido de su porvenir.* Mexico City: Fondo de Cultura Económica, 1977.

Olivier, Guilhem. *Mockeries and Metamorphoses of an Aztec God: Tezcatlipoca, "Lord of the Smoking Mirror".* Boulder: University Press of Colorado, 2003.

Ong, Walter. *Orality and Literacy: The Technologization of the Word.* London: Methuen, 1982.

Origen. *Contra Celsum*. Trans. Henry Chadwick. Cambridge: Cambridge University Press, 1953.

Ortner, Sherry B. "Is Female to Male as Nature Is to Culture?" In *Women, Culture, and Society*, ed. Michele Rosaldo and Louise Lamphere, 67–87. Stanford: Stanford University Press, 1974.

Osorio Romero, Ignacio. *La enseñanza del latín a los indios*. Mexico City: Universidad Nacional Autónoma de México, 1990.

Panaccio, Claude. "Intuition, abstraction et langage mental dans la théorie occamiste de la connaissance." *Revue de Métaphysique et de Morale* 97:1 (1992): 61–81.

Panofsky, Erwin. *Perspective as Symbolic Form*. Trans. Christopher S. Wood. New York: Zone Books, 1991 [1927].

Parish, Helen Rand, and Harold E. Weidman. *Las Casas en México: Historia y obra desconocida*. Mexico City: Fondo de Cultura Económica, 1992.

Pratt, Mary Louise. *Imperial Eyes: Travel Writing and Transculturation*. London and New York: Routledge, 1992.

Procesos de indios idólatras y hechiceros. Mexico City: Publicaciones del Archivo General de la Nación, 1912.

Putnam, Hilary. *The Many Faces of Realism*. LaSalle, IL: Open Court, 1987.

Quijano, Aníbal. "Coloniality of Power, Eurocentrism, and Latin America." *Nepantla: Views from the South* 1:3 (2000): 533–580.

Quine, Willard Van Orman. *Ontological Relativity*. New York: Columbia University Press, 1969.

———. *Word and Object*. Cambridge: MIT Press, 1960.

Quiñones Keber, Eloise, ed. *Codex Telleriano-Remensis: Ritual Divination and History in a Pictorial Aztec Manuscript*. Facsimile edition. Austin: University of Texas Press, 1995.

Rabasa, José. "Colonial/Postcolonial Studies." In special issue on "Subaltern Studies," ed. Gustavo Verdesio. *Disposition* 52 (2005): 81–94.

———. "Ecografías de la voz en la historiografía nahua." *Historia y Grafía* 25 (2006): 105–151.

———. "In the Mesoamerican Archive: Speech, Script, and Time in Tezozomoc and Chimalpahin." In *Without History: Subaltern Studies, the Zapatista Insurgency, and the Specter of History*, 205–229. Pittsburgh: University of Pittsburgh Press, 2010.

———. *Inventing America: Spanish Historiography and the Formation of Eurocentrism*. Norman: University of Oklahoma Press, 1993.

———. "Utopian Ethnology in Las Casas's *Apologética*." In *Re/Discovering Colonial Writing*, ed. René Jara and Nicholas Spadaccini. *Hispanic Issues* 4: 261–289. Minneapolis: Prisma Institute, 1989.

———. *Without History: Subaltern Studies, the Zapatista Insurgency, and the Specter of History*. Pittsburgh: University of Pittsburgh Press, 2010.

———. *Writing Violence on the Northern Frontier: The Historiography of Sixteenth-*

Century New Mexico and Florida and the Legacy of Conquest. Durham: Duke University Press, 2000.

Ricard, Robert. *La conquista espiritual de México*. Mexico City: Fondo de Cultura Económica, 1986.

Robertson, Donald. *Mexican Manuscript Painting of the Early Colonial Period: The Metropolitan School*. New Haven, CT: Yale University Press, 1959.

Rojinsky, David. *Companion to Empire: A Genealogy of the Written Word in Spain and New Spain, c. 550-1550*. Amsterdam: Rodopi, 2010.

Román Gutiérrez, José Francisco, and Guilhem Olivier. "Tezcatlipoca y la guerra del Miztón." In *Las vías del noroeste II: Propuesta para una perspectiva sistémica e interdisciplinaria*, ed. Carlo Bonfiglioli, 131-147. Mexico City: Universidad Nacional Autónoma de México, 2008.

Sahagún, Bernardino de. *Colloquios y doctrina christiana con que los doze frayles de San Francisco enbiados por el papa Adriano sesto y por el Emperador Carlo quinto convirtieron a los indios de la Nueva España en lengua Mexicana y Española*. Facsimile edition and trans. Miguel Leon-Portilla. Mexico City: Universidad Nacional Autónoma de México, 1986 [1564].

———. *Florentine Codex: General History of the Things of New Spain*. 13 parts. Ed. and trans. by Charles E. Dibble and Arthur J. O. Anderson. Salt Lake City and Santa Fe: University of Utah and the Museum of New Mexico, 1954-1982 [ca. 1579].

———. *Historia general de las cosas de Nueva España*. 3 vols. Ed. Miguel Acosta Saignes. Mexico City: Editorial Nueva España, 1946.

———. *Primeros memoriales*. Facsimile edition. Norman: University of Oklahoma Press, 1993 [1561].

———. *Psalmodia Christiana (Christian Psalmody)*. Bilingual edition. Trans. Arthur J. O. Anderson. Salt Lake City: University of Utah Press, 1993.

Searle, John. *The Construction of Social Reality*. New York: Free Press, 1995.

Seed, Patricia. *Ceremonies of Possession in Europe's Conquest of the New World, 1492-1640*. Cambridge: Cambridge University Press, 1995.

Sepúlveda, Juan Ginés de. *Democrates Alter/Tratado sobre las causas justas de la guerra contra los indios*. Spanish/Latin edition. Trans. Marcelino Menéndez y Pelayo. Mexico City: Fondo de Cultura Económica, 1941 [1547].

Sepúlveda, Juan Ginés de, and Bartolomé de Las Casas. *Apología*. Trans. Ángel Losada. Madrid: Editorial Nacional, 1975 [ca. 1550-1551].

Shackelford, Laura. "Counter-Networks in a Network Society: Leslie Marmon Silko's *Almanac of the Dead*." *Postmodern Culture* 16:3 (2006). Internet publication.

Silko, Lesley Marmon. *Ceremony*. New York: Penguin, 1986.

Sommer, Doris. *Proceed with Caution, When Engaged by Minority Writing in the Americas*. Cambridge: Harvard University Press, 1999.

Spinosa, Charles, and Hubert Dreyfus. "Two Kinds of Antiessentialism and Their Consequences." *Critical Inquiry* 22 (Summer 1997): 509-535.

Spivak, Gayatri Chakravorty. "Can the Subaltern Speak?" In *Marxism and the Interpretation of Culture*, ed. Cary Nelson and Lawrence Grossberg, 271–313. Urbana: University of Illinois, 1988.

———. *A Critique of Postcolonial Reason*. Cambridge: Harvard University Press, 1999.

———. *Death of a Discipline*. New York: Columbia University Press, 2003.

Sterrett, Susan G. "Pictures of Sound: Wittgenstein on Gramophone Records and the Logic of Depiction." *Studies in History and Philosophy of Science* 36 (2005): 351–362.

Taussig, Michael. *Mimesis and Alterity: A Particular History of the Senses*. New York: Routledge, 1993.

———. *Shamanism, Colonialism, and The Wild Man: A Study in Terror and Healing*. Chicago: University of Chicago Press, 1987.

Tello, Antonio. *Crónica miscelánea de la Sancta Provincia de Xalisco. Libro Segundo*. 2 vols. Guadalajara, Jalisco: Gobierno del Estado de Jalisco; Universidad de Guadalajara; IJAH; INAH, 1968 [1653].

———. *Fragmentos de una historia de la Nueva Galicia*. In *Colección de documentos para la historia de México*, ed. Joaquín García Icazbalceta, 2:375–438. Facsimile edition. Mexico City: Editorial Porrúa, 1971 [1858–1866].

Toussaint, Manuel. *Pintura colonial en México*. Mexico City: Universidad Nacional Autónoma de México, 1990.

Townsend, Camilla. "Burying the White Gods: New Perspectives on the Conquest of Mexico." *American Historical Review* 108:3 (2003): 659–687.

Trésor de la langue française. http://atilf.atilf.fr/.

Valadés, Diego. *Retórica cristiana*. Facsimile bilingual Latin-Spanish edition with an introduction by Esteban J. Palomera. Mexico City: Fondo de Cultura Económica, 2003 [1579].

Valtón, Emilio. *Cartilla para enseñar a leer, México, Pedro Ocharte, 1569. Estudio crítico, bibliográfico e histórico*. Mexico City: Porrúa, 1977.

Vera Cruz, Alonso de la. *De dominio infidelium et justo bello. Relectio eduta per Reverendum Patrem Alfonsum a Vera Cruce, Sacrae theologiae magistrum, Augustinianae familiae priorem, et cathedrae primariae eiusdem facultatis in Academia Mexicana regentem. 1553-1554*. In *The Writings of Alonso de la Vera Cruz*, vol. 2, ed. and trans. Ernest J. Burrus, S.J. Rome and St. Louis: Jesuit Historical Institute, 1968 [1553–1554].

———. *De Justo Bello contra Indios*. Ed. and trans. C. Baciero et al. Madrid: Consejo Superior de Investigaciones Científicas, 1997.

Wake, Eleanor. "Sacred Books and Sacred Songs from Former Days: Sourcing the Mural Paintings at San Miguel Arcángel Ixmiquilpan." *Estudios de Cultura Nahuatl* 31 (2000): 95–121.

Wallace, David. *Premodern Places: Calais to Surinam, Chaucer to Aphra Behn*. Malden, MA: Blackwell, 2004.

Weber, Max. "Science as a Vocation." In *From Max Weber: Essays in Sociology*, ed. H. H. Gerth and C. Wrights Mills, 129–134. London: Routledge, 1991.

Weckmann, Luis. *La herencia medieval de México*. 2 vols. Mexico City: El Colegio de México, 1984.

White, Roger M. *Wittgenstein's Tractatus Logico-Philosophicus*. London: Continuum, 2006.

Whorf, Benjamin. "The Relation of Habitual Thought and Behavior to Language." In *Language, Thought and Reality*, 134–159. Cambridge: Technology Press of the Massachusetts Institute of Technology, 1956.

Wittgenstein, Ludwig. *Culture and Value*. Trans. Peter Winch. Chicago: University of Chicago Press, 1984.

———. *Philosophical Investigations*. Trans. G. E. M. Anscombe. New York: Mac-Millan, 1968.

———. *Tractatus Logico-Philosophicus*. Trans. D. F. Pears and B. F. McGuinness. London: Routledge and Kegan Paul, 1974 [1921].

Wolfe, Eric. *Europe and the People without History*. Berkeley: University of California Press, 1982.

Wolter, Allan B. *The Philosophical Theology of John Duns Scotus*. Ithaca: Cornell University Press, 1990.

Womack, John, Jr. *Zapata and the Mexican Revolution*. New York: Vintage Books, 1970.

Wood, Stephanie. *Transcending Conquest: Nahua Views of Spanish Colonial Mexico*. Norman: University of Oklahoma Press, 2003.

Wyclif, John. *Tractatus de apostasia*. Ed with an intro. Michael Henry Dziewicki. New York: Johnson, 1966 [1889].

Žižek, Slavoj. "Melancholy and the Act." *Critical Inquiry* 26 (Summer 2000): 657–681.

Zumárraga, Juan de. *Doctrina breve cristiana: en que en suma se contiene todo lo principal y necessario que el cristiano debe saber y obrar. Y es verdadero cathecismo para adultos que se han de bautizar: y para los nuevos baptizados necessario y saludable documento: y lo que mas conviene predicar y dar a entender a los indios: sin otras cosas que no tienen necesidad de saber. Ympressa en Mexico por mandado del Reverendissimo Señor: Don Fray Juan Çumarraga: primer Obispo de Mexico. Del consejo de su Magestad, etc.* (ca. 1545).

———. *Doctrina cristiana cierta y verdadera para gente sin erudicion y letras: en que contiene el catecismo o informacion pa indios con todo lo principal y necessario que el cristiano deue saber y obrar. Impressa en Mexico por mandado del Reverendissimo señor Don fray Juan de Çumarraga: primer Obispo de Mexico.* Mexico: 1546.

Zupančič, Alenka. "The Subject of the Law." In *Cogito and the Unconscious*, ed. Slavoj Žižek, 41–73. Durham: Duke University Press, 1998.

INDEX

Note: Italic page numbers refer to figures.

Acosta, Joseph de, 111, 170–171
Adorno, Theodor W., 173
Agamben, Giorgio, 93, 131, 132, 207n4, 232n13
alphabetical writing: in Codex Telleriano-Remensis's Spanish annotations, 27; collecting verbal performances with, 11, 88, 111, 112, 113, 114, 116, 117, 121–122, 123, 152, 154–155, 156; and colonizing Mesoamerican habitus, 14, 36; and comparativism, 179–181; exappropriation of, 116; as mimetic device, 121; and Nahuas' telling story of conquest, 107, 121; and pictorial texts, 11–12, 27, 109, 113, 117, 123–124, 126, 127, 224n19; and Sahagún's ethnographic inquiry, 88–89; *tlacuilo*'s incorporation of, 21, 194; and translation of Nahuatl iconic script, 109; tyranny of, 121, 220n34; and wild or savage literacy, 14, 36, 68, 111, 114, 121, 154, 156; and writing-versus-orality binary, 111, 112, 113
Alvarado, Pedro de, 26, 27, 29, 30, 48, 96
amatl (native paper), 22, 23, 153
Amerindians. *See* indigenous subjects
amoxtli, 2, 7, 23–24. *See also* pictorial texts

Ankersmit, F. R., 38, 162, 172–173, 177, 207n5
appropriation: and comparativism, 188–189, 190; hybrid or transcultural instances of, 14
Aquinas, Thomas: central concepts of, 78–79; and Dominican order, 34; and Marx, 157; and meaning of *habitus*, 8, 14, 160; on theological science, 70, 75–76; and Vera Cruz, 161. *See also* Thomism
Aristotle, 78, 79, 80, 190
Augustine, 80
Augustinians, 69, 79, 91
authorship, multiple sense of, 112, 126, 153, 154, 156

background. *See habitus* or *background*
Badiou, Alain, 224n16, 228n7
baptism debate: and Dominican/Franciscan doctrinal inconsistencies, 4, 7, 8, 26, 30, 32, 33–34, 45, 48, 53, 58–59, 61–62, 65–67, 68, 69, 70, 71, 74–77, 84–85, 91, 94–95, 101, 102, 147, 148, 188; and Las Casas, 30, 32, 33, 34, 53, 57, 59–60, 101, 148; and messianism, 34, 67, 72, 204; and Motolinía, 34, 57, 59–60, 66–67, 72, 101; and Paul III's 1537 bull, 65, 66; and *tlacuilo*'s depiction of missionaries,

Casas on compatibility of Meso-american life-forms with, 45; missionaries' dream of Nahuatlizing of, 10; multiple versions of, 78; universal history of, 8, 30, 196, 199
Clifford, James, 194, 208–209n13, 230n2
Codex Aubin, 111, 115
Codex Bodley, 208n7
Codex Colombino, 208n7
Codex Mendoza, 18–19, 126, 154, 221n42
Codex Mexicanus, 111
Codex of Tlatelolco, 111, 112–116, *112*, 123, 124, 125
Codex Ríos, 126–127, *128*, 208n7
Codex Selden, 208n7
Codex Telleriano-Remensis
— folio 3v, 117
— folio 8v, 27, *28*
— folio 13v, 45
— folio 27r, 22, 23
— folio 30r, 2, *3*
— folio 44v, 5, *5*, 35
Codex Telleriano-Remensis, folio 46r: as album, 5, 46, 55, 104, 132, 133; ancient culture documented in, 20–21; book form of, 22, 24, 38, 146; colonial order produced from *elsewhere*, 131; colonization of mind of *tlacuilo* in, 21; dating systems in, 2, 15, 21–23; deities in, 20, 26–27, 28, *31*, 42, 45, 46, 55, 84, 95; depicted objects in, 26; Dominican in full ceremonial dress, 2, 7, 26, 35, 37, 45, 46, 47–48, 50, 52–53, 54, 58–59, 95, 96, 103, 194–195; early years of conquest removed from, 125, 126; effect on Dominican friars, 4, 5; *elsewheres* identified in, 5, 162, 163; ethnosuicide promoted in, 12; events on, 25–34; Francis-

can friar in frontal perspective, 2, 5, 7, 26, 33, 35, 37, 44–50, 52–53, 54, 57, 58–59, 61, 78, 90, 185, 195; and genres of Mesoamerican pictorial texts, 20; habitus investigating habitus in, 14, 146; history of, 19; hybrid verbal and pictorial texts in, 11; and Indian walking in 1542, 34; as inquiry into Mesoamerican culture, 134; and Judeo-Christian dates, 136, 138; juxtaposition of apostle and apostasy, 30, 32–33, 35, 54, 59–61, 62, 93, 94–96, 102–103, 116, 195, 196; manuscript studies of, 208n7; and Mesoamerican calendar, 21, 22, 41, 136, 138, 222n9; mestizo scribes' glosses on, 27, 29, 45, 46, 116, 127; and Mixtón War, 59, 60, 62; and Nahuas' telling story of conquest, 110; performative force of, 1, 14, 27, 213n1; pictographic writing of, 19–20, 23, 25, 30, 40–41, 131–132, 154; and plurality of worlds, 89; profile of subjects in, 7, 50, 52; Ríos's glosses on, 27, 28, *31*, 45–46, 47, 62, 63, 104, 116, 117, 127; Ríos taking over production of, 47, 57, 63, 116, 125, 126–127, 193; scenes under discrete years, 21–22, 136, 164; signifying forms of, 10, 25; Spanish glosses on, 3, 10, 20, 21, 24–25, 26, 27, 28, 29, *31*, 38, 44–45, 46, 55, 88, 104, 109, 116, 117, 127, 138, 161, 203; subjectivities of, 20, 25; sun in, 27, 33, 35, 48. *See also tlacuilo* (native painter-scribe of Codex Telleriano-Remensis)
Codex Telleriano-Remensis, folio 49r, *63*
Codex Vaticanus A, 126–127, *128*, 208n7

coevalness, 139, 143, 144
College of Santa Cruz de Tlatelolco, 88
Colloquios y doctrina christiana
   (Sahagún), 12, 74, 133
colonial Mesoamerica: authority in,
   100–101; and domesticated glyphs,
   111, 114; fragility of, 125–126;
   and heterogeneity of Indians, 125;
   heterogeneous temporalities in,
   143; incorporation of European
   life-forms, 11; Indians' accommodation within, 114, 116; and indigenous habitus, 150; and insurgency,
   32–33, 196; and limits of evangelical practices, 10; and medieval
   Mexico, 141–147, 155, 156, 224n19;
   and Mixtón War, 27, 29, 32; and
   modernity, 139, 141, 223n15; and
   Nahuas' telling story of conquest,
   106, 107, 113–114, 124, 129; and
   native political administration,
   140, 151; pictorial texts in, 111,
   123–124; preservation of colonial
   regime, 157; repatriating ancient
   pictographic manuscripts of, 18,
   209n1; and replacement of habitus, 146; and return of gaze, 129;
   and temporal displacement, 139;
   tlacuilo's making sense of, 4–5, 7;
   tlacuilo's objectification of, 46, 131,
   194, 197, 198; and *tlacuilo*'s pictorial vocabulary, 35, 184, 193, 196;
   and *tlacuilo*'s use of perspective, 25,
   26; and universal system of *anno
   Domini*, 21, 136–137, 138
colonization of knowledge, 175–176,
   202
Columbus, Christopher, 164, 175, 189
communal lands, sale of, 158
comparativism: and appropriation,
   188–189, 190; and colonial studies,
   162; critique of, 224n19; and defamiliarization, 185; and domes-

tication of alterity, 185; epistemic
   violence of, 143, 165; and existence
   of background, 163–164; and familiarization, 185; and family resemblance concept, 174–175, 176;
   and globalatinization, 177–178;
   and *habitus* or *background*, 162,
   163–167, 173, 182, 183, 192; and
   juxtaposition and montage, 164,
   165, 176, 182, 185, 188; and Kant,
   167–174, 185; and language games,
   174, 176, 184; limits of, 162, 163;
   and medieval parallelism, 144; mimetic component in, 183–184; and
   naming of centrisms, 167–168,
   172, 173, 190–191; and objectivity,
   167, 174, 180–181, 189–190; and
   observer observed, 188–189; and
   periodization, 161; and present as
   background, 182; and reading indigenous pictorial and alphabetical texts, 179–181; teleology in,
   166, 170, 172, 174, 175, 176, 178,
   182–185, 186, 190; and teleopoeisis,
   186–187; third terms in, 166, 176,
   177, 182, 183; and transcendental
   subject, 167–168, 172, 173, 174;
   and translation, 191; and use of indigenous knowledge, 175–176; and
   witchery, 180–182; and Wittgenstein, 174–175, 176
conquest: and comparativism, 162,
   171, 181, 182, 188, 189; Dominican
   friars' indictment of, 126, 127; and
   Duns Scotus's view of historical
   evolution, 81, 89; effect on indigenous habitus, 83, 89; Las Casas on,
   30–31, 32, 60, 97–98, 103, 126;
   missionaries' place in, 78; and periodization, 131, 134, 136, 142; Roman and other forms of, 130; subaltern condition as effect of, 146;
   and Tenamaztle, 97–98, 103, 196;

Elliot, J. H., 123

elsewheres: and border dialogue, 229n41; and colonial texts, 65; and comparativism, 163; concept of, 1, 4–5, 9, 16, 93, 141, 195–196, 228n7; and conquerors-as-ancestors, 62, 214n12; desiring of, 200–201; exhaustion of, 179; exposing limits of empire, 12, 195, 199; and globalatinization, 194; and globalization, 16, 179, 181–182; to Greco-Abrahamic tradition, 108, 193, 195, 197; and *Historia Tolteca-Chichimeca*, 153; intuition of, 1, 4, 7, 17, 207n4; and melancholia, 107; Nahuas' call to commit ethnosuicide from, 13; Nahuas' telling story of conquest from, 108; and Nahuatl *Exercicio quotidiano*, 149; and negation, 1, 16, 17; and nonmodern, 144–145, 146, 147, 150, 151, 156; and regimes of truth, 139; and Sommer's rhetoric of particularism, 3–4; suffering and confusion produced by, 15; and *tlacuilo* perspective, 1, 4, 10, 12, 16, 17, 25–26, 50, 93, 131, 133, 135, 162, 182, 193, 195, 197, 199; and translation, 218n7; and worlds with different pasts, 205

encomiendas, 32, 98–100, 103, 158, 216n15, 221n42

Enlightenment, 141, 171, 183, 185, 230n41

Erasmus, 64

ethnogenesis, emerging from ethnosuicide, 13, 14, 166, 189

ethnographic inquiry: and belief systems, 77, 78, 82, 83–84, 86, 88–89; of Dominican friars, 8, 9, 10, 56, 78–79, 82–85, 89, 139; ethnosuicide involved in training informants, 13, 14, 140; and fantasy,

103; of Franciscan friars, 8, 56, 78, 80, 81, 82, 85–86, 88, 132–133, 139; and Nahuas' telling story of conquest, 12, 117; and reading, 112; and Sahagún, 78, 81, 84, 86, 88–89, 117; and Scholasticism, 77–82; and translation of indigenous narratives to Spanish, 155

ethnosuicide: and catechism, 12, 13; and collection of objects, 12–13; colonial divide seeking to implant narrative of, 131, 199; contemporary research projects promoting, 71; ethnogenesis emerging from, 13, 14, 166, 189; European writing and painting promoting, 147; failed narrative of, 54, 93, 193; and globalization of Christianity, 129; and homogeneous temporality, 21; and indigenous informants, 12, 13, 14, 21, 140; inevitability narratives of, 192; and internalization of phrase regimens, 163; and internalizing epistemological break, 105; and limits of empire, 21, 54, 56; limits of narrative of, 124–125; and periodization, 133, 140; primordial demand in narrative of, 110; and *tlacuilo*, 13, 131, 196, 198–199; in training informants, 13, 14, 140

Euro-American background, 164, 174, 175–176, 187, 227–228n4

Europe: incorporation of America into consciousness, 135; incorporation of European life-forms in colonial Mesoamerica, 11; and modernity, 141, 223n15; multiple regimes of truth in, 139; thinking in Indian categories, 106, 108, 110, 116, 127, 135, 203

exappropriation, 11, 116, 135

Eze, Emmanuel Chukwudi, 168–169, 171

146; Nahuas' awareness of, 8, 10, 14, 36; Scholastic meaning of, 8, 9; of *tlacuilo*, 5, 7, 8, 12, 17, 134, 162, 184; *tlacuilo* recording of habitus of Dominicans and Franciscans, 9–10, 11. *See also* indigenous habitus

Hakluyt, Richard, 19

Hallen, Barry, 175–176, 202–203

Hamy, E. T., 19, 208n7

Hegel, G. W. F., 168, 197, 200, 202, 227n4

Heidegger, Martin, 15, 174, 189–192, 197, 211n9

Hispanicization, 10, 122, 140

Historia de las Indias (Durán), 85, 219n10, 219n18

Historia de Tlatelolco (in *Anales de Tla-telolco*), 111, 112, 113–114, 115, 121, 123, 226n42

Historia general de las cosas de Nueva España (Sahagún). *See Florentine Codex* (Sahagún)

Historia Tolteca-Chichimeca, 12, 147, 152–156

historical consciousness, and com-parativism, 165, 167

history: and baptism, 95; bewitching the living, 181; concept of, 93, 102, 103; defining ancient history, 138–139, 145; limits on accessing figure of apostate, 94; reading, 4, 21; sub-jectivity of historian, 167; trans-historical understanding of, 153; universal history of Christianity, 8, 30, 196, 199

Holsinger, Bruce, 143–144, 225n26

Hugh of Saint Victor, 24, 25, 80, 210n10

Huitzimengari, Antonio, 91

hybrid "in-betweenness," 107, 110

ideal types: in botanical illustrations, 37, 41; and collecting objects,

42–43; and *tlacuilo*'s depiction of Dominican and Franciscan friars, 48

ignoratiam invincibilem, concept of, 154, 156–161

Illich, Ivan, 24, 209–210n10

indigenous conquistadors, 29, 210n15

indigenous habitus: in album-codices, 46–47; and belief systems, 83, 88–89; and colonial Mesoamerica, 150; Dominican belief in extirpa-tion of, 45; and ethnographic in-quiry, 82–90; goal of colonization as destruction of, 14–15; as object of observation, 184; transforma-tion of, 8

indigenous informants: and album-codices, 46–47; and comparativ-ism, 175; and ethnosuicide, 12, 13, 14, 21, 140; and interpreta-tion of pictorial texts, 11; mourn-ing of, 110; and periodization, 134; and Sahagún, 88, 121, 217n1, 220n27; silencing of, 155; train-ing of, 14, 140. *See also* Nahuas telling story of conquest; *tlacuilo* (native painter-scribe of Codex Telleriano-Remensis)

indigenous languages, 84–85, 122, 139–140, 203, 223n13, 231n5. *See also* Nahuatl language

indigenous subjects: attitude toward evangelical programs, 65–66, 77; and catechism, 67–68, 70; con-temporary, 143; contributions to national identity, 142; effect of plagues on, 158; and Franciscan friars' ethnographic inquiry, 81; heterogeneity of, 125; Las Casas on conversion of, 32, 60–61, 72–73; and learning, 187; orality of, 111; as receptors of medieval culture and practices, 142–143; relationship to Spanish Crown, 99–100; represen-

Mohanty, Satya, 218n7, 231n6
Molina, Alonso de, 81, 84, 85–86, 109, 218n8
mondialisation (world-forming), 100, 101, 129, 178–179, 221n46, 229n33
Moteuczoma (Tenochca ruler): in Nahuas' story of conquest, 109–110, 218n9; as tyrant, 159
Motolinía, Toribio de Benavente, 34, 57, 59–60, 66–67, 72, 101
multiculturalism, 162, 163, 231n5
Multiple, and One, 165, 228n7
Mundy, Barbara, 211n12, 221n42

Nahuas: awareness of *habitus* and *background*, 8, 10, 14, 36; bilingual confessional manuals objectifying own culture, 12, 208n11; and conventions and techniques of perspective, 51–52; critical consciousness of missionaries' contradictory conceptualization, 13; Dominican friars' awareness of habitus, 46; Dominican friars' indoctrination of, 5; and Franciscan friars' ethnographic inquiry, 80, 82, 132–133; Franciscan friars on deception of, 8, 82, 86, 89; Franciscan friars on obligation to accept Creed, 74; and Franciscans' demand for ethnosuicide, 132; manuscript culture of, 152–156; missionaries recording knowledge of, 10, 11; and Sahagún's texts, 12; *tlacuilo*'s depiction of, 20, 47, 184, 188; and *tlacuilo*'s depiction of missionaries, 53–54, 55; and trompe l'oeil, 51, 212n21; use of three-dimensional perspective and phonetic script, 36, 51–52, 53
Nahuas' telling story of conquest: and articulation of failure of magic,

105, 124, 125, 127, 129; and domesticated glyphs, 111, 112, 114, 115, 123; early years removed from Codex Telleriano-Remensis, 125, 126–127; and *elsewhere* perspective, 108; and ethnographic inquiries, 12, 117; and ethnosuicide, 13, 21, 124, 131; and gaze of indigenous subjects, 107; and melancholia, 107–111, 114, 115, 124, 129, 218n8, 219n10; as response to demand, 20–21, 110–111, 116–118, 120–121, 127, 129, 188; and Sahagún, 106, 109–110, 117–118, 120, 121, 217n1, 220n33, 226–227n42; and thinking about Europe in Indian categories, 106, 108, 110, 116, 127; and topology of conversion and conquest, 2, 30, 35–36, 54–55, 91, 93, 94–95, 103, 105, 116, 140–141, 195, 204; and wild or savage literacy, 110–111, 112, 113, 121, 123
Nahuatl *Exercicio quotidiano*, 13, 146–151, 155–156, 161
Nahuatl language: categories of, 203, 205; doctrinal texts in, 68; and grammars, 121–123, 139–140, 223n13; and *Historia Tolteca-Chichimeca*, 152; incorporating European systems of representation in, 107; as lacking syntax, 122; lack of standard orthography for, 36; and melancholia, 109–110, 218n8; and metaphor, 188; missionaries recording, 11, 29; notarial documents in, 221n42; and Sahagún, 81–82, 85, 86, 88, 89, 109, 118, 120–121, 122, 127, 217n1; Sahagún's psalms in, 74–77, 214–215n30; texts written outside supervision, 110–111, 154; translation of, 108–109, 118, 120–121;

Western forms in Nahuatl semantic space, 110

Nancy, Jean-Luc: and background, 192; and *elsewheres*, 15, 179, 207n4; and globalatinization, 127; and Greco-Abrahamic tradition, 195; and Kant, 174; and mode of finite infinite, 166, 228n8; and *mondialisation*, 100, 178–179, 221n46, 229n33

native informants. *See* indigenous informants

Nebrija, Antonio de, 123

nepantla, 83–84, 90

New Laws of 1542, 98, 216n15, 221n42

Nietzche, Friedrich, 227n1

nonmodern: defining of, 142, 144; and *elsewheres*, 144–145, 146, 147, 150, 151, 156; modernities' coexistence with, 16, 132–133, 134, 145, 163, 182, 196; and Nahuatl *Exercicio quotidiano*, 149, 155–156

Nowotny, Karl Anton, 224n19

Nuevas Leyes of 1542, 98, 216n15, 221n42

Nuño de Guzmán, 30, 32, 33, 97

objectivity: and comparativism, 167, 174, 180–181, 189–190; history of, 41–42, 46, 55; impossibility of, 167, 174; in stories, 181; as witchery, 180–181, 189, 190

observer observed: and comparativism, 188–189; and habitus investigating another habitus, 14, 46–47; and Nahuas' telling story of conquest, 107, 110, 226–227n42; and *tlacuilo*, 7, 116–117, 193

Ockham, William of, 34, 57, 78, 79, 81, 86

O'Gorman, Edmundo, 57, 133–134, 135, 223n15, 227n4

Ometochtzin, Carlos, 56–57, 62, 65–66, 69, 77, 82, 89–90

Oñate, Juan de, 97

One, and Multiple, 165, 228n7

Ong, Walter, 210n10

Origen, 127

Other, mirroring effect with Same, 4, 16, 141, 195

Panofsky, Erwin, 25, 26, 35, 48–49, 50

Parish, Helen Rand, 59

Paul III (pope), 65, 66

periodization: and colonial texts, 65; dwelling outside, 200–201; *elsewhere* complicating, 131; and ethnosuicide, 133, 140; and European invasion, 129, 130, 141–142; limits of, 132, 134; and medieval Mexico concept, 141–147, 224n19; of Middle Ages and Renaissance, 130, 132, 134, 139–140, 141, 142, 222n1; and modernities, 130, 145, 161; multiple configurations of, 136; and narrative of Euro-America, 135; and narratives, 132, 199; and perpetual tutelage, 139–140; and subalterns, 151, 226n33

perpetual tutelage, 139–140

photography, writing compared to, 113

phrase regimens, 163, 165

pictorial perspective: in Codex Telleriano-Remensis, 20, 25; debates on, 49; link between linear and illusionistic perspective, 51; and missionaries, 52, 53, 212n25; multiple forms of, 39; ontological status of, 50; and representation, 44; and signification, 184; symbolic forms in West, 48–49, 51; three-dimensional, 5, 12, 20, 21, 25, 26, 35, 39; *tlacuilo*'s *elsewhere* perspective, 1, 10, 12, 16, 17, 25–26, 50;

syncretism, and Dominican friars, 10, 77, 84

Taussig, Michael, 54, 181–184, 188
Tello, Antonio, 29, 102
Tenamaztle, Francisco: *elsewhere* perspective of, 131, 195, 201; historicization of, 93–94; as insurgent, 29, 30, 196; and juxtaposition of apostle and apostasy, 95, 96, 102–103; and Las Casas, 33, 60–61, 93, 96–100, 101, 103, 104, 210n19, 216n15; Mendoza's battle with, 2, 30, 38, 59, 62, 91, 95, 96, 131, 204; and periodization, 131; and verbal texts telling story of conquest, 116
Tezcatlipoca (Smoking Mirror), 30, 31, 44, 62, 95, 214n12
Tezozomoc, Fernando Alvarado, 94, 153
Thevet, André, 19
Thomas à Kempis, 149
Thomism, 8, 57, 64, 68, 75, 78, 79, 82–83. *See also* Aquinas, Thomas
thought experiments, in reading history, 4, 21
tlacuilo (native painter-scribe of Codex Telleriano-Remensis): and assumptions of Western thought, 8, 12, 162; depiction of Nahuas, 20, 47, 184, 188; Dominican friars' surprised by, 5, 46, 193, 195; *elsewhere* perspective of, 1, 4, 10, 12, 16, 17, 25–26, 50, 93, 131, 133, 135, 162, 182, 193, 195, 197, 199; and ethnosuicide, 13, 131, 196, 198–199; and evil eye, 52–53, 55; and Franciscan friars' powers of observation, 44; gaze of, 5, 7, 197; habitus of, 5, 7, 8, 12, 17, 134, 162, 184; minority writers distinguished from, 3–4; and modernity, 129, 139; neutralizing power of orders, 47, 53–54,

55; objectification of colonial order, 46, 54; objectification of missionaries, 13, 139, 188, 211n5; objectification of own culture, 7, 46, 131, 139, 163, 164, 166, 184, 188, 193; objects produced as actors, 13; pictographs of deities, 41, 46, 55, 211n5; pictorial vocabulary of, 4, 7, 9–10, 11, 17, 20, 25, 27, 30, 35, 38, 40–41, 54, 58, 90, 91, 95, 103–104, 105, 116–117, 135, 140–141, 166, 182, 184, 193, 196, 226–227n42; playfulness of, 46; questions posed by, 7; radical alterity of, 17; recognition of self, 25; recording of habitus of Dominicans and Franciscans, 9–10, 11, 45, 46–47, 56, 184, 189; relativization of ethnographic and evangelical programs of missionaries, 9, 47, 53, 55, 57, 62, 69, 77, 78, 82, 89, 91, 125–126, 134, 139, 182, 188, 196, 201, 212n25; removal from project, 47, 57, 77, 116, 125, 193; replica of Mesoamerican pictorial system, 19–20; representation of Mesoamerican world, 41; return of the gaze, 5, 15, 35–36, 47, 54, 77, 78, 90, 116–117, 129, 164, 184, 185, 188, 189, 193, 195, 196, 205; as second-degree observer, 134; self-portrait of, 2, 3; Spanish authorities' trust in, 123; and Spanish system of representation, 20, 25, 36; subjectivity of Mesoamerican life-forms, 7, 38, 193; and topology of conversion and conquest, 2, 30, 35–36, 54–55, 91, 93, 94–95, 103, 105, 116, 140–141, 195, 204; use of perspective, 5, 20, 21, 25, 26, 35, 49–50, 52–55, 57, 90, 116, 139, 194, 212n25, 220n27. *See also* Codex Telleriano-Remensis, folio 46r
Tlatelolcas, story of conquest, 110,

111, 112–113, 124, 125, 217n1, 226n42

tonalamatl (book of the days), 22, 27, 136

tonalpohualli (count of the days), 20

Torquemada, Juan de, 111

Tovar, Juan de, 155

Townsend, Camilla, 214n12

transition-to-capital narratives, 144, 225n26

transmodernity, 151

trompe l'oeil, 51, 212n21

truth: conflicts over universal truth, 196, 197; modernity's claims to, 151; multiplicity of European regimes of, 139; Plato on, 198; revealed truth, 8, 73, 74, 76, 79, 80, 86, 148; self-evident, 159

Valadés, Diego, 38, 70, 81

veintena (feasts of the twenty months), 22, 27

Velasco, Luis de, 96–97

Vera Cruz, Alonso de la, 73, 91, 92, 101–102, 146–147, 156–161, 187

verbal performances, indigenous intellectuals' collection of, 11, 88, 111, 112, 113, 114, 116, 117, 121–122, 123, 152, 154–155, 156

Vitoria, Francisco, 59, 73, 101

Weckmann, Luis, 142, 146, 156

Western thought: and appropriation, 188, 190; and Dominicans' demands of *tlacuilo*, 10; *elsewhere* as alternative to will for mastery

and dominion, 5, 17, 200–201, 207n4; *elsewhere* destroying, 15; *elsewhere* disrupting, 1; and Euro-American background, 164; and Judeo-Christian calendar, 138; symbolic function in Nahuatl semantic space, 110; teleology in, 178; *tlacuilo*'s habitus showing assumptions of, 8, 12, 162

Whorf, Benjamin, 81

wild or savage literacy: and alphabetical writing, 14, 36, 68, 111, 114, 121, 154, 156; and indigenous subjects, 68, 69, 70; and Nahuas' telling story of conquest, 110–111, 112, 113, 121, 123

without, signifying absence and outside, 93, 94–95

Wittgenstein, Ludwig, 15, 37–40, 42–44, 174, 176, 210nn3–4

Wolter, Allan, 80, 81

Wood, Stephanie, 221n42

writing-versus-orality binary, 111–112, 115–116, 127, 219n11

xiuhamatl (book of the years), 22–23, 35, 198, 222n9

xiuhpohualli (count of the years), 20, 222n9

Zapatistas, 90, 151, 198

Zumárraga, Juan de: on doctrine, 33–34, 61–64, 65, 66–67, 70; inquisitorial powers of, 5, 6, 35, 61, 66

www.ingramcontent.com/pod-product-compliance
Ingram Content Group UK Ltd.
Pitfield, Milton Keynes, MK11 3LW, UK
UKHW041911060225
454777UK00001B/230